A Revolution Unfinished

The Mexican Experience
William H. Beezley, *series editor*

A Revolution Unfinished

The Chegomista Rebellion and the
Limits of Revolutionary Democracy
in Juchitán, Oaxaca | *Colby Ristow*

University of Nebraska Press | Lincoln and London

© 2018 by the Board of Regents of the University of Nebraska. All rights reserved. ♾

Library of Congress Cataloging-in-Publication Data
Names: Ristow, Colby, author.
Title: A revolution unfinished: the Chegomista rebellion and the limits of revolutionary democracy in Juchitán, Oaxaca / Colby Ristow.
Description: Lincoln: University of Nebraska Press, [2018] | Series: The Mexican experience | Includes bibliographic references and index.
Identifiers: LCCN 2017052548
ISBN 9781496203656 (cloth: alk. paper)
ISBN 9781496207821 (pbk.: alk. paper)
ISBN 9781496208958 (epub)
ISBN 9781496208965 (mobi)
ISBN 9781496208972 (web)
Subjects: LCSH: Juchitán de Zaragoza (Mexico)—History. | Mexico—History—Revolution, 1910–1920. | Oaxaca (Mexico: State)—History.
Classification: LCC F1391.J92 R57 2018 | DDC 972.08/16—dc23 LC record available at https://lccn.loc.gov/2017052548

Set in Lyon Text by E. Cuddy.

For my mom and dad

CONTENTS

List of Illustrations   viii
List of Tables   viii
Acknowledgments   ix

Introduction: The Chegomista Rebellion and the Limits of Revolutionary Democracy   1

1. The *Barrio de Arriba* and the *Barrio de Abajo*: A Tale of Two Cities in Porfirian Juchitán   25

2. "The Rebirth of an Old Political Party": Liberal Politics and the Rise of the Chegomista Movement   75

3. "They Imagined That the Horse and the Rider Were One": The Chegomista Rebellion   117

4. "It Is Not Possible with the Stroke of a Pen to Suppress the Jefaturas": State Sovereignty and the Peace Process in Juchitán   151

5. "More Ignorant Than Guilty": A "Counterinsurgent" Narrative of the Chegomista Rebellion   193

Conclusion: Political Assassination and the Limits of Revolutionary Democracy   231

Notes   249
Bibliography   273
Index   287

ILLUSTRATIONS

1. Oaxaca in Mexico   15
2. Juchitán in Oaxaca   17

TABLES

1. Ethnic classification of Juchitán   62
2. Outside-born population of Juchitán   62
3. Education in Juchitán   63
4. Employment in Juchitán   65
5. Industrial employment in Juchitán   66

ACKNOWLEDGMENTS

Conducting the research for this book would have been impossible without the support of many institutions. At the University of Chicago, I owe thanks to the Division of the Social Sciences, the Department of History, and the Center for Latin American Studies. I am especially grateful to the Andrew W. Mellon Foundation, the Tinker Foundation, the William and Flora Hewlitt Foundation, and the Fulbright-Hays Program for putting me in and around the archives for many years. And I would like to thank Hobart and William Smith Colleges for keeping me there in recent years. The support of these institutions and of the U.S. Department of Education has been fundamentally important.

While working on this book I spent the better part of a decade in Oaxaca and Mexico City, and along the way I accrued many debts. While the personal debts are far too many to list here, I want to thank the staffs and archivists at the Archivo General del Poder Ejectivo de Oaxaca, the Biblioteca Francisco de Burgoa (Penélope Orozco, in particular), the Fundación Bustamante Vasconcelos, the Instituto Cultural de Oaxaca (especially Lucero Topete), the Hemeroteca Pública de la Ciudad de Oaxaca, the Archivo General de la Nación, and the Biblioteca Miguel Lerdo de Tejada. Without exception, I enjoyed my experience in the archives and libraries, in no small part because of the tremendous service and courtesy provided by those who work there. I also benefited from working in a region with an exceptionally vibrant intellectual community, particularly in the field of history. Despite my tendency toward aloofness, Francisco José Ruiz Cervantes, Carlos Sánchez Silva, and Daniela Traffano received me warmly and always made themselves available for advice and conversation. Francie Chassen-López was especially helpful, with her remarkable knowledge of all things Oaxacan. I also owe a debt of gratitude to my good friend Soid Pastrana, a remarkable artist who also served as my guide to Juchitán. During my time in Oaxaca, I had the good fortune of participating (both formally and informally) in the Oaxaca Summer Institute, organized by William Beezley. Here, as an impressionable young graduate student, I learned about the craft of history and the world of academia from a roster of extraordinary historians and anthropologists, including Bill French, Gil Joseph, Alan Knight, Ann Blum, Peter Guardino, Patricia Pessar, John Hart, and Paul Vanderwood among others. The conversations I had at the Summer Institute were as valuable as any classroom experience I've ever had.

Among those at the University of Chicago whom I wish to thank, I must begin with my graduate school advisers, Friedrich Katz and Claudio Lomnitz. Professor Katz's greatness as a historian was surpassed only by his kindness as a man. I was blown away by his humility and his generosity the first time I met with him, and the last time I met with him. While I was officially his last student, I know that so long as his work survives there will be *Katzistas* for generations to come. Nobody has had a greater, more direct impact on my work than Claudio Lomnitz. In class, conversation, and writing he has consistently inspired me, transforming the way I think about Mexican history. His influence is evident on every page of this book. I only hope it reflects even a fraction of his intuition and creativity. I would also like to thank Chris Boyer, whose insight and recommendations were critical not only to finishing the dissertation but also to shaping this book in its current form. I am also indebted to all of my graduate school teachers at the University of Chicago: William Sewell, Tamar Herzog, Dain Borges, Emilio Kourí, Javier Garciadiego, Suzanne and Lloyd Rudolph, and Dipesh Chakrabarty.

So many fellow graduate students outside the field of Latin American history helped me broaden my intellectual horizons, ask bigger questions, and maintain my mental health. Among them are Aaron

Hill, Michael Stamm, Ani Sarkissian, Michael Brillman, Steve Sawyer, Mark Loeffler, Dana Simmons, and Emmuelle Saadia. I was especially lucky to have such a great cohort of Latin American historians. In workshops, reading groups, and late nights at the Regenstein, they talked to me, listened to me, and helped me think through new ideas and seeming dead ends. So many thanks to Paul Ross, Ana María Serna, Mac James, José Angel Hernández, Jovita Baber, Rueben Zahler, Jaime Pensado, and Ann Schneider. Special thanks are owed to Luis Barrón, for taking me under his wing in my first years of graduate school, and to Ev Meade, for everything—without his endless generosity it is doubtful this book would even exist.

This project began a long time ago, at Michigan State University. Sadly, my original adviser and mentor did not live to see its completion. When I met David Walker, I was a nineteen-year-old who had never read a book cover to cover in his life. He sparked my interest in Latin America and made me believe it was something I could make a career out of. I cannot imagine where I would be now if not for Professor Walker. At Michigan State, I also had the tremendous good fortune of taking classes with Peter Beattie, Dagmar Herzog, and Steve Averill, all of whom influenced the kind of history I wanted to study and, later, write.

Since graduate school I have taught at several institutions—Carleton College, the University of California–San Diego, and Winona State University (all of which were tremendously supportive)—before settling at Hobart and William Smith Colleges. At HWS, I have benefited from the support and generosity of my colleagues in the History Department and across campus, including Matt Crow, Maureen Flynn, Derek Linton, May Farnsworth, Laura Free, Lisa Yoshikawa, Clif Hood, Dan Singal, Will Harris, Sarah Whitten, Janette Gayle, and Judy Mahoney-Benzer. I owe special thanks to Matt Kadane for his insight and his friendship. Provosts Titi Ufomata and Teresa Amott have provided the generous and timely support needed to finish this book.

I am eternally grateful to Bridget Barry, my editor at the University of Nebraska Press. She has provided advice, assistance, and patience in guiding me through the publication process. I am also grateful to the editorial staff at the University of Nebraska and the anonymous reviewers who offered invaluable recommendations and have made this a better book.

Finally, and most importantly, I thank my family for all of their patience and support over the years. My brothers, Alan and Tony, suffered the slings and arrows of growing up at my side and have now become good friends. By example, our parents, Susan and Hugo Ristow, taught us the value of sacrifice, hard work, and integrity, and the importance of not taking any of it too seriously. This book is dedicated to them.

 # Introduction

The Chegomista Rebellion and the Limits of Revolutionary Democracy

On November 6, 1911, Francisco Madero arrived at the Chamber of Deputies to be sworn in as Mexico's first democratically elected president in four decades. The occasion marked Madero's second victory march in five months: in the first days of June, he had arrived in Mexico City at the head of the revolutionary army that had toppled the regime of Porfirio Díaz after more than thirty years of authoritarian rule. Then, as now, "cheering throngs" rallied to greet his arrival, but the enthusiasm of Madero's inauguration could not match the euphoric jubilation of five months prior, when he had been heralded as the "Apostle of Democracy" and the earth literally moved upon his arrival (there was an earthquake). Then, victory had come swiftly for the revolutionaries, sparked by Madero's call to armed revolution, driven by a groundswell of popular protest, and held together by the promise of democratic restoration, suppressed but not forgotten during the dictatorship. Now it was increasingly obvious that victory had done little to stem the tide of popular violence that spread through the countryside, exposing deep ideological rifts between disparate revolutionaries. As popular revolutionaries pushed for more radical reform, Madero entrusted a conservative provisional regime to pacify rebellious regions and prepare the grounds for free and democratic elections. Five months of increasingly conservative rule and military repression tore at the seams of the patchwork revolutionary coalition and fueled the fires of popular mobilization. By the time Madero assumed office, the revolutionary zeal that greeted his arrival in June had given way to pessimistic anxiety, and his increasingly vocal critics had begun to question both his capacity to fulfill the promises of the Revolution and to halt the nation's descent into anarchy.

Just as Madero was being sworn in as president, hundreds of miles away in Juchitán, a relatively large, predominantly Zapotec rail town in the state of Oaxaca, a small contingent of federal soldiers pushed out from their bunker in the local barracks, in search of food. For four days, waves of indigenous rebels had laid siege to the barracks, cutting off the federal army from reinforcements and forcing them to eat their own horses. Days of intense combat at close quarters had transformed the city into a "theater of dreadful carnage," as both sides settled in for a battle of attrition.[1] On the fourth day a detachment of federal reinforcements arrived with heavy artillery, forcing the "rebellious Indians" to abandon their positions under intense cannon fire. The colonial aspect of this reconquest of Juchitán was not lost on one participant who analogized that the cannon, "which created a thunder like no one had ever heard," was "unknown to [the people of Juchitán] until now . . . as the horse was unknown to the valiant soldiers of Moctezuma when the army of Hernán Cortés appeared, for they imagined that the horse and rider were one."[2] On November 6, as thousands of rebels melted away into Juchitán's rugged interior, federal soldiers immediately set about burning the hundreds of bodies that lined the streets in various stages of putrefaction. The smoke from the bodies mingled with that of smoldering buildings to form a billowing cloud that could be seen more than twenty miles away, in Salina Cruz, where refugees who managed to escape the carnage looked on in horror. The following day news of the conflict in Juchitán began to trickle in to the capital, stealing headlines from Madero's inauguration and providing a solemn reminder that, even as it reached its seeming culmination, the Revolution was, as yet, unfinished.

The eruption of violence in Juchitán came after months of escalating political tensions, dating back to the victory of the Revolution, and centered around the local office of *jefe político* (political boss). Mobilized by the revolutionaries' promises of democracy and restored local autonomy, and emboldened by the rapid spread of popular protest, during the summer of 1911 the poor and indigenous majority of Juchitán's southern neighborhoods came together to support the candidacy of José F. Gómez, or "Che" as he was known locally, for the office of jefe político of Juchitán. The highest office in the district, the *jefatura política* was not an elected position but was under the legal jurisdiction of the state government of Oaxaca, who appointed jefes políticos in consultation with President Díaz, rather than public opinion. In uniting behind the candidacy of Che Gómez, the popular classes of Juchitán sought to break the cycle of imposition by asserting their right to self-determination and political representation, and enunciated these rights in the same language of liberal republicanism that Madero's coalition had used to justify the Revolution. Specifically, in the name of popular sovereignty the Chegomistas called on the "republican principle of the dominion of the majority" to demand that the position of jefe político be filled in consultation with public opinion and in accord with the popular will. Anything less, Gómez warned the governor of Oaxaca, "would be the same as considering the revolution unfinished."[3]

In lieu of democratic institutions by which to effectively gauge public opinion, the Chegomistas demonstrated popular will by informal means, such as mobilizing massive public demonstrations and circulating petitions to collect signatures—the "noisy apparatus" of the masses.[4] Through strength of numbers, Che Gómez and his supporters usurped local political functions from the dominant clique of elites, and with the assistance of the revolutionary army, forced the *gente bien* (the middle and upper classes) of Juchitán to evacuate the city along with the federal army. The new, revolutionary government of Oaxaca, eager to consolidate its authority in the peripheral districts, rejected the Chegomistas' popular interpretation of liberal democracy and moved to break their grip in Juchitán. With the support of the provisional federal government, just days before Madero assumed power, Governor Benito Juárez Maza appointed a new jefe político and sent him to Juchitán at the head of five hundred federal soldiers, commissioned to wrest control from Gómez and his people. The violent standoff that ensued came to be known as the Chegomista Rebellion.

The timing of the Chegomista Rebellion, in the final days before Madero assumed the presidency, heightened the conflict's symbolic importance for the new revolutionary regime. For the first month of Madero's presidency the conflict in Juchitán dominated the pages of national newspapers, drawing the rapt attention of the Mexican public to the new regime's efforts to restore order in Juchitán, transforming the region into a public test case for the revolutionary regime's particular brand of democratic consolidation. As a massive popular movement, composed almost exclusively of poor *indígenas* and devoid of radical social demands such as land reform, the Chegomista Rebellion gave Mexico's moderate revolutionary coalition a public stage on which to articulate its response to the unresolved "Indian problem" and provided the public with a sounding board against which to project its very real concerns about revolutionary disorder and the changing role of the poor and indigenous population in Mexican society. It was here in Juchitán, in November 1911, that the Madero regime worked out its version of liberal-democratic rule in indigenous Mexico, in response to the challenge of popular liberalism, and in conflict with a deeply divided revolutionary coalition.

The Chegomista Rebellion brought into sharp relief the political challenge facing the Madero regime as it took office in November 1911. Madero's call for the revival of nineteenth-century liberal principles through armed revolution had liberated a multitude of disparate political actors who had previously been controlled by the political system, particularly the rural, indigenous masses, and brought them into the public sphere in distinctly undemocratic terms, through collective and often violent direct action, frequently led by personalist leaders, known as *caciques*, who used their prestige and political patronage to build large followings among the popular classes. The persistence of popular violence and the resurgence of personalist authority in the form of *caciquismo* roused the anxieties of Mexico's gente bien about the extension of citizenship rights to the nation's poor and indigenous population, reflecting a particular understanding of popular politics that dominated Mexican political discourse of the moment. Specifically, the popular classes were widely acknowledged to lack both the necessary intellectual capacity to participate rationally in political life and the political virtue needed to sublimate their collective interests in pursuit of the common good. As such, the popular classes were understood to be proto-citizens, in need of the guidance of an enlightened state to mediate their participation in the public sphere and elevate them to the status of true citizens. However, by exposing the vulnerable masses to liberal-democratic principles before they could be redeemed, the regime's critics feared that Madero had made them available to the seductions of predatory caciques—demagogues who took advantage of the naïveté of the ignorant masses to advance their own self-interest against that of the nation. Caciquismo, in the political discourse of 1911, represented the antithesis of democracy and the greatest obstacle to the consolidation of democratic rule: by appropriating public functions for private use, caciques not only circumvented the redemption of the popular classes by breaking their dependence on "good society" but also reinscribed corporate identities based on socioeconomic and ethnic status by articulating their collective interests in the public sphere, thereby corroding national unity and exacerbating social disintegration.[5] If Madero had, as Porfirio Díaz famously insinuated, "let the tiger out of the cage" by politicizing the masses, the task of putting the tiger back into the cage required Madero and his co-revolutionaries to strike a delicate balance between the lofty ideological promises of revolution and the pragmatic necessities of order.

Faced with persistent popular violence and the growing prevalence of caciquismo in provincial political life, the revolutionary regime relied on the disciplinary structures of the Old Regime to restore order and impose social control in recalcitrant rural districts. Specifically, in the absence of democratic institutions, the revolutionary regime continued the Porfirian practice of using the jefatura política to mediate access to the public sphere on the nation's indigenous periphery.

Invested with extraordinary legal and extralegal powers of supervision, surveillance, and discipline, jefes políticos represented the face of the state (and its eyes and ears) in the nation's remote districts. As appointed officials, detached from public opinion, by the eve of the Revolution the jefatura política had become a lightning rod for critics of the Díaz regime, who regarded it as a reservoir of centralist power that constrained municipal autonomy, corroded civil society, and impeded the expansion of citizenship rights.[6] However, once in power, Díaz's liberal opponents proved reluctant to relinquish the state's primary means of mediating conflicts between competing local interest groups and controlling access to political and economic power. Rather than eliminate the jefatura altogether—a common goal that had once unified Díaz's liberal opposition—the Madero regime sought to inject the office with the spirit of democracy. In negotiation with the Chegomistas, Madero called on state governors to temper their use of legal authority in the districts and, in the name of social harmony, to appoint jefes políticos in consultation with public opinion and in accord with the will of the people. In so doing, Madero harked back to the days before Díaz, when a comparatively weak Mexican state negotiated political rule in the rural districts, and entered into informal "pacts" with local political leaders (often caciques), that afforded indigenous communities a degree of autonomy in exchange for loyalty to the government. While Madero's recommendations were intended to be general, he specifically called on the state government of Oaxaca to remove the appointed jefe político of Juchitán, and appoint a new one, in harmony with the will of the people.[7]

The state government of Oaxaca, comprised in the majority by liberal revolutionaries, jealously guarded its political authority and rejected Madero's interference in local politics as a violation of state sovereignty. Led by Governor Juárez Maza, the Oaxacan government staunchly defended its right to appoint jefes políticos, with or without consent. Despite his previous promises to eliminate the jefatura in the state, Juárez Maza's refusal to name a new jefe político in Juchitán galvanized Madero's growing opposition, particularly among federalists, who feared the Madero regime's expanding executive authority. As the voice of protest reached a crescendo in the press, the halls of congress, and the streets of Oaxaca City, the state government threatened to withdraw its recognition of the federal government, resurrecting the specter of national disintegration. Faced with diminishing public support and the possibility of civil war, the Madero regime capitulated, abandoning its commitment to democratic reform in Juchitán. By the end of 1911 the old status quo had been restored: under the jurisdiction of the state government, the federal army seized control of the district, forcing remaining rebels from their interior encampments back to work in the neighboring fields; the state-appointed jefe político remained in power, regaining control of local political functions and solidifying the state government's sovereignty; and Che Gómez had been taken into custody, where he was killed under the aegis of the infamous *ley fuga*. His assassination brought a temporary end to the Chegomista Rebellion and transformed Benito Juárez Maza into a revolutionary hero. The divergent fates of Gómez and Juárez Maza stand as a symbol of the failure of Mexico's first twentieth-century liberal-democratic experiment.

Using the Chegomista Rebellion as a lens, this book will examine the limits of revolutionary democracy, forged in conflict with resurgent popular liberalism. For forty days beginning in early November, the Chegomista Rebellion took center stage in Mexican politics, and the debate surrounding its resolution touched on a several issues central to the political history of the nation. Specifically, the Chegomista Rebellion illuminates three interrelated factors that prevented the consolidation of liberal democracy in Juchitán: Mexico's ambivalent nineteenth-century liberal inheritance, which had not adequately worked out the proper role of local autonomy in the consolidation of political rule, especially in indigenous Mexico; the peculiar form of Porfirian "modernization" that hardened and collapsed corporate solidarities of ethnicity and class and facilitated the emergence of forms of popular representation that reinscribed these corporate identities and sectoral interests; and the emergence of a discourse of caciquismo—a public articulation of deep-seated elite fears of low politics and social dissolution that excluded the poor and indigenous masses from the domain of the political and, in denying them agency in their own political actions, denigrated the value of popular will in democratic rule. By examining the confluence of these factors at their nexus in the local politics of Juchitán, this book not only illuminates the sources of Mexico's liberal elite's inability to integrate the poor and indigenous majority as anything other than dependents but also brings to light the practices and discourses by which the revolutionary regime attempted to consolidate a liberal-democratic state, while restricting political liberties to a small minority.

The Chegomista Rebellion and the Historiography of Juchitán

Largely lost in the shadows of Zapatismo, the Chegomista Rebellion has long confounded historical classification. Until recently historians ignored popular participation in the Revolution in Oaxaca, arguing broadly that the state had been "bypassed by the tides of modernization" and thus lacked the requisite material conditions to generate the level of discontent necessary for sustained popular revolutionary activity.[8] Beginning in the 1980s, however, historians began to reevaluate Oaxaca's place in the Revolution, uncovering a more diverse and robust history of development, discontent, and upheaval than had previously been acknowledged.[9] No region of the state attracted more scholarly attention than Juchitán, where the Chegomista Rebellion stood as the largest and most powerful popular response to the Revolution, despite the region's supposed lack of acute discontent. As scholars sought to explain Juchitán's seemingly counterintuitive rebellion the historiography grew, divided broadly into two interpretative camps, one "horizontal" and one "vertical." The horizontal interpretation of the Chegomista Rebellion, written from a local perspective primarily (but not exclusively) by local intellectuals, locates the strength of the Chegomista Rebellion in horizontal relations of shared ethnicity and common class interest, unique to Juchitán. In this interpretation the Chegomista Rebellion represented but one moment in a long history of resistance to outside encroachment, enabled by Juchitán's historically "closed" status, which protected the region from social stratification and cultural distinction—forces that elsewhere corroded unity and undermined communal solidarity.[10] The vertical interpretation, on the other hand, downplays the exceptionality of the rebellion, situating it in the context of revolutionary politics and comparing the Chegomistas to contemporaneous popular but vertically oriented movements. Emphasizing the hierarchical (and reciprocal) dimensions of popular rebellion, particularly the importance of caciquismo, this interpretation deemphasizes the centrality of ethnicity and class in explaining the rebellion.[11] While the two interpretations have carved out a space for the Chegomista Rebellion in the revolutionary and regional historiography, a more accurate account of the rebellion and its role in the Revolution must combine elements of both.

The horizontal interpretation of the Chegomista Rebellion has been indelibly attached to the political successes of another indigenous movement in Juchitán, the Coalición Obrera-Campesina-Estudiantíl del Istmo (COCEI). A social movement that imbued a radical political agenda with ethnic revivalism, the COCEI won municipal elections in 1980, making Juchitán not only the first urban center in Mexico to be controlled by a leftist opposition group under the PRI but also a political *cause célèbre*, vaulted to international prominence as the site of one of Latin America's most successful indigenous movements.[12] The COCEI's extraordinary political success was aided and punctuated by a spike in local intellectual and cultural production aimed at mobilizing direct action around ethnic pride. This "Zapotec Renaissance" entailed a broad reimagining of local history from the perspective of the region's poor and indigenous majority, intended to counterbalance "official histories." Transmitted through political speeches, scholarly works, and a vibrant artistic and literary scene, the COCEI's explicitly political rendering of Juchitán's past emphasized the region's historical "rebelliousness in the face of oppression" and represented the COCEI as "the most recent link in an unbroken chain of rebellions, resistance, and defense of Zapotec culture dating back to precolonial times."[13] No link in Juchitán's "unbroken chain of rebellions" figured more prominently in the *coceista* political imagination than the Chegomista Rebellion.

As tensions between the COCEI and the Mexican state heightened, coceista intellectuals articulated the history of the Chegomista Rebellion as a political rallying point—a symbol of Juchitán's "spirit of rebelliousness"—and in so doing transformed Che Gómez into "the central figure of coceista continuity" with the past.[14] COCEI histories, most notably the work of Victor de la Cruz, represented the Chegomista Rebellion as a unified defense of Juchitán's ethnic identity and socioeconomic interests against the commercial interests of the landed oligarchy in the Valley of Oaxaca and their government allies. In this interpretation, the Chegomista Rebellion became a symbol of the struggle of Mexico's poor and indigenous population to maintain its identity and control of its resources in the face of encroaching modernity, and Che Gómez became an authentic representative of Mexico's marginalized masses, ideologically akin to more famous popular revolutionaries, like Emiliano Zapata.[15] As such, Che Gómez and the rebellion that bore his name functioned as a reflection of how the COCEI saw itself, or at least sought to represent itself. In particular, the violent repression of the Chegomistas by the federal government and Che Gómez's martyrdom at the hands of the state government made the Chegomista Rebellion the ideal symbol of Juchitán's historical conflict with the outside world and a parable for the ongoing treachery of the regime. By mobilizing the Chegomista Rebellion as a symbol of continuity, the COCEI sought to foster solidarity and facilitate collective action by underscoring a history of conflict rather than collaboration. This strategic appropriation of the Chegomista Rebellion proved to be politically expedient, and its impact on the historiography of Juchitán was profound.

Drawn to Juchitán by the COCEI's cultural renaissance, in the 1980s and 1990s scholars from around the world transformed the study of Juchitán into something of an intellectual cottage industry.[16] While focusing primarily on contemporary issues, these outside studies excavated the region's past in search of a social scientific explanation for the COCEI's unprecedented success and, more broadly, "a historical understanding of the uniqueness of Juchitán."[17] Perhaps unsurprisingly, then, the bulk of these histories reproduced the horizontal (and teleological) interpretation articulated by coceista intellectuals. At the core of this teleology is an image of Juchitán as a traditional "closed corporate community," historically unified in its resistance to the penetration of the outside world. This "closed" paradigm of Juchitán's past is based on an understanding of the town and the region as geographic periphery where, protected from the full impact of Spanish colonialism, Juchitán preserved "a strong sense of ethnic distinctiveness and a hostility toward all non-Zapotecs" that predated Mexico's independence from Spain.[18] Thus, in the nineteenth century, when the forces of state and capital threatened to penetrate Juchitán and engulf the region in wider political and economic networks, the people could draw on horizontal relations of shared ethnicity and class to defend their cultural boundaries, and "the culture of Zapotec resistance to state power and other encroaching outsiders was fully established at Juchitán." According to John Tutino, this paradigm of conflict, pitting "ethnically unified Juchitán" against all forms of outside encroachment, transformed Juchitán into "a center of adamant resistance to state power, the role it maintains to this day."[19] As Tutino's parallel suggests, once Juchitán was established as a site of resistance, safeguarded from the corrosive influence of social stratification and cultural distinction, the next 150 years become an inexorable process of identity formation culminating in coceista victory.

While this horizontal interpretation has empowered local indigenous political activity and helped to put Juchitán in bold letters on the cultural map of Mexico, it has done so at the expense of misrepresenting the Chegomista Rebellion and its role in the Mexican Revolution. In applying an inside-outside (or closed-open) dichotomy to the history of Juchitán, this interpretation divorces Juchitán's historical trajectory from that of the nation, reducing all acts of historical resistance in Juchitán into indistinguishable links in an "unbroken chain of rebellions," made possible by Juchitán's closure from national politics; privileges conflict with the outside as the primary mover in the region's history, obfuscating other types of center-periphery relations that also characterized Juchitán's relationship with the state; reifies Juchitán as an ontological entity with a unified voice achieved by communal consensus—a reflection of shared ethnic identity and socioeconomic interest—rather than the product of internal competition and raw power relations; and ignores a long history of internal distinction and social stratification in Juchitán, itself the product of a complex relationship with the outside world that defies simple closed-open typologies. Ultimately, the historical image of Juchitán as a relatively closed corporate community fails to recognize that the Chegomista Rebellion did not pit "unified Juchitán" against outside "forces of oppression" but was instead experienced primarily as an internal conflict, reflecting deep fissures associated with the region's participation in the open fields of state and market.

The second interpretation of the Chegomista Rebellion locates the rebellion firmly in the comparative context of widespread revolutionary violence. In his tome on the Mexican Revolution, Alan Knight laid the groundwork for this more vertical interpretation by fitting the Chegomista Rebellion into the broad milieu of *serrano* movements. According to Knight, in juxtaposition with popular "agrarian" movements, serrano rebellions were bound together by vertical ties of patronage rather than shared ethnicity or class interests; they were "politically ambivalent and opportunistic" rather than ideologically unified; and they mobilized for primarily political ends—self-government and the end of political impositions—rather than for control of land and resources.[20] Knight's inclusion of serrano movements in the mosaic of popular revolutionary protest challenged the existing populist narrative of the Revolution, which privileged agrarian movements and fetishized (horizontal) "peasant" unity as the authentic expression of popular discontent. His work helped to expand the dominant narrative of the Revolution to include popular movements previously marginalized as ill-defined at best, or non-revolutionary at worst, and place caciquismo at the center of studies of revolutionary violence.

According to Knight, communities on the geographic periphery often invoked "powerful local patrones" to defend their shared interests and serve as bulwarks against the "construction of a strong centralised state." These patrons "readily contented themselves with a revived caciquismo of the old style," consolidating their authority locally through networks of patronage, ritual kinship, unequal reciprocity, and "the diagnostic threat and practice of violence," rather than formal institutions or the rule of law. While their followers invested in them the authority to defend their perceived (and inherently defensive) collective interests, and serrano caciques were "probably more sensitive than other caciques," *cacical* rule was personalist and arbitrary, and caciques often used their authority to advance their own self-interest.[21] Within this paradigm, according to Knight, the Chegomista Rebellion had "all the ingredients" of a prototypical serrano movement: it was clearly popular, politically oriented, aimed at local autonomy rather than land redistribution, and led by an opportunistic, old-style cacique.[22]

More recently, Jennie Purnell fleshed out Knight's vertical interpretation, adding two critical caveats. First, Purnell notes that while Gómez was an "old-style" cacique who used "ties of kinship, locale, and patronage" to consolidate his authority locally, the rebellion that bore his name was "not anti-state in character, but rather aimed at seizing control of the state apparatus at the local and district level."[23] Second, Purnell recognizes that the rebellion did not unify Juchitán in resistance to the outside world but was experienced primarily as an internal power struggle between two local factions. By placing factionalism at the center of her analysis in place of ethnicity and class, Purnell explicitly rejects the horizontal interpretation of the rebellion. "Factions in Juchitán," she writes, "were defined in terms of families, ritual kinship, patronage, and possibly neighborhoods, rather than by class, ethnicity, ideology, or organizational membership."[24] Thus, Purnell's interpretation runs directly counter to the prevailing "image of Che as the representative of the pueblo as a whole, and the embodiment of ethnic and regional solidarity in the face of external threats."[25] Instead, Purnell sees factional conflict in Juchitán in purely political terms, and the Chegomista Rebellion as a conflict between elite families and their patronage networks.

Purnell's explanation of the Chegomista Rebellion is convincing on several counts: Che Gómez was a cacique who used traditional forms of informal authority to seize control of the state apparatus in Juchitán and advance his own interests and those of his family in direct competition with local political rivals. However, in dismissing horizontal explanations of the rebellion, Purnell loses sight of those who comprised the rebellion itself. While she acknowledges a possible spatial dimension in the development of local political factions, Purnell does little to excavate local spatial divisions, ignoring the extent to which the urban space of Juchitán had become imbued with ethnic and socioeconomic identities. In this book I will argue that the changing spatial dynamics of Juchitán, the product of rapid economic and demographic growth, provide the keys to understanding the formation and the repression of the Chegomista movement, and bring horizontal factors, such as ethnicity and class, back to the center of the historiographical debate. Ultimately, if Che Gómez failed to represent "the pueblo as a whole," he did embody the collective identity of one sector of the pueblo, its poor and indigenous majority.

Cultural Distinction, Collective Identities, and Caciques

The narrative of Juchitán's historical development as a relatively "closed," peripheral community, safeguarded from the effects of social stratification and internal cultural distinction, is predicated on two factors. First, the climate of Juchitán is notoriously inhospitable. Located on the Isthmus of Tehuantepec in the southeastern corner of the state of Oaxaca, Juchitán is unbearably hot during the dry season, and the rainy season yields inconsistent rainfall, making droughts in the region quite common. More often dry than not, eight rivers run from the Sierra Oriente mountain system to the Gulf of Tehuantepec,

Fig. 1. Oaxaca in Mexico. Wikimedia Commons.

dividing the district into two parts—the Pacific plain in the southern half, and the Sierra Oriente to the north. The district *cabecera* (head town), also called Juchitán, and the other larger settlements in the district are located in the flat, dry lowlands, while the mountainous zone has historically been sparsely settled, with little communication and transportation infrastructure. Before the nineteenth century the paucity of water inhibited the development of commercial agriculture and kept the population density low.[26]

The second factor can be traced to the region's ethnic origins and, more specifically, to pre-Columbian patterns of spatial organization. Since their arrival in the mid-fourteenth century, Isthmus Zapotecs have comprised the vast majority of Juchitán's population.[27] Before the arrival of the Spanish, Zapotec society was organized according to socioeconomic status, with nobles and commoners organized into regional cabeceras and tributaries, respectively. On the Isthmus the cabecera, Tehuantepec, collected tribute from thirty-one tributary villages, including Juchitán. The economic and cultural gap between

Introduction 15

nobles and commoners was massive, and as a result, according to ethnographer Joseph Whitecotton, territorial relationships subsumed ethnic affiliation: "Zapotec ethnicity, on a larger level, was of little consequence, as there were few, if any, social forms that gave it unity."[28] Following the conquest in the sixteenth century, Spanish efforts at colonization exacerbated this disjuncture by centralizing administrative authority, spiritual power, and commercial interest in Tehuantepec, now the official cabecera. As Spanish penetration of *istmeño* society deepened in the seventeenth century and Spanish magistrates, priests, and landowners displaced Zapotec authorities, power and wealth became increasingly concentrated in Tehuantepec. As power and wealth became associated with Spanishness, Zapotec nobles in Tehuantepec began to conform to Spanish culture (most notably language), while Juchitán and the other tributaries developed as undifferentiated reservoirs of indigenous people and identity.[29]

However, while ethnic distinction and social stratification in Juchitán and other tributaries on the Isthmus were likely minimal at the time of Independence, during the nineteenth century Juchitán clearly set itself apart. As conservatives and liberals battled for control of the Isthmus and its abundant economic potential, commercial development schemes increasingly targeted Juchitán, transforming it into the second-largest population center in the state and, according to a U.S. businessman, "the most industrious and thrifty town on the Pacific plains."[30] In response to the swelling population, in 1857 the state government officially elevated Juchitán from pueblo to villa, and the following year removed it from the jurisdiction of Tehuantepec, naming Juchitán its own political district. Encompassing eighteen *pueblos* and forty-three *ranchos* and *haciendas*, and covering 11,133 square kilometers, the district of Juchitán was, and still is, the largest in the state of Oaxaca.[31] The official recognition of Juchitán as the district's cabecera set the table for its transformation into a "modern" Mexican city.

The modernization schemes of the Porfiriato, particularly the expansion of the nation's transportation infrastructure, introduced

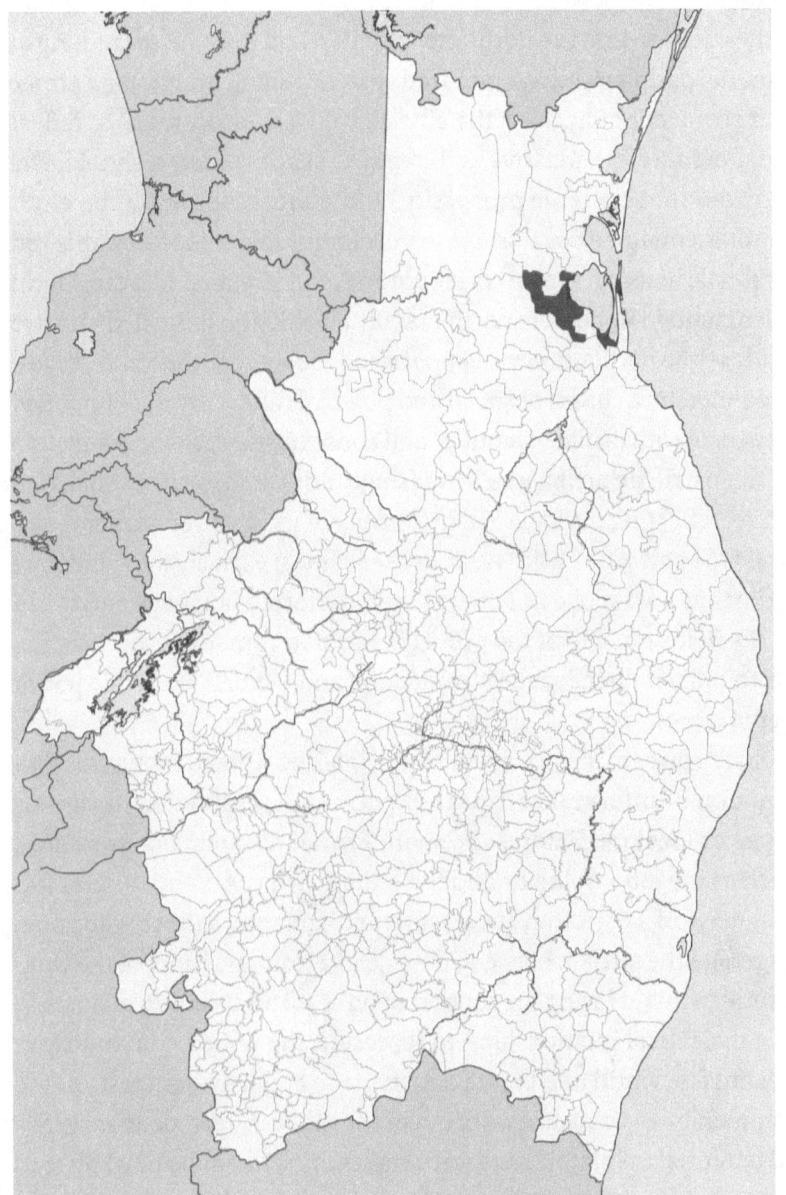

Fig. 2. Juchitán in Oaxaca. Wikimedia Commons.

intense social stratification, unprecedented ethnic distinction, and sustained state power to Juchitán. The 1890 census demonstrates that only a decade into the Porfiriato, Juchitán had become something of a model peripheral city, organized spatially along overlapping ethnic and socioeconomic axes: the city center was transformed to reflect ideal modernity—massive architecture, spatial order, technological innovation, economic prosperity, and education—while the city's southern margins became a reservoir for traditional Mexico, marked by simple housing, spatial chaos, poverty, and illiteracy. Bleeding down the mountain slope from north to south, Juchitán was divided into two worlds—the northern *barrio de arriba* and the southern *barrio de abajo*—separated by a chasm of social and political difference and inhabited by people with distinct identities and consciousnesses. The population of the barrio de arriba was increasingly educated, professional, and white, reflecting the idealized modernity of its material surroundings, while the barrio de abajo was inhabited almost exclusively by illiterate indígenas who spoke Zapotec as their preferred language and toiled in the fields outside of town.[32] This peculiar form of modernization profoundly influenced the introduction and mediation of state power in the region.

State power in Mexico's rural municipalities worked through a combination of informal networks of patronage, embodied in various types of local mediators, and more formal disciplinary structures, such as the jefes políticos and the federal army. Among the less formal networks of power, successful mediators were those who could negotiate the tension between outside interests and those of the community without losing the support of either. The authority to mediate this dialectical relationship—to represent the reified community to the outside world and create and manage collective interests of the community—was achieved not by consensus but by competition. While all potential mediators in Mexico's pueblos walked the line between the collective interests of the community and the interests of outside power networks, in communities with extensive resources and social stratification, competition produced divisions between distinct types of local intermediaries: cultural mediators, whose authority stemmed from prestige within the community, and power brokers, who derived their authority from their influence in political administration or the control of economic resources. Max Weber broadly recognized this as the difference between social power and class or political power, or power derived from prestige and popularity (status) versus the power derived from the control of wealth or political power.[33] Both types of intermediaries had legitimate claims to authority within the community: local power brokers derived power from engaging in broader national and regional debates, while cultural mediators (who functioned as "organic intellectuals") won prestige by articulating community interests, values, demands, and histories in the public sphere and identifying themselves in solidarity with those members of the community shut off from class and political power (and thus unauthorized to speak in the public sphere).[34] In this competition, Florencia Mallon has argued that the primary function of the power broker was to act as an agent of surveillance and discipline for larger networks of power; an "enforcer of more dominant forms of political culture who brings these more 'official' discourses back into village politics."[35] Derived primarily from outside sources, the authority of power brokers expanded at the expense of more popular cultural mediators and was experienced by subordinates as a form of imposition, consolidated through vertical relations of patronage and in collaboration with more formal agents of discipline and surveillance, most notably jefes políticos. In short, the authority of power brokers was hierarchical and coercive, as it stifled more "organic," popular forms of political expression.

In Juchitán, the successful implementation of Porfirian economic schemes clearly favored the authority of local power brokers associated with the barrio de arriba, at the expense of mediators who identified in solidarity with the interests of the poor and indigenous of the barrio de abajo. As elsewhere in Mexico, mediating the advent of "modernity"—the influx of capital that accompanied the arrival of more efficient transportation—brought together a close-knit network of elites (a *camarilla*) in Juchitán and Mexico City, known locally as the *partido rojo*. Bound by friendship, family, and economic interest, the partido rojo (or *camarilla roja*) used close connections within the Díaz regime to monitor the growth of the city and control the influx of commerce and technology into Juchitán, using its expanding wealth to ensure the cooperation of local political officials, most notably the jefe politico (who also got rich in the process). During the Porfiriato, local elites, the jefe político, and the complicit middle class became the informal caretakers of Porfirian progress, forming a composite apparatus of dominance, while their subordinates—almost exclusively poor and indigenous—were denied access to political and economic resources. Like other regional camarillas, the partido rojo used informal networks of patronage to establish links with the marginalized classes but understood that the exploitative relationship between the small minority of local elites and middle classes (capital) and the vast majority of poor indígenas (labor) could function only under the close watch of the state's increasingly ubiquitous disciplinary apparatus (the federal army). When Porfirio Díaz reconfigured national troop allocations, he took care to place a federal army garrison in Juchitán, while transforming nearby San Jerónimo into one of the biggest garrison towns in Mexico. Rather than the manufacture of consent, the partido rojo consolidated its authority through the constant supervision of the state, maintaining peace and the free flow of commerce for the bulk of the Porfiriato.

Despite its promises of redemption for the indigenous lower classes, increased participation in urban life did not provide a panacea for the lingering effects of the nation's "Indian problem." Rather than dissolve colonial caste distinctions and the "premodern" forms of sociability that held them in place, the Porfirian model of urbanization reinforced sub-local (not communal) group solidarities and identities. On the one hand, while indigenous participation in the market economy expanded, accelerating the process of social stratification—a process typified by emerging peripheral cities like Juchitán—class distinction did not replace that of caste, especially in less formal realms. Even as they dismantled the legal structures that held colonial caste hierarchies in place, the liberal gente bien never relinquished the Spanish idealization of whiteness, maintaining a bipolar understanding of society. When indigenous populations moved to the city and became integrated into economic cycles of production, class distinction was grafted onto enduring colonial racial hierarchies. Thus, as the term *indio* disappeared as a juridical category, Claudio Lomnitz notes that Indianness "became synonymous with a combination of material poverty and cultural 'backwardness.'" On the other hand, the reorganization of urban space—a process itself informed by these neocolonial distinctions—created new networks of solidarity among the poor and indigenous population, based on residential segregation, compounding class and ethnic identities into one composite identity. As such, Juchitán became a microcosm of Mexico's "dual society": one consisting of the *masa general*, which included mestizos, and had whites as its apex (the barrio de arriba); and the other consisting of those "collectivities most recalcitrant to enter fully into a capitalist economy of wage labor, private property, and free enterprise"—the indigenous population (the barrio de abajo).[36] Relegated to the physical margins of the city and barred from access to political office and economic resources, the nearly exclusively indigenous *gente de abajo* developed their own "domain of sovereignty," separate from the material realm of capital, statecraft, and technology controlled by the gente bien and politicized by the shared experience of exploitation and alienation.[37] By allowing for (or, indeed, planning for) the development of separate and deeply unequal social worlds, the Porfirian version of modernity obstructed the assimilation of the indigenous pueblos into the fabric of city life, pushing the unresolved "Indian problem" below the surface of public politics, where it would remain until 1910.

The internal distinction that accompanied Porfirian "modernization" did not inhibit, but actually facilitated, Juchitán's participation in the coming Revolution. When revolutionaries introduced the language of democracy and citizenship into local politics, the unified popular classes of the barrio de abajo were easily mobilized. However, rather than join political parties formed around universalist legal order and abstract political ideologies, the collectively identified gente de abajo gravitated toward "renegade politicians" like Che Gómez, who, unlike other elite political leaders in the region, was unafraid to appeal directly to the collective interests of Juchitán's poor, indigenous majority. Gómez publicly defended the right of the poor indígenas of the barrio de abajo to political representation in the name of popular sovereignty, and organized them into an informal political "party," the *partido verde*, essentially occupying the political space that liberal revolutionaries hoped would be filled by formal political parties.

The emergence of popular liberalism in the context of expanding revolutionary violence violated the political sensibilities of Mexico's more urbane liberal revolutionaries, greatly reducing the chances for democratic consolidation in Juchitán. First, the liberal republican model of democracy favored by most revolutionaries did not allow for the representation of sectoral interests, whether they be those of social class, ethnicity, or locality, but sought to subjugate these interests to those of the nation (the singular "common good").[38] The presence of corporate identities in the public sphere was anathema to liberal revolutionaries, who broadly understood corporate forms of sociability to impede the growth of rational individualism and political ideology. Liberal revolutionaries saw corporate identities as obstacles to political "modernization" and the creation of a virtuous citizenry, capable of electing responsible leaders, intent on advancing public (rather than private) interests. Second, the expansion of personalist authority in the form of caciquismo came at the expense of more rational, reliable, and legal means of expressing and gauging public opinion, and blocked the expansion of citizenship rights in the countryside by impeding the growth of formal political parties. And finally, Mexico's elites were simply unprepared to see poor, illiterate indígenas participating in the public sphere in any independent capacity. They broadly agreed that the population of the indigenous periphery had not yet achieved the level of civilization needed for self-government, and feared the destabilizing effect that popular sovereignty could have on Mexican political life, especially in the midst of revolutionary upheaval. Ultimately, elite revolutionaries sought to implement liberal-democratic reform that served the unified interest of the nation, not the private interests of its competing sectors (and especially its most vulgar sectors), and thus could not satisfy the Chegomistas' legitimate demands for autonomous political representation. Instead, the revolutionary regime sought to restrict political liberties to a small, enlightened minority, capable of discerning the national interest, and defending it from the misguided attacks of the poor and indigenous masses, and their caciques.[39] While this project appealed to Mexico's political classes, eager to put the tiger back in the cage, it presented the revolutionary regime with a difficult dilemma: how to contradict the popular will without compromising its commitment to democratic consolidation.

In November 1911 the Mexican press constructed a narrative of the Chegomista Rebellion, easily legible to the nation's elite and middle classes, that resolved the contradiction between elite and popular interpretations of revolutionary democracy. Embedded in centuries-old concepts and discourses of civilization and racial inferiority, this narrative blamed the conflict in Juchitán on the "pernicious influence" of Che Gómez, a selfish and ambitious "demagogue" who prayed on the naïveté of the "unconscious multitudes" to advance his own self-interest, against that of the nation. Beginning in early November, for forty days news of the Chegomista Rebellion dominated the front pages of all of Mexico's national newspapers, focusing not on the ideology or motivations of the rebels but on their character. By accentuating the coarse and uncivilized nature of the Chegomistas, newspaper correspondents, editorialists, and politicians denigrated the political value of popular will. They argued, often implicitly, that if the popular classes were unconscious, illiterate, "rudimentary" beings, then they were unfit for self governance, and it made no sense for the government to respect their will. Rather, it was the duty of the educated, enlightened classes (the *gente sensata*) to discern the will of the people and protect the poor indígenas from the influence of vicious, predatory elites, such as Gómez, who used his status and false promises to seduce them, and sever them from the bonds of "good society," which offered true redemption. Only by participating in a civil society invigorated by the renewed spirit of democracy, as breadwinners and wage laborers, would the poor and indigenous masses elevate themselves from their degraded state and transform themselves into virtuous citizens capable of sublimating self-interest, working toward the common good, and defending the interest of the nation.

This "counterinsurgent" narrative of the Chegomista Rebellion, articulated in national newspapers as anxiety about the persistence of popular violence reached its zenith, doubled as a parable for the nation, warning Mexico's reading public of the dangers not only of caciquismo but of the volatile and degraded majority population upon which revolutionary leaders had been called to build a democratic society. As such, the narrative of the Chegomista Rebellion undermined the legitimacy not only of Che Gómez but of all popular (and populist) revolutionary leaders. Perhaps more importantly, the national discourse of caciquismo, sparked by the Chegomista Rebellion, defined the nation's popular classes as pre-political and excluded popular mobilization from the domain of the political. By denying the poor and indigenous majority agency in its own political actions, the discourse of caciquismo underwrote the government's attempts to restore order in the countryside and restrict access to the public sphere, and allowed the regime to do so without compromising its own liberal-democratic credentials. This was the very limit of revolutionary democracy.

1 The *Barrio de Arriba* and the *Barrio de Abajo*
A Tale of Two Cities in Porfirian Juchitán

On November 7, 1911, as federal forces in Juchitán worked to pick up the pieces of a city in ruins, Juan Sánchez wrote President Francisco Madero, hoping to shed light on the inequalities that had led to the city's destruction. "Half of Juchitán has lined-up streets," wrote Sánchez, "the straw huts have completely disappeared and the blocks are well laid out, existing in this part of town the best buildings and as a result all government offices." The other half of town, he continued, "does not have streets, they live like a tribe and all the houses are made of very primitive palm." This spatial division carried important social implications: "in the first live all of the thinking people [gentes pensantes], almost all of whom know how to read and write and whose party . . . has always dominated public affairs [la cosa pública]"; while in the other half, "the people are in their majority illiterate, resistant to all progress and have always opposed material improvements which they reject at first glance." Juchitán emerges from Sánchez's letter as two cities in one, divided between the wealthy and the poor—the "barrio de arriba" and the "barrio de abajo," respectively—and organized into two competing political factions. In the midst of a popular revolution, the dangers of such stark contrasts seemed so self-evident that one could have easily forgotten that only a short time before, Juchitán—despite its disparities—had been considered a thriving rural metropolis and a reflection of the successes of Mexico's rapid economic development: one of Porfirio Díaz's modest "monuments of progress."[1]

Beginning in the 1880s, as new roads and railroads connected Juchitán to surrounding markets and transformed the city into a regional transportation hub, the city center was reordered to "stage" modernity, while relegating the remnants of Old Mexico to the physical margins. Ostentatious government buildings, foreign businesses, new technologies, and rectangular blocks lined with houses of brick and adobe marked the barrio de arriba, which bled up the mountainside to the north, while scattered huts dominated the descending landscape of the barrio de abajo, where the roads simply did not go. The material wealth of the barrio de arriba was matched by an increasingly educated, professional, and white population, while the impoverished barrio de abajo was inhabited almost exclusively by illiterate indígenas, who worked the fields outside of town and spoke Zapotec as their preferred language. By separating the middle and upper classes from the poor and indigenous population, Porfirian urban planners hoped to preserve the modern aspects of city life for the gente bien, while containing the social degeneracy of the popular classes, and by registering, regulating, and monitoring them, gradually transforming them into modern citizens through the regime's distinct brand of redemptive discipline. On the eve of the Revolution, Juchitán stood as a symbol not only of modernity (with all of its disparities) but also of national redemption.

Between 1876 and 1911, under the authoritarian rule of Porfirio Díaz, Mexico lifted itself from the morass of political instability and economic depression that characterized its first fifty years as a nation, and achieved prolonged political stability and consistent economic growth. By building a strong, effective state, subsidized by foreign investment, the Pax Porfiriana was heralded as the end of Mexico's "age of chaos," when political outcomes were determined by force and endemic warfare and rebellion led the nation down the path of disintegration. Increasingly, Mexico's bourgeoisie blamed the nation's chronic instability on the imposition of imported concepts of natural rights and popular sovereignty—citizenship—in a society still predominantly governed by "premodern" forms of sociability: corporate loyalties, collective solidarities, personal relations, and dense webs of patronage. With the emergence of a strong, centralizing state, the fetish of material progress submerged that of citizenship, and faith in the state supplanted social unity as the key to national redemption. In place of "metaphysical" ideals, technocratic state builders offered order, administered by a progressive state and an enlightened elite who would gradually instill the poor and indigenous population with the civic virtue necessary to unlock their potential as autonomous individuals and rational, responsible citizens. Often, however, Porfirian state builders eschewed political modernization in the face of material progress, leaving the popular classes isolated, their "redemption" incomplete. This form of social order had critical implications for political development in Juchitán.

Economic development during the Porfiriato introduced unprecedented socioeconomic stratification and ethnic distinction to Juchitán, transforming the city's social and spatial structure. Rather than dissolve the corporate identities of Juchitán's barrio de abajo and inculcate its inhabitants in "modern" forms of sociability, social segregation and ethnic distinction actually collapsed and hardened "premodern," sub-local identities and solidarities, bound by ethnicity, class, and residential proximity, and reinforced personalist forms of sociability that "modernity" was supposed to supersede. During the Porfiriato, the gente bien of the barrio de arriba lived in a world apart from the gente de abajo, who established a "domain of sovereignty" separate from the material world of the gente bien and held together by a shared sense of alienation. The development of separate identities and political consciousnesses produced competing forms of cultural mediation: that based on solidarity with and the public articulation of the demands of the poor and indigenous majority, and that of regional power brokers, whose mediating position stemmed from their influence in political administration or control of economic resources. These competing forms of mediation were embodied in the formation of two informal political factions: the partido verde and the partido rojo. State patronage during the Porfiriato favored the latter, and the partido rojo dominated access to political authority and economic resources through an extensive network of personal and economic ties to the Díaz regime. As such, the *rojos* became the regime's primary agents of surveillance in Juchitán, and enforcers of the status quo, while the partido verde and its poor and indigenous constituents were proscribed from participation in public political life.

Ultimately, despite the Porfiristas' commitment to replacing traditional politics of personalism and patronage with rational administration, the Porfirian state remained dependent on informal networks of clientelage to maintain political order and prolonged peace. That it did so without resorting to mass violence was one of the regime's proudest achievements. Despite the lack of bloodshed, however, the Pax Porfiriana did not transcend the politics of force, at least not in Juchitán. The inequality between the partido rojo and the partido verde required the constant vigilance of the state's streamlined disciplinary apparatus. By augmenting the powers of state-appointed local authorities, the jefes políticos, and increasing the efficiency and coverage of the federal army, the Díaz regime maintained Juchitán's delicate political equilibrium, while bringing the region into its increasingly vast purview. While the bulk of the Pax Porfiriana passed in Juchitán without recourse to violence, it was still characterized by force without consent.

After Spanish Rule: The "Second Conquest" of the Isthmus?

After three centuries of colonial rule, independence from Spain left the formation of the Mexican state in the hands of a political elite deeply divided by economic and regional interests as well as political ideology. Of the two main coalitions, the centralists saw themselves as preservers of the colonial order and defended the system of corporate rights and privileges (*fueros*) for the church, the army, and indigenous villages established by the Spanish Crown. Their opposing coalition, the federalists, saw themselves as heirs of the insurgents who broke with the Crown, and sought to dismantle the corporate order by increasing participation in sovereignty and expanding individual rights. Over time a more coherent liberal program absorbed the federalist coalition and called for a full-scale repudiation of the colonial system, including the subordination of the church to the state, the abolition of corporate privileges, freedom of trade, and the "rationalization" of property held in common. The struggle between these two competing factions to determine who would control the direction of the nation's political and economic development engulfed the nation in fifty years of prolonged political instability and economic depression, as the state's expenditures grew to accommodate a swollen military budget at the same time constant warfare disrupted mineral and agricultural production in the countryside, reducing state revenues.

As federalist governments came to power in the provinces, liberal principles increasingly came to guide state-building projects, bringing the state into increased conflict with the indigenous pueblos. While Spanish colonials (and some conservatives) saw indigenous society, organized into far-flung, autarchic communities, as something to be overseen, the dominant liberal ideology of the mid-nineteenth century construed it as "something to be overcome."[2] In order to resolve the burgeoning "Indian problem," liberal state builders sought to transform indigenous villagers from protected wards of the state into autonomous individual citizens by removing the corporate privileges of the colonial *repúblicas de indios*, while increasing state revenues by selling off communal and unused resources to private citizens, who could take advantage of reduced trade restrictions to maximize production. This imposition of "equality" reduced the autonomy of the pueblos, integrated them into the state tax structure, and divested them of their communal landholdings while denying them usufruct access to natural resources, thereby representing what some historians have called a "second conquest" of indigenous Mexico.[3]

The history of Juchitán, and of Oaxaca in general, during the first fifty years of Independence tells a different story. While Oaxaca's liberal elite was surely interested in eliminating corporate identities and increasing the commercial exploitation of natural resources, it seems that the indigenous pueblos, particularly on the Isthmus, wielded considerable power vis-à-vis the weak Oaxacan state. As the conflict between liberals and conservatives extended to the Isthmus, the people of Juchitán took up arms in support of one or another of Mexico's warring factions to defend traditional forms of natural resource exploitation. The state's chronic economic shortfalls, limited enforcement apparatus, lack of transportation infrastructure, and constant need of the political and military support of the popular classes all combined to temper the "modernization" of the Isthmus and ensured a modicum of political and economic autonomy in the pueblos.[4] Nowhere on the Isthmus, nor in Oaxaca, was the response to encroaching liberalization more powerful than in Juchitán, where, despite the privatization of natural resources, there was little the state could do to abrogate communal patterns of resource allocation and exploitation in the face of armed collective action.

During the colonial period the Crown's protection of Indian lands and the fluctuating nature of the agricultural economy inhibited the development of haciendas and plantations on the Isthmus. Following the conquest of Mexico the Crown granted conquistador Hernán Cortés personal sovereignty over the Marquesado del Valle de Oaxaca, a massive network of livestock haciendas that encompassed the southern Isthmus of Tehuantepec. However, the demographic decline of the indigenous population due to foreign disease and fluctuations in the silver economy prevented sustained commercial development of the Marquesado and rendered large landholding on the Isthmus too risky. Moreover, the Crown granted indigenous communities legal title to their original lands and allowed them to receive additional land, and the Isthmus Zapotecs consistently used colonial courts to defend their land and labor rights. As a result, the Oaxacan elite shifted to a mercantile system of exploiting the indigenous populations—exporting the products of indigenous villages rather than monopolizing land and directly exploiting indigenous labor. Even as a boom in the international dye market increased the production and exportation of cochineal and indigo on the Isthmus in the mid-eighteenth century, it did not require the expropriation of indigenous land, but rather the seasonal and supplemental labor of indigenous villagers. By the end of the colonial period, indigenous communities continued to be, by far, the largest landowners on the Isthmus (and Oaxaca), and the

Spanish presence in the region remained low, particularly outside of the district cabecera, Tehuantepec.[5]

Independence from Spain brought to the Isthmus the first sustained threats to the economic base of the region's indigenous inhabitants. The first state constitution of Oaxaca called for the privatization of all natural resources within the state, challenging communal access to salt flats and pastures that the indigenous communities of the Isthmus had enjoyed "from time immemorial." Salt had always been a critical part of the Isthmus Zapotec diet, both as a condiment and a preservative, but by the late colonial period it had also become integral to the region's commercial economy, as Isthmus Zapotec villagers traded salt illegally to Guatemala in exchange for British and French textiles. In part to stem the tide of contraband trade, in 1825 the state government declared its intention to privatize the salt flats of the district of Tehuantepec (which, at the time, included Juchitán), ostensibly to put them in the hands of "an individual who would be able to exploit the salt more economically than the Indians." However, rather than sell to a private investor, in the early 1830s the state government monopolized profits from the salt deposits, adding approximately 25,000 pesos annually to its coffers. The state government's "centralization" of salt profits sparked resistance in Juchitán and drew the attention of the federal government, itself in desperate need of revenue. In 1843 the federal government contravened the state's monopoly and sold Juchitán's salt deposits to a powerful merchant from Veracruz, Francisco Javier Echeverría, for 250,000 pesos. The federal government's intervention did not sit well in Juchitán or in the state capital.[6]

Meanwhile, the Marquesado del Valle, now known as the Haciendas Marquesanas, was also changing hands, spurred by the drive to increase agricultural production and a major decline in the international dye market. The increased production of cochineal in Guatemala and indigo in India created a glut in the dye market, driving down international prices. With the collapse of the Isthmus's export economy the owner of the Marquesanas, the Duke of Monteleone, looked to sell his Oaxacan properties. In 1836, two Europeans, Frenchman Juan José

Guergué and Italian Esteban Maqueo, purchased the Marquesanas, intent on restoring them to profitability. However, they would quickly learn, as would Echeverría, that on the Isthmus purchasing property and asserting one's claim to it were two different things entirely.[7]

The privatization of natural resources sparked resistance from the indigenous population of the Isthmus, who defended their natural right to exploit the salt deposits and graze their livestock on the pastures of the Marquesanas, as they had under Spanish rule. Led by José Gregorio Meléndez, in 1834 the people of Juchitán joined Juan Álvarez's Plan de Texca—a widespread indigenous rebellion that stretched from the state of Guerrero to the Isthmus—and took up arms in rejection of the state government's appropriation of the salt flats. Meléndez, born in 1793 on a ranch just outside of Juchitán, had joined the insurgent army during the Wars of Independence and earned his stripes helping to defeat the Spanish royal army on the Isthmus. A mestizo of "dashing demeanor" with a "natural intuition," Meléndez parlayed his success in battle into a prosperous career as a rancher, and by 1834 he had become "the undisputed leader of the indigenous peoples of the Isthmus," to whom he was known as Che Gorio Melendre. While the rebellion of 1834 was short-lived and resulted in a brief jail stint for Meléndez, in its wake the villagers of Juchitán continued to illegally graze their livestock on Marquesana lands and extract salt without paying taxes on it, establishing a pattern of conflict with the region's landowners that would hold for years.[8]

In 1847, national political events transformed the pattern of low-intensity conflict in Juchitán into full-scale rebellion. In the midst of a U.S. military invasion in February, a group of conservatives in Mexico City, known derisively as *polkos*, rebelled against the federal government, protesting the state's efforts to build its war chest by appropriating church assets. In Oaxaca, the state's conservative coalition, led by the co-owner of the Marquesanas, Juan José Guergué, showed its support of the "Polko Rebellion" by toppling the liberal government of Oaxaca. Conservative control was short-lived, both in Mexico City and Oaxaca, where the conservative government quickly crumbled under pressure from liberal forces, including Meléndez in Juchitán. As the liberal faction seized control of the state government, culminating in the appointment of Benito Juárez as governor, the U.S. Army occupied the nation's capital, forcing the new governor into a defensive position. To defend the state's borders from foreign invasion, Juárez needed to ensure unity in the state, while at the same time increasing revenues in order to sustain a sizable militia. On the Isthmus Juárez found himself caught in the play of powerful local interests: Meléndez and his followers, whose defense of the liberal cause entitled them to continue exploiting salt and pasture; large commercial interests, led by Echeverría, who demanded the military support of the state in order to enforce their private property rights; and the still-powerful conservative faction, led by Guergué, which needed to be placated to ensure stability.[9]

In an attempt to balance these competing interests, Juárez named Meléndez head of the local garrison of the National Guard, appointed a conservative governor to the Isthmus, and requested from Echeverría that he sell his salt deposits to the state government. By placing the blame on Echeverría for "privileging his own interests to those of the community," while offering usufruct access to the salt flats to the inhabitants of Juchitán, Juárez moved to sacrifice Echeverría in favor of increasing state revenues and maintaining political stability. In offering usufruct access to the salt flats only after the conclusion of the harvest, Juárez sought not only to placate Meléndez and his supporters but also to defend the property rights of the owners of the Marquesanas, Guergué and Esteban Maqueo, the leader of Oaxaca's conservative coalition and a close family friend of Juárez's Italian wife, respectively. Despite Juárez's shrewdness, the plan failed. Echeverría refused to sell, Meléndez rejected his position as head of the National Guard, and after a few local skirmishes the people of Juchitán organized an armed movement that seized military control of the region, while calling for the separation of the Isthmus from the state of Oaxaca. For the next two years the people of Juchitán continued to ignore tax and property law to extract salt and graze livestock, much to the chagrin of the local elite, who loudly protested Juárez's preference for negotiation over force.¹⁰

In April 1850 Juárez finally capitulated to the demands of local landowners, sending four hundred federal soldiers to Juchitán to help enforce property laws. On May 18, after a small skirmish between Meléndez and Echeverría's personal guard left ten dead, Juárez ordered the army to occupy Juchitán. Facing resistance on the outskirts of town, the federal detachment dispersed Meléndez and his men, penetrating Juchitán and setting fire to its complex of straw huts. As the fire spread the army continued to pelt the town from its perimeter with cannon fire. The people evacuated the town as it smoldered behind them, and Meléndez and three hundred of his men took brief shelter in neighboring Chiapas. All told, the federal army burned down over one-third of the houses in Juchitán, killing sixty and injuring many more. Juárez infamously blamed the spread of the fire on the strong winds of the Isthmus.¹¹

Having tasted defeat, Meléndez returned from exile later that year with a new political strategy. In the face of the state government's recalcitrance, Meléndez understood that his only hope for survival was to make allies at a national level. Extra-local alliances would not only open up access to arms and ammunition but would lend his movement (already maligned as "criminal" and "seditious") an air of political legitimacy. With the spread of cholera in Oaxaca monopolizing the state government's funds and attention, Meléndez declared the Plan de 20 de Octubre, a sweeping political plan aimed at winning support in the nation's capital. The plan blended aspects of both liberal and conservative agendas, supporting a federalist government and free trade while defending the colonial fueros of the church, military, and indigenous pueblo. Later, Meléndez's movement added a critical element to its agenda: the separation of the Isthmus from the state of Oaxaca. While the plan initially rejected the centralist regime of President Mariano Arista, when conservative general Antonio López de Santa Anna returned from exile in 1852, Meléndez found a willing patron for his movement. In 1853 Meléndez seconded Santa Anna's conservative coup, reiterating his desire to secede from Oaxaca, and explicitly recognizing Santa Anna as the *jefe del ejército libertador*. In April, Santa Anna seized control of the federal government for the eleventh and final time, sending Juárez into exile and putting Meléndez in control of the Isthmus. On May 29 the federal government officially recognized the Isthmus of Tehuantepec as a federal territory, denying the state of Oaxaca one of its most productive economic regions and bringing a temporary end to the violence in Juchitán. Ironically, on the very night that the Meléndez rebellions reached their culmination, José Gregorio Meléndez died of poisoning, supposedly administered by the husband of one of his lovers.[12]

While some historians have represented the Meléndez rebellions as a foundational moment in the formation of Juchitán's distinct cultural identity—an ethnically unified defense of Zapotec culture in the face of outside encroachment—Francie Chassen-López has argued that this period of rebellion was rather a defense of a colonial, "pactist" interpretation of citizenship, germane to the nation's indigenous pueblos. Mexico's indigenous population broadly subscribed to a Spanish colonial model that interpreted society as a "social pact" between unequal sovereign corporations (rather than individuals), based on reciprocal obligation. During the colonial period the Crown generally recognized the sovereignty of the indigenous pueblos, so long as they met their tribute obligations. While this model held for centuries, it allowed little room for the centralization of authority, as new impositions generated new obligations, violating the sovereignty (or the moral economy) of the pueblos. With Independence and the ascent of liberal republicanism, the new Mexican state became increasingly intrusive in the political life of the pueblos, drawing resistance from the popular classes. In defense of a social contractual imaginary in which they served the nation and paid their taxes in exchange for a modicum of autonomy, indigenous pueblos withdrew their loyalty from the state and entered new pacts with entities that promised to protect their sovereignty—liberals or conservatives, federalists or centralists, local caciques or regional caudillos. This was the crux of the "Indian problem."[13]

In this sense the Meléndez rebellions were more typical than exceptional, representative of the myriad indigenous pueblos that took up arms against the centralizing state. The rebellions in Juchitán were not a unified, anti-capitalist defense of traditional values, nor did they strictly follow the logics of political partisanship or ideology: Meléndez and his supporters defended free trade and private property while actively aligning with both liberal and conservative factions, and did so in contention with local elites, often outsiders to the region. Moreover, the conflicts that generated constant instability and intermittent violence in Juchitán were the very same as those that plagued the nation at large: the elite factional conflict that resulted in the arming and mobilization of the popular classes; the conflict between the federal government, state governments, and municipalities over the location of sovereignty; the inability of the state to enforce its authority, exacerbated by constant economic shortfalls; the privatization of communal land and the prohibition of the customary forms of resource exploitation—all led to endemic violence and the proliferation of popular rebellions that tore at the seams of the nation in the first half of the nineteenth century, and all were exacerbated by the presence of an expansionist foreign power to the immediate north.

That is not to suggest that the mid-nineteenth-century rebellions in Juchitán had no lasting impact or were indistinguishable from other popular rebellions of the time. The Meléndez rebellions marked the beginning of a long tradition of istmeño separatism, born in mutual antagonism between Juchitán and the state government of Oaxaca. In collusion with the oligarchy of Oaxaca's central valley (the so-called Vallestocracia), the state government had begun to probe the economic fertility of the Isthmus, eyeing the region as a potential source of revenue. Yet Juchitán remained geographically isolated, culturally alienated, and economically aloof from Oaxaca's central valley, engendering jealousy in the state capital. For the next half century the cloud of separatism—both real and perceived—hovered closely over local politics, shading each side's interpretation of the other's motivations, often prompting the intervention of the federal government. If the Meléndez rebellions are proof of Juchitán's propensity for resistance—"the Juchitecan seed of revolt," as Miguel Covarrubias put it—this seed was sown not in the region's distinct ethnic identity but in its political and geographic relationship to the state capital.[14]

The Era of National Emergency: The Rise of Popular Liberalism

By midcentury the sense of humiliation at the disintegration of the national space following the war with the United States made Mexico's political elite acutely aware of its failure to sufficiently resolve the "Indian problem." Faced with foreign invasion, the indigenous pueblos remained apathetic or mobilized in defense of their own collective interests rather than the nation's, making clear that decades of applying liberal theory on the nation's periphery had failed to dissolve the corporate identities and ethnic divisions that defined colonial rule. Conservative ideology coalesced around the perceived inadequacy of the liberal republican principles that had guided the nation's early formation, intensifying political polarization and sending Mexico into ten years of civil war, first between liberals and conservatives in the wars of La Reforma, then between liberals and a conservative-French alliance during the French Intervention. In need of manpower to build an army capable of defeating conservative and interventionist challenges, national liberal leaders cast a wide net in constructing regional coalitions, making deals with groups whose vision of society was not wholly commensurate with, and sometimes directly contradictory to, national liberal policy. The necessities of national emergency resulted in a high period of "popular liberalism" in which national liberal leaders forged closer relationships than ever before with their poor and indigenous constituencies, and by doing so defeated the conservative and interventionist threat.[15]

The national liberal coalition was a loose network of regional political alliances that encompassed two distinct and often competing visions of the liberal project, broadly defined as "elite" and "popular" liberalism. According to Florencia Mallon, in those areas in which the intersection of regional and local interests and state apparatuses was controlled by landowners, merchants, and entrepreneurs, liberalism based on "the right to accumulate and invest capital without the restrictions represented by such neocolonial institutions as the Catholic Church or the Indian community" subordinated liberalism based on the expansion of citizenship rights. Here, the practice of political mobilization was generally exclusive and vertical, drawing on elite networks of clientelage to ensure popular support. In those areas where this intermediate space was controlled by irregular forces—National Guard and guerrilla units drawn from the popular classes— "liberalism represented the right of all individuals to citizenship—defined broadly as the just exercise of property rights, equitable access to resources and revenues, and the right to elect representatives and hold them accountable for their actions." Participation in irregular forces made all responsible for the defense of the national territory, regardless of class or ethnicity, reinforcing horizontal relations of reciprocal obligation and fostering among National Guardsmen and guerrillas a sense of entitlement—the right to have their demands recognized and met—based on their military service to the liberal cause. While these two forms of liberalism coexisted during the period of national emergency, the elite version of liberalism was always more compatible with national liberal policy.[16] Once the liberal faction had consolidated its victory, contradictions between the two liberalisms came to the surface, and liberal leaders sought to distance themselves from their popular contingents, and distance them from the political apparatus by falling in line with elite liberalism to repress the popular liberal impulse.

During the period of national emergency, Juchitán maintained an alliance with the national liberal coalition. In the wars of La Reforma, the French Intervention, and the Plan de la Noria the people of Juchitán mobilized irregular forces recruited from the popular classes against the enemies of the national liberal faction, and by 1872 they had established liberal authority on the Isthmus. Their armed support was critical to liberal victory on the Isthmus. National Guardsmen and guerrillas mobilized in exchange for the recognition and satisfaction of their collective demands—political independence from Tehuantepec, increased autonomy over public offices and funds, and equitable access to natural resources, such as salt and pasture. So complete was their dominance in combat that popular leaders drawn from the ranks of Juchitán's irregular forces continued to control local politics even after the expulsion of the French.

When civil war spread to the South with the wars of La Reforma, on the Isthmus it was difficult to disentangle political factionalism from ancient enmities. Liberal-conservative conflict on the Isthmus was filtered through the historical antagonism between Juchitán and Tehuantepec, giving way to full-scale intervillage warfare. Since pre-Columbian times, Juchitán had been a tributary village, subordinate to the cabecera of Tehuantepec, the regional seat of both Isthmus Zapotec and Spanish authority. As the state of Oaxaca reorganized its territory following Independence, Juchitán remained under the political jurisdiction of Tehuantepec, as a municipality in the district of Tehuantepec. As Juchitán grew in the first half of the nineteenth century, so did its resentment of Tehuantepec, which it came to regard as a hispanized holdover of colonial wealth, and to which it owed taxes and compulsory labor. When liberal General Juan Álvarez launched the revolution of Ayutla in 1854, Juchitán took up the liberal cause, at least in part to break the regional hegemony of Tehuantepec, a consistent bastion of conservative support. Led by Captain Pedro Gallegos, the National Guard of Juchitán rebelled against the conservative government of Santa Anna, launching a series of armed attacks against conservative forces stationed in Tehuantepec. After six months of pitched battle, Gallegos's National Guardsmen forced the surrender of the Isthmus's conservative government and seized control of Tehuantepec. As a reward, Benito Juárez reintegrated the Isthmus into the state of Oaxaca, only now with Juchitán as its own separate political district. While Juárez hoped that this repartition would bring peace to the region, fighting between Juchitán and Tehuantepec continued, though usually with lower intensity.[17]

Again in the 1860s, Juchitán mobilized irregular forces in support of the national liberal coalition, this time against the joint interventionist forces of the French and their conservative collaborators. In collusion with Mexican conservatives, the French imperial army invaded Mexico, occupying Mexico City in 1862, and driving the liberal republican government to the North. Two years later, when the interventionists captured Oaxaca City, Juchitán remained one of the few centers of republican support in the state, defending itself with one battalion of the regular army and six companies of guerrilla volunteers, the latter drawn from the lower rungs of Juchiteco society. Wearing traditional peasant garb in lieu of uniforms, volunteers received a small daily wage, usually paid in rations, outnumbered the regular army two to one (approximately 800 to 400), and were armed with spears, slings, and a consignment of two hundred machetes, paid for by the regular army. On September 5, 1866, the conservative government of Tehuantepec joined forces with the French, launching an invasion of Juchitán. The interventionist army briefly occupied Juchitán before a guerrilla counterattack forced them to retreat from town on the royal highway, which had been washed out by seasonal rains. Bogged down in the swamps of Juchitán, the interventionists abandoned their heavy artillery and guerrilla units descended, defeating them in mostly hand-to-hand combat. Still commemorated as a local holiday, the Battle of Juchitán, as it came to be known, set the stage for similar defeats throughout Oaxaca, sounding the death knell for the French imperial project. By early 1867 the French had fully withdrawn from Mexico, leaving the nation firmly in the hands of its liberal faction.[18]

Five years later, Juárez once again called on his allies in Juchitán to defend his liberal government from attack. Jilted after losing to Juárez in national elections for the second time, liberal general Porfirio Díaz denounced Juárez's reelection as fraudulent and called for a nationwide rebellion against the Juárez regime. The rebellion petered out before becoming a serious threat, but it did draw support from much of the military high command, who seized a few important cities. Nowhere was the rebellion more powerful than in

Díaz's home state of Oaxaca, where his brother Félix used the state militia to capture Oaxaca City and much of the surrounding Central Valley. Hoping to isolate pro-Díaz forces in the Central Valley, Juárez specifically requested the services of former guerrilla commander Albino Jiménez to reconvene his forces and secure the Isthmus for his government. Jiménez had established his reputation as a brave and dependable commander in over twenty years of combat, earning his Zapotec nickname, Binu Gada (Nine Lives), first alongside Meléndez, and later against the French, whom he fought in both the Battle of Puebla and the Battle of Juchitán. In the latter conflict he commanded two companies of Juchitán's guerrilla contingent, which were crucial to the defeat of the French. Now in exile in Chiapas, Binu Gada resurrected his guerrilla army and led them on an invasion of the Isthmus, wresting the region from Díaz's supporters with little resistance. Jiménez's dominance was so thorough that the governor of Chiapas reported that by January 1872 there was "no longer one enemy soldier on the Isthmus."[19]

The precise political nature of Juchitán's armed support of the liberal coalition is difficult to discern, though we get a general sense of its demands by looking at the concessions they won from national liberal leaders, especially Benito Juárez. Following their mobilization in support of the Plan de Ayutla, Juárez upgraded Juchitán's official status from pueblo to villa and officially recognized Juchitán as the cabecera of its own political district, the largest in the state. By removing it from the administrative and economic supervision of Tehuantepec, the state government of Oaxaca granted Juchitán increased political autonomy and independent access to tax revenues, explicitly "in consideration for the good services that the people of Juchitán have lent to the cause of liberty in the Revolution of Ayutla."[20] Ten years later, following the expulsion of the French, Juárez contravened the authority of Governor Félix Díaz by satisfying local petitions for usufruct access to the salt mines and grazing pastures. Finally, in 1872, after Jiménez's forces had eliminated the pro-Díaz threat on the Isthmus, Juárez himself arranged a meeting between Juchitán's guerrilla leaders and the new governor of Oaxaca, in which he granted the guerrilla leaders a virtual monopoly of public office in Juchitán and named Jiménez commander of two contingents of the local militia.[21]

In alliance with the national liberal coalition, "through blood and fire" the people of Juchitán won their political independence from Tehuantepec, autonomous control of public funds, communal access to natural resources, and the right to be governed by one of their own, selected more by the ability to mobilize people than by popular election. This was not necessarily exceptional: while many regions with similar social and economic conditions sided with conservatives in self-defense against the liberal assault on public lands, many other indigenous communities supported the liberal cause. These communities, not unlike Juchitán, developed "popular" forms of liberalism that were incorporated into the national liberal coalition, despite their tension with the core tenets of liberal doctrine. However, once war with the French was over, the contradictions between popular and elite versions of liberalism came to the surface. As liberals consolidated and centralized their authority in the nation, national-level liberals turned on their "popular" allies, demobilizing and even repressing irregular forces, and distancing popular liberal leaders from the political apparatus.[22] This would not be the case in Juchitán, where elite liberal discourses and centralizing political structures would not subordinate popular liberalism for another decade. Popular liberalism in Juchitán withstood the assault of national-level liberals after the war because of Juchitán's alliance with Benito Juárez, which, in turn, was based on the region's geography, which made it a particularly valuable political commodity.

By the mid-nineteenth century, Juchitán's enormous economic value remained speculative. Located on the narrow corridor of the Isthmus of Tehuantepec, Juchitán—the largest district in the state—figured prominently in Mexican development schemes as a key transportation hub. Both as a roadway connecting Mexico to Central America and as an interoceanic passageway, Juchitán and the Isthmus, more broadly, represented a potential wellspring of revenue for both private investors and the state. However, by the mid-nineteenth century, chronic instability, fiscal decline, and the devastation of war thwarted the development of the nation's transportation infrastructure, leaving the Isthmus's economic potential as yet unrealized. Even as the commercial economy of the Isthmus began to expand slowly after Independence, the region remained almost completely isolated from the state capital. This did not stop speculation in the region's wealth, presupposing the arrival of dependable roads and railroads.[23] As a result, liberal leaders and conservatives alike coveted the Isthmus as both a thoroughfare and a font of future wealth. This gave popular political leaders in Juchitán tremendous bargaining power in their dealings with the national liberal coalition.

Three factors, all related to the Isthmus's value as a political commodity, explain the relative strength and durability of popular liberalism in Juchitán. First of all, the nearby presence of Tehuantepec as a competing regional political and economic center, and a bastion of conservatism, was a critical determinant in Juchitán's alignment with the liberal coalition. For liberals, Juchitán represented the only counter to the economic strength and manpower of Tehuantepec. As a result, liberal leaders—most certainly Benito Juárez—were more flexible and even generous when dealing with Juchitán. On the flip side, Juchitán's historical subordination to Tehuantepec gave liberal leaders a powerful bargaining chip in mobilizing support in Juchitán: by offering to remove Juchitán from the administrative and economic jurisdiction of Tehuantepec, liberal leaders could concede some of Juchitán's demands for political autonomy and economic independence at practically no political cost. While publicly Juárez was "animated by the sincerest desire for the reestablishment of peace and to the reconciliation of ancient differences" between Juchitán and Tehuantepec, he also exploited the conflict to his benefit.[24] Second, given the region's isolation from the state capital and its tradition of separatism—the Isthmus was, after all, an independent federal territory from 1853 to 1856—Juchitán could use the threat of separation, on the one hand, to bring the state government to the table, and on the other, to unify its popular classes. Maintaining the Isthmus under the jurisdiction of the state government was a paramount political concern for Oaxaca's liberal politicians, who needed the region's revenues to finance their ongoing war effort. Even in times of peace, as the jefe político of Tehuantepec noted in 1872, the idea of separatism remained a threat "that could serve to mobilize rebels at any moment."[25]

Finally, by the third quarter of the nineteenth century, Juchitán had not experienced the level of social stratification necessary for the development of an elite version of liberalism strong enough to subordinate its more popular iterations. Despite the expansion of commercial livestock and an active salt trade, Juchitán did not have a large, ethnically distinct upper and middle class to occupy the intermediate position between state apparatuses and the poor, indigenous majority. That is not to suggest, however, that there were no conflicts in Juchitán, or that popular mobilization ruled in Juchitán by default. In 1870, conflicts emerged in Juchitán between regular and irregular forces over the demobilization of guerrilla units and the fixing of public office. In the wake of the French Intervention, regular army forces led by Colonel Marcos Matus decommissioned irregular forces, monopolizing political positions and freezing out and even persecuting irregular veterans. When a group of former guerrillas resisted, led by Albino Jiménez, Oaxacan governor Félix Díaz led a massive punitive expedition to occupy Juchitán. Díaz's expedition took on the character of a modern counter-insurgency campaign: federally commissioned forces burned down the houses of nonparticipants, pursued refugees into the surrounding forest, executed prisoners, and forced rebel leaders into exile. Critically, Díaz's punitive expedition was not without willing collaborators in Juchitán. According to Jiménez, the expedition's atrocities "were all carried out by Juchitecos themselves, and the governor tolerated it."[26] By 1870 an alliance between liberal governor, Félix Díaz, and former commanders of Juchitán's regular army contingent (the Zaragoza Battalion)—all veterans of the liberal Republican Army—had suppressed irregular forces and their collectivist program. However, owing to the necessities of popular support, the elite liberals' victory was short-lived. The following year, when Porfirio Díaz arose to challenge Juárez's election, Juárez called on the former guerrillas, now in exile in Chiapas, to shore up his support in Oaxaca. Afterward, it was Jiménez and his colleagues, all members of Juchitán's irregular, volunteer army, who would dominate politics in Juchitán. Elite liberals would have to wait a decade before economic development could produce a competing version of liberalism strong enough to subordinate Juchitán's popular liberal impulse.[27]

The Pax Porfiriana I: Economic Development

Between 1876 and 1910 Porfirio Díaz imposed the first stable and long-lasting government since Independence. The political stability of the Pax Porfiriana depended on the construction of a powerful and effective state, subsidized by consistent economic growth. The Díaz regime's economic strategy was predicated on the intertwined objectives of reducing exorbitant shipping costs by expanding the nation's transportation infrastructure and increasing state revenues by luring foreign capital. The regime was wildly successful on both counts. By the end of the century the Díaz regime had laid fourteen thousand kilometers of railroad tracks, and brought in $1.2 billion in foreign capital. The massive influx of capital allowed the state to increase its revenues without raising taxes, leading to an unprecedented annual growth rate of 8 percent, allowing Mexico to balance its budget for the first time and to improve its international credit rating. At the same time, the expansion of roads and railroads throughout the countryside triggered a boom in the export sector, primarily in mining and commercial agriculture. The proceeds from this new development, essentially, paid for sustained peace.[28]

The poor (and often indigenous) population of Mexico's rapidly transforming periphery paid the costs of economic modernization. The increased profitability of agricultural enterprise produced a regressive movement in the distribution of property as well as a sharp disparity between Mexico's export and domestic sectors. By reducing transportation costs and connecting previously isolated areas with distant markets, railroads made landownership more profitable than ever before, transforming land and labor into precious commodities. As a result, railroads ushered in an era of land concentration and increased labor exploitation, as the nation's largely indigenous rural municipalities lost their land base and were forced onto expanding estates.[29] Those areas unfit for export production languished in underdevelopment, untouched by the promise of technological improvement and financial windfall. Until recently, historians had long considered Oaxaca to be one of these areas "bypassed by the tides of modernization."[30] However, more contemporary studies of the region have revealed a more complex economic picture of Oaxaca in general and Juchitán specifically.[31]

Given its location on the narrow corridor of the Isthmus of Tehuantepec, Juchitán had long been the focal point for various trans-Isthmian transportation schemes. For centuries Europeans and Americans had coveted the region as the ideal place to connect the Atlantic and Pacific Oceans, but not until after Independence were they able to secure concessions from the Mexican government. Groups of speculators and investors visited the Isthmus at midcentury, but because of Mexico's instability they were able to do little more than open a road from Coatzalcoalcos (Veracruz) to Tehuantepec. By the 1860s foreign transportation schemes had bottomed out, but they would be reinvigorated in the coming decades under more stable conditions.[32]

By the end of the Porfiriato, two rail lines traversed the district of Juchitán: the Pan American Railway, which connected Mexico to Central America, and the Tehuantepec National Railway, which connected the Atlantic and Pacific Oceans from Veracruz to the port of Salina Cruz. The Pan American Railway was built between 1902 and 1904 on a concession to American investors, and Porfirio Díaz sat on its board of directors. Though not the most efficient track, it passed through multiple settlements in the district of Juchitán (including the city of Juchitán) and connected the district to Mexico City through its spurs. Construction of the Tehuantepec National Railway was financed by the British engineer and oil baron Weetman Pearson, whose plans also included the development of two port cities, Puerto México in Veracruz, and Salina Cruz in Oaxaca. Progress was tough, but despite setbacks the railroad was completed by 1907 and was inaugurated by Porfirio Díaz himself. In its first five months of operation, 123,000 tons of merchandise had traveled by land from the Gulf of Mexico to the Pacific Ocean, loaded and unloaded in two new, booming ports. Between the two lines, railroad stations sprang up in many of the settlements in the district of Juchitán, including Juchitán, Rincón Antonio, San Jerónimo, and Unión Hidalgo.[33]

As elsewhere in Mexico, the arrival of more efficient transportation to Oaxaca attracted foreign investment, which stimulated the growth of commercial agriculture and the privatization of public and communal lands. Laws against communal landholding had long been on the books in Oaxaca, but little had been done to divest communities of their holdings. The arrival of the railroads and foreign capital sped up the process of privatization by transforming previously marginal lands into commercially viable commodities. Primarily between 1889 and 1903 haciendas and plantations sprang up throughout Oaxaca, harvesting a variety of commercial crops. By 1910 Americans had invested more capital in Oaxaca than in all but four other states, and the number of haciendas in the state had jumped from 123 in 1874 to 450 in 1910. However, unlike other regions in Mexico, land concentration did not necessarily entail the displacement of the state's rural population or its transformation into a dependent labor force. Despite the steep increase in commercial estates, approximately 85 percent of the population of Oaxaca continued to live in free rural villages, and 92.3 percent of Oaxacan villages continued to own some communal land. Moreover, land tended to concentrate in the hands of small and medium-sized producers, rather than the massive *latifundias* that characterized other regions: only 10.7 percent of Oaxaca's commercial properties were larger than five thousand *hectares*. However, the effects of land concentration and foreign investment were not felt evenly throughout the state, and the district of Juchitán, in particular, became a regional center of export agriculture.[34]

Land speculation began in Juchitán long before it did elsewhere in the state, proceeding hand in hand with early transportation schemes. As early as 1857 land was appropriated in the district and auctioned off to the French consul on the Isthmus, Henry de Gyves. As development plans petered out so did interest in buying land. Weetman Pearson's purchase of the Tehuantepec National Railway in the 1890s renewed interest in the region, especially from American enterprises. Protecting the Isthmus as a vital zone for U.S. national security, American investors began buying up land in the region hoping to offset British transportation dominance, and in the process transformed the Isthmus into "Uncle Sam's district." American agricultural enterprises multiplied on the Isthmus, exporting sugar, coffee, and bananas and cultivating the largest orange groves in Mexico. Due in part to this increased interest, the district of Juchitán came to house the largest estates in Oaxaca, producing the widest variety of crops. Of the five properties of over 40,000 hectares in the state, four were in Juchitán. The Maqueo Castellanos family of Juchitán was the largest landowning family in Oaxaca, boasting the Sugar Mill of Santo Domingo (77,500 hectares) and the Hacienda La Venta (41,000 hectares). Juchitán was also the largest cattle-producing district in the state by far, an indication of the district's rapidly growing population.[35]

However, much like the rest of the state, expanding commercial agriculture did not displace a large number of rural villagers, nor did it convert them into a population of dependent laborers. This was due primarily to the large size and subsequently low population density of the district. Encompassing 11,133 square kilometers, despite the growing population, the district of Juchitán continued to be the state's most sparsely populated, with a population density of 5.8 people per square kilometer. As a result, while estate agriculture expanded, villages generally remained intact, a conclusion borne out by looking at agricultural labor relations. In 1907, 12,818 *jornaleros* worked in the district of Juchitán, the second most in the state. However, these jornaleros maintained their communal land base, worked seasonally, and had a great deal of leverage in labor negotiations; the average wage in Juchitán was seventy-five centavos per day, which was twenty-five centavos more than any other district in Oaxaca. Ultimately, Juchitán remained at its base a traditional peasant community, but one that had been transformed into a critical transportation hub and a regional economic center.[36]

The Pax Porfiriana II: The Politics of Patronage

Porfirio Díaz centralized power by dominating the national congress and engineered his own reelection five times, while maintaining internal stability and prolonged peace. In so doing, he faced the daunting task of transcending the endemic violence that haunted Mexico's post-Independence past. In the first fifty years after Independence, the popular classes began to participate increasingly in public politics, guided by corporate loyalties, personalist leaders, and networks of clientelage, and often with the effect of destabilizing the political order. Rather than electoral participation, direct action—mass demonstrations, street agitation, and rural rebellion—became the preferred mode for expressing popular opinion and effecting political change. To break the cycle of popular violence, Porfirian state builders aimed to reduce the importance of personal relations in politics and replace them with a technocratic state administered by an enlightened elite who could dispassionately manage the play of political interests in the name of the common good. Behind the mantra "order and progress," Porfirian liberals imposed stability by increasing the state's administrative and disciplinary capacity. Owing to the necessities of pacification, however, while the state's disciplinary and administrative apparatus swelled, so too did its dependence on traditional social networks to maintain political order. Contrary to Porfirian propaganda, administration did not replace, but actually augmented politics. While the regime could boast of unprecedented success in establishing and maintaining political order at the price of minimal bloodshed, the real strength of the Porfirian brand of so-called political modernization was built on state surveillance and traditional clientelist social networks.[37]

Faced with widespread instability, Porfirio Díaz undertook the wholesale restructuring of the state's military establishment. Despite reducing the number of active soldiers from thirty thousand to fourteen thousand, Díaz expanded the presence of the federal army throughout the countryside. With the help of his minister of war, Díaz reorganized the federal army into a comprehensive grid of military zones and *jefaturas de armas*, designed to maximize their coverage through the use of modern transportation and communication technologies, such as railroads and telegraph lines. The president determined the locations and troop allocations of the new command centers and took care to place federal garrisons and appoint military commanders in strategic trouble spots. Moreover, Díaz was committed to professionalizing and modernizing an army that had once been a source of national embarrassment. He allocated higher budgets for the army, approved higher pay for soldiers, and imported European arms, uniforms, and techniques, hoping to instill the army with a renewed pride, and loyalty to the *patria*. However, ever mindful of the dangers of a renegade army, Díaz also expanded the state's paramilitary apparatus, in part to counterbalance the growing strength of the federal army. The *rurales*, a national police force outside of the army's command structure, enjoyed a 90 percent increase in personnel and a 400 percent increase in federal funding during Díaz's first term in office. More often than not, it was the more effective rurales that Díaz called upon to contain disorder in the countryside. While the jury is still out on whether the new disciplinary apparatus actually reduced crime and banditry, by the 1880s its ubiquity and perceived effectiveness provided Mexico with the illusion of order at a time when such an illusion was at a premium. There can be little doubt, however, that the state's purview in the countryside had expanded, and with it the not-so-oblique threat of state violence.[38]

The extension of the state's long arm into the countryside generated discontent among powerful regional and local caciques, who resisted the state's muscling in on their territory. Díaz replaced those caciques who challenged his authority with loyalists, but allowed and even encouraged deposed caciques to enrich themselves by working as intermediaries for foreign investors looking to sink capital into their respective regions. Nonetheless, these caciques represented a potentially destabilizing influence. To balance their power, Díaz expanded the scope and powers of the jefatura política. The jefe político was a political boss, appointed to the cabecera of every political district by the state governors. The office was created by the Constitution of Cádiz in 1812 and modified by subsequent federal constitutions, but the regulation and appointment of the jefes políticos generally fell under the legal jurisdiction of the individual states, resulting in some variation in their powers from state to state. Nonetheless, two broad trends emerged during the Porfiriato. First, the appointment of jefes políticos became increasingly subjected to executive approval. While the president's intervention in the naming of local officials had begun under Juárez, Díaz routinely handpicked jefes políticos, and state governors generally took care to select candidates who would satisfy Díaz's criteria. Second, the powers of the jefes políticos were systematically expanded following the ratification of the Constitution of 1857, submerging the authority of existing local political institutions, such as the *ayuntamiento* (town council) and the municipal president. With the regime's increasing focus on law and order, during the Porfiriato the jefes políticos obtained nearly unlimited power in peripheral districts.[39]

The expansive powers of the jefes políticos were directly commensurate with the range of their duties, both formal and informal. The primary formal responsibilities of the jefes políticos were to oversee the day-to-day functioning of the ayuntamiento and other municipal councils, supervise elections on a local level, enforce building codes, and administer local police forces. Informally, the jefes políticos, over three hundred in all, became Díaz's eyes and ears on the ground, trusted to provide the president with reliable information on municipal affairs. They constituted the regime's most critical check on the power of local political machines, and as such they were expected to ensure the loyalty of municipal presidents and caciques while steering the outcomes of local elections and maintaining social order. Such power and responsibility, however, during a time of rapid economic development presented the jefes políticos with nearly endless opportunities for graft. In such cases, the real currency of the jefes políticos was the distribution of rewards and punishments, which they bartered in equal measures, often colluding with local political machines or building their own. Public funds, public works, and government concessions were all at the disposal of the jefe político, making him an indispensable tool for local power brokers, and allowing him to get rich in the process. On the other end of the spectrum, the jefes políticos' police powers were nearly unlimited, giving them the capacity to dole out punishments—jail time, fines, and manual labor—to all who crossed their path. The jefes políticos used their authority to advance their own interests and those of their allies, aloof from public opinion, but by and large remained loyal to the regime, helping to maintain stability.[40]

The stabilizing power of the Díaz regime was not invested solely in its formal disciplinary apparatus or local political officials, but depended greatly on informal networks of patronage, known as camarillas. Camarillas were networks of elites, bound by economic interest, friendship, and family, that permeated all levels of Mexican political life under Díaz. On a local level, camarillas constructed political machines by drawing both upward and downward on patron-client networks—using personal connections with high-level agents in the regime to ensure their control of political power and privileged access to growing economic resources, while exploiting paternalist authority or extended social and familial networks to maintain order and stability among the popular classes. As such, male heads of powerful families became the principal arbiters of social mobility in peripheral Mexico, capable of mobilizing both bread and stick to manipulate their followers and determine political outcomes. Dependent on the political favor of Díaz and his cabinet and consistent access to foreign capital, powerful regional and local camarillas became the most important enforcers of order, capable of absorbing middle- and lower-class discontent in their dense webs of patronage. For all his talk of modernization and the reduction of politics, Díaz's strength in the provinces depended on a decidedly "premodern" mode of politics. Camarilla political culture—the "ideology of hierarchy"—saturated Mexican society, replacing "metaphysical" principles and working hand in glove with the state's ubiquitous administrative apparatus, especially the jefes políticos.[41]

The investment of state power in the federal army, appointed officials, and elite patronage networks came at the expense of the poor and indigenous populations of the countryside, who had their local autonomy compromised and their municipal governments stripped of any real authority. Lacking vertical connections (save those of the patron-client variety), the rural masses either stifled their discontent, or funneled it through more formal (and less effective) channels, such as local elections. While the pacification of the anarchic countryside provided Porfirian ideologues with one of their proudest achievements, pacification did not equal "modernization," nor was it effected as seamlessly as the Porfirians would have us believe.[42]

The Pax Porfiriana did not happen overnight, nor was political authority so easily centralized that it did not require some recourse to mass violence. Between 1877 and 1884 the regime's attempts to consolidate political power combined with the rapid commercialization of the countryside to generate tremendous discontent in provincial Mexico. Díaz's initial strategy of political centralization focused on controlling states and villages by co-opting existing officials or imposing new ones who would collaborate unconditionally with the regime—a practice that proved effective but frequently had to be enacted at the end of a bayonet. Moreover, by increasing land prices, the coming of the railroads generated "the most widespread agrarian disturbances in nineteenth-century Mexico," as the rural poor resisted the negative consequences (especially land expropriation) that always accompanied the arrival of new tracks.[43]

In Juchitán a rebel movement coalesced in 1882 around the collective repudiation of the terms and effects of Porfirian political and economic development. As plans for an interoceanic railway began in earnest, local landowners, most notably the Maqueo Castellanos family, conspired with the jefe político to expand its control of the region's natural resources, at the expense of the popular classes, who resisted by organizing a protest movement led by Ignacio Nicolás. Known locally as Mexu Chele (Zapotec for Brave Blonde), Nicolás earned his reputation and his nickname as a guerrilla commander under Albino Jiménez, first in the Battle of Juchitán and again in 1871. Now, as then, Mexu Chele's movement represented the demands of Juchitán's poor and indigenous majority, protesting the arrival of the railroad, the obstruction of communal access to natural resources, and the abuses of a jefe político unresponsive to popular opinion. Failing to gain redress for their demands, on August 9 Nicolás and a small group of allies organized a short revolt, killing the municipal president and a few local notables, including the parish priest.[44]

The jefe político of Juchitán, Francisco León, responded by organizing a punitive expedition of about three thousand men, composed of volunteers from Juchitán and the Seventeenth Battalion of the federal army, while Nicolás and his followers took up positions on the outskirts of town. For the next two months the two armies remained deadlocked, with the federal forces occupying the city center and the rebels dominating the countryside. This stalemate persisted, despite the influx of two more detachments of the federal army, which swelled the ranks of the federal forces to as many as eleven thousand soldiers. To break the stalemate, León ordered all of the livestock from nearby ranches (sparing those of his allies) relocated to a corral in town, where it would be used exclusively to feed the soldiers quartered there, and forcibly relocated the wives and mothers of suspected rebels to San Miguel Chimalapa, leaving behind their children and the elderly. Shortly thereafter, starving and fearing for the safety and well-being of their families, rebels began returning to Juchitán. Upon surrender, León's conditions of amnesty were steep: rebels were required to turn in a rifle upon their surrender or pay a fine of one hundred pesos (the cost of a new rifle).

If they could do neither (most could not), they were forced to work off their debt, toiling in public works. Mexu Chele himself retired to Veracruz, where he lived the rest of his days.[45]

The punitive expedition of 1882 signaled the end of popular liberalism as a public force in the shaping of politics in Juchitán. With the unflagging support of the federal government, elite liberals interested in expanding their investments used the expedition to consolidate their influence over the region and conjure popular, collectivist articulations of liberalism from the public sphere. For the remainder of the Porfiriato, politics in Juchitán would be contested between two rival factions, the partido rojo and the partido verde. The use of red and green in local politics dated back to the wars of La Reforma, when it marked liberal and conservative factions, respectively, but by 1876 the color red had been appropriated by the local pro-Díaz faction. As Díaz consolidated his authority, Mexu Chele and his supporters took to wearing green as an indicator of their opposition to the regime, rather than as an ideological marker of conservatism. The colors stuck, and in the wake of the punitive expedition the partido rojo established itself as the dominant local camarilla, excluding the partido verde from public politics. While the partido verde ceased to function as a public political entity, the deep-seated animosity of political factionalism simmered just below the surface of Porfirian peace. While Juchitán remained relatively tranquil for the remainder of the Porfiriato, the submerged political identities of 1882 resurfaced with the arrival of the Revolution.[46]

By subordinating popular forms of liberalism to more elite interpretations, the punitive expedition of 1882 completed the task left incomplete by Félix Díaz in 1870. The success of the 1882 punitive expedition can be explained by two related factors. First, national emergencies were a necessary condition for the emergence and relative success of popular liberal movements. Unlike Juárez in 1871, once Díaz had consolidated his power he did not face any national-level challenges to his authority, and thus did not need to align his regime with popular, regional political movements to defeat political opponents. Second, the pending arrival of the railroad inflated the economic ramifications of political conflict on the Isthmus, ensuring the federal government's alignment with nominally liberal landowners, merchants, and entrepreneurs over grassroots political movements. In the name of material progress, the Díaz regime was committed to providing international investors and local elites with the order and stability necessary to facilitate the accumulation and investment of capital. The punitive expedition of 1882 provided local elites with the muscle necessary to consolidate their authority and impose social order. When the expedition withdrew, they left behind a permanent garrison of about five hundred federal soldiers in Juchitán, relocated the Ninth Military Zone to nearby San Jerónimo, transforming it into "one of the biggest garrison towns in Porfirian Mexico," and granted Francisco León nearly unlimited power as the jefe político of Juchitán. A distinguished businessman, schoolteacher, and veteran, León had a reputation as an energetic and stern boss. With a massive pool of unpaid labor at his disposal, it was he whom Díaz entrusted to oversee the modernization of Juchitán.[47]

A Tale of Two Cities I: The *Barrio de Arriba* and the *Barrio de Abajo*

During the Porfiriato, cities became "monuments of progress" and veneers of modernity. Fueled by economic development and increasing mobility, rural populations migrated to more prosperous areas, and urban centers sprang up throughout the countryside, becoming crucial links between the center and the periphery. As such, provincial and peripheral cities were organized (or reorganized) to reflect a growing developmentalist ethos, promoted by the burgeoning middle class. Urban space was reordered to showcase the hallmarks of Porfirian modernity, while relegating to the margins the remnants of Old Mexico. By separating the so-called gente bien from the poor and indigenous populations, the Porfirian middle class hoped to preserve the modern aspects of city life for themselves while containing the social degeneracy of the popular classes and gradually transforming them into modern citizens. In this respect, by the 1890s Juchitán had become something of a model Porfirian city: the city center had been transformed to reflect ideal modernity, while the city's southern margins became a reservoir for traditional Mexico. However, rather than strip the poor and indigenous population of the southern barrio de abajo of its corporate identities and inculcate them in modern forms of sociability, social segregation and cultural distinction actually reinforced and even compounded "premodern" identities of class and ethnicity, and their social and political forms.

Unencumbered by chronic instability and spurred by a modest increase in the standard of living, the population of Mexico ballooned during the Porfiriato. From 1877 to 1895 the annual mean of population growth more than doubled, from 0.7 percent to 1.6 percent, and by 1910 the total population had grown from nearly ten million at the start of the Porfiriato to over fifteen million. The population increase, economic growth, and the new mobility afforded by improved transportation led to rapid urbanization. While the old cities of the nation's center grew at a consistent pace, provincial cities experienced a population boom, growing by 88 percent over the course of the Porfiriato, and new urban centers sprang up on the periphery, usually following the rail lines. These peripheral and provincial cities came to represent the experience of modernity for the majority of Mexicans, nearly three-quarters of whom continued to live in rural pueblos and, as such, were organized to represent an inverse reflection of rural life. In short, peripheral cities were meant to represent that which the countryside was not, and in so doing, provide their rural correlates with a model of modernity.[48]

As new cities emerged on the periphery, city people began to imbibe a new, developmentalist ethos. Developmentalism stressed hard work and moral rectitude, providing incipient capitalism with an ideological justification while explicitly fetishizing modernity. The protagonists for this new ethos were the old elite and the "new people" of the Porfiriato—educated people who worked their way into the middle class through the expanding bureaucracy and new business opportunities in the export sector. Upwardly mobile members of the new bourgeoisie identified themselves with the gente bien and sought to separate themselves from the uneducated and uncultured lower classes (especially Indians). As a result they produced a number of new forms for ordering Mexican society in a manner best suited for achieving modernity (in distinctly capitalist terms): the inculcation of a new time discipline, a renewed emphasis on female domesticity, and most importantly for this study, a new organization of urban space. The gente bien throughout Mexico "staged" modernity through urban planning, building and renovating city centers with spectacular and ostentatious architecture, public parks and gardens, government buildings reflecting a vibrant civic culture, and new roads organized along a linear grid, reflecting their emphasis on visual order and the efficient use of time and space. The city center was to be preserved for the gente bien, and all those who did not fit the description were to be removed. By passing new laws regulating the use of public space, city planners rid the central precincts of "degenerate" populations, especially the poor and Indians, and relocated them to the physical margins of Mexico's cities.[49]

Relegated to particular wards, the poor could be identified and regulated, registered by the census, and subjected to the Porfirian brand of redemptive discipline. In theory, their vices would be moderated, they would be disciplined through public education, and taught to read and write (in Spanish); they would be inculcated with civic virtue, and transformed into modern citizens—hardworking, autonomous individuals, willing to sacrifice personal (or corporate) interest to the common good, and no longer bound by personal relations, outdated notions of honor, and collective loyalties. Once transformed into virtuous citizens, they could be integrated into society and legally enfranchised.[50] In reality, however, redemption was slow in coming, the institutions of indoctrination often nonexistent, and the commitment of the gente bien to redeeming the socially degenerate wanting. In the meantime, segregation and discipline took precedence over integration and participation, reinforcing the cultural isolation of the nation's poor.

In Oaxaca, the annual rate of population growth was slightly lower than the national average. By the end of the Porfiriato the state claimed over one million inhabitants, up from 761,000 in 1885. Population growth spiked in areas with intense economic development, especially along the railways, and urban centers and networks emerged throughout the state. None grew larger than the Isthmus, where the population of Juchitán swelled to over ten thousand early in the Porfiriato and reached nearly fourteen thousand by 1910. Combined with neighboring Tehuantepec, the population of the istmeño urban network rivaled that of Oaxaca City. In the 1880s, Juchitán embarked on a project of urban development, guided by the firm and steady hand of Francisco León. Mobilizing a massive pool of pressed labor, León supervised the building of nine new roads, connecting Juchitán to the surrounding municipalities; the extension of modern technologies to Juchitán, including electricity and telegraph and telephone lines; and the architectural renovation of the city center, highlighted by the construction of an opulent municipal palace. The building of the new municipal palace—Juchitán's first "modern" building—illustrates the ethos that informed urban planning.[51]

Construction on the palace began on May 26, 1882, based on plans drawn up by Italian architect Esteban Cioti. The manual labor was provided by the rebels of Ignacio Nicolás, who as part of their amnesty agreement were forced to work off a hundred-peso fine doing construction. Raw materials and skilled labor had to be imported, as up to that point all the buildings in Juchitán were made of mud, straw, and cane, with a palm roof, and thus there were no masons or carpenters who knew how to make brick and adobe, or work with wood. After a year and a half of toil, the massive new palace was inaugurated on October 14, 1883. Running north-south to cut the winds that whipped through town, the new palace took up 1,520 square meters in the center of town, running 102 meters from north to south, facing the central plaza. Once inaugurated, the municipal palace became the center of municipal life, housing a bustling market on the ground floor and all government offices on the second floor (the treasury, police station, circuit court, and civil registry). The following year, Juchitán's first public clock was installed on the palace's flag tower, a reminder of the new time discipline. From this point forward, as the city's renovation proceeded, all buildings in the center of town would be built in this new "modern" image.[52]

Another important function of the municipal palace was to informally divide the city into two halves, the north and the south. The north side of town, situated on higher ground, included the central precincts and became known as the barrio de arriba, while the south side, which descended into the lagoons that bordered the city, became known as the barrio de abajo. This division, which brought together almost perfectly the socioeconomic and ethnic axes of distinction, was codified in the city's spatial grid in December 1889, when Juchitán was officially recognized as a city. The city was divided into nine numbered *secciones* (wards), beginning in the north and moving south, most with their own nicknames based on occupational patterns or ethnic composition. The first, northernmost ward was the wild cherry ward, as the majority of the young women of this neighborhood would travel to the mountains to collect wild cherries to sell in the market. The second ward was the iguana ward, because the women sold iguanas, both live and cooked, in the central market. The third and fourth wards, the most centrally located, accommodated the "gentes pensantes" of the upper and middle classes in homes of brick and adobe on clean, well-lit streets conveniently located near the municipal palace, the market, and a spate of new shops. The barrio de abajo began with the fifth ward, known for its bright green coloring due to the abundance of lime trees (and its support of the partido verde). The seventh ward (*la séptima*) was called the loincloth ward—a comment on the attire of the neighborhood men and a clear marker of their ethnicity. The eighth ward, known as Cheguigo, was held in similar regard to the seventh, and both ran along the banks of the symbol of their marginality, the usually dormant Río de los Perros—so named for the volume of dead dogs left behind on the riverbed after heavy rains. The population of the ninth and final ward, El Cerrito, was split between the city and a ranch of the same name. Together, the southern wards provided a stark contrast to the center of town, as noted by Juán Sánchez: "The barrio de abajo has no streets, they live like a tribe and all of the houses are very primitive palm huts."[53]

A detailed analysis of the 1890 census paints a vivid picture of internal distinction in Juchitán. Ethnic distinction was already mapped on to the city's spatial grid a decade into Porfirian rule. In the census, 5.7 percent of Juchitán's population was classified as white, and 87.0 percent as indigenous. However, an examination of table 1 shows that all four of the city's northern wards were less than 87.0 percent indigenous, while the first and the third wards were more than one-quarter white and mestizo. While the first and fourth wards both had nearly double the average white population of Juchitán, the third ward was a full 23.8 percent white. In all, 86.0 percent of Juchitán's white population lived north of the municipal palace, with 63.0 percent located just in the two central wards. On the other hand, all five of the city's southern wards were over 87.0 percent indigenous, with 98.5 percent of those in the three southernmost wards classified as indigenous and with less than 1 percent of the population characterized as white. The white areas of town tended to be the most "cosmopolitan" areas as well. As table 2 shows, migration to Juchitán both from other districts in the state, and from outside of Oaxaca, was much more prominent in the northern and especially the central wards. In fact, migration into the southern wards was almost nonexistent, with nearly 100 percent of the south side's population in 1890 having been born in Juchitán. Ethnicity was mapped onto Juchitán in a manner commensurate with the developmentalist ethos, with the white population in the city center and the indigenous population on the margins.

A Tale of Two Cities 61

Table 1. Ethnic classification in Juchitán

Ward	Total population	White population	Percentage white population	Mestizo population	Percentage mestizo population	Indigenous population	Percentage indigenous population
First	1,162	106	9.1	263	22.6	793	68.2
Second	785	8	1.0	117	14.9	660	84.0
Third	751	179	23.8	24	3.2	548	73.0
Fourth	1,365	138	10.1	62	4.5	1,165	85.3
Fifth	1,258	27	2.1	84	6.7	1,147	91.2
Sixth	980	25	2.6	74	7.6	881	89.9
Seventh	1,214	9	0.7	7	0.6	1,198	98.7
Eighth	906	10	1.1	12	1.3	884	97.6
Ninth	392	0	0.0	0	0.0	392	100.0
Total	8,813	502	5.7	643	7.3	7,668	87.0

Source: Archivo General del Poder Ejecutivo de Oaxaca, Censos y Padrones, Distrito: Juchitán, 1890, legajo 1, expediente 1.

Table 2. Outside-born population in Juchitán

Ward	Population born in another district in Oaxaca	Population born outside Oaxaca
First	46	5
Second	25	7
Third	43	23
Fourth	44	19
Fifth	39	9
Sixth	19	3
Seventh	12	0
Eighth	2	1
Ninth	0	0
Total	230	67

Source: Archivo General del Poder Ejecutivo de Oaxaca, Censos y Padrones, Distrito: Juchitán, 1890, legajo 1, expediente 1.

Table 3. Education in Juchitán

Ward	Read only	Read and write	Some education	Percentage with some education	Primarily Castellano speakers	Percentage of primarily Castellano speakers
First	58	85	143	12.3	70	6.0
Second	42	44	86	10.9	45	5.7
Third	35	101	136	18.1	96	12.8
Fourth	75	121	196	14.3	95	6.9
Fifth	22	45	67	5.3	69	5.5
Sixth	20	63	83	8.5	2	0.2
Seventh	4	12	16	1.3	0	0.0
Eighth	12	16	28	3.1	5	0.6
Ninth	16	9	25	6.4	0	0.0
Total	284	496	780	8.9	382	4.3

Source: Archivo General del Poder Ejecutivo de Oaxaca, Censos y Padrones, Distrito: Juchitán, 1890, legajo 1, expediente 1.

The map of ethnic distinction in Juchitán corresponded perfectly with that of literacy and education. Juan Sánchez observed in 1911 that "all of the thinking people live in [the barrio de arriba], [where] almost everyone knows how to read and write," but in the barrio de abajo "the majority are illiterate, resistant to all progress."[54] The hyperbole and cultural subjectivity of this observation notwithstanding, the basic distinction was already borne out by the 1890 census. The literacy rate in Juchitán was about one-third the national average—5.6 percent of the population was fully literate, and 8.8 percent could at least read. However, these numbers fluctuated greatly between the neighborhoods. As table 3 shows, in each of the northern four wards of the city more than 10 percent of the population had some education, with the third ward leading the way with 18.1 percent of the population being minimally literate—over double Juchitán's average. On the other hand, all of the southern five wards were under the local average. The seventh ward had only 16 semi-literate people out of a population of 1,214. Unsurprisingly, higher literacy rates were directly correlated with the Spanish-speaking population. According to the census, only 4.3 percent of the population of Juchitán was classified as primarily "Castellano" speakers in 1890, spiking in the north and tapering in the south. In fact, in the southern four wards only seven of over three thousand inhabitants were classified as Spanish speakers.

An examination of employment patterns in Juchitán suggests that socioeconomic status corresponded with ethnic status and literacy. By 1890, 162 people classified as "professionals" lived in Juchitán, the majority of whom were state employees (33.3 percent), merchants (27.2 percent), and musicians (17.3 percent). As table 4 shows, professionals were concentrated in the wards of the barrio de arriba, all of which demonstrate an above-average percentage of professionals. All told, 81.5 percent of Juchitán's professionals lived in the barrio de arriba. Not surprisingly, the third ward, the whitest and most educated of Juchitán, defined 10.5 percent of its working population as professionals—over double the city's average. Conversely, the five southern wards of Juchitán all registered well under the local 4.0 percent average for professionals, with under 1 percent of the working population in the seventh, eighth, and ninth wards defined as professional. A brief survey of local administration indicates that while the third and fourth wards housed thirty-three state employees alone, the four southernmost wards had five state employees combined. Agricultural labor exhibits similar patterns, though not in such exaggerated form—37.9 percent of Juchitán's working population was classified as "agricultural laborers" (a vast majority *labradores*, with a minority of jornaleros),[55] but this number is significantly lower in the third and fourth wards, where about one-quarter of the population were cultivators. All five of the southern wards exceeded the local average, with the fifth and sixth wards peaking at around or over half the population.

While the distribution of Juchitán's professional and agricultural workers reflects the ethnic and educational grid nearly perfectly, mapping out the artisan and industrial population is a little more complicated. Fifty-eight percent of Juchitán's working population engaged in arts, industry, and manufacturing, and with the exception of the fifth and sixth wards, there seems to be little variation. According to table 4, the whiter central wards show a slightly higher percentage of industrial laborers, but the indigenous southern wards are less than ten percentage points lower. However, not all industrial work was regarded equally. Upon closer inspection, table 5 demonstrates that a vast majority of the seventh, eighth, and ninth wards' industrial workforce were women, engaged in the production of foodstuffs (78.7, 68.1, and 80.7 percent, respectively; more than double the ratio of the central and northern wards). On the hierarchy of industrial labor, *tortilleras* and *molenderas* occupied the bottom rung, and the vast majority were the wives of agricultural laborers. In fact, the occupational standard in the seventh, eighth, and ninth wards was that the paterfamilias (officially classified as *jefe*) worked in the fields and his wife made tortillas, reflecting the prevalence of the traditional peasant household. This was not at all the case in the central and northern wards.

Table 4. Employment in Juchitán

Ward	Total working population	Professionals	Percentage of working population	Agricultural laborers	Percentage of working population	Art, industry, and commerce	Percentage of working population
First	558	34	6.1	177	31.7	347	62.1
Second	304	12	3.9	133	43.8	159	52.3
Third	370	39	10.5	93	25.1	238	64.3
Fourth	723	47	6.5	201	27.8	475	65.6
Fifth	495	13	2.9	242	48.9	240	48.5
Sixth	334	9	2.7	176	52.7	149	44.6
Seventh	564	3	0.5	228	40.4	333	59.0
Eighth	506	4	0.8	201	39.7	301	59.4
Ninth	193	1	0.5	83	43.0	109	56.5
Total	4,047	162	4.0	1,534	37.9	2,351	58.1

Source: Archivo General del Poder Ejecutivo de Oaxaca, Censos y Padrones, Distrito: Juchitán, 1890, legajo 1, expediente 1.

Table 5. Industrial employment in Juchitán

Ward	Population employed in arts, industry, and manufacturing (AIM)	AIM workers in food production (tortilleras and molenderas)	Percentage of total working population	Percentage of AIM workers
First	347	32	5.7	9.2
Second	159	29	9.6	18.2
Third	238	77	20.8	32.4
Fourth	475	225	31.1	47.3
Fifth	240	71	14.3	29.6
Sixth	149	69	20.7	46.3
Seventh	333	262	46.5	78.7
Eighth	301	205	40.5	68.1
Ninth	109	88	45.6	80.7
Total	2,351	1,058	26.1	45.0

Source: Archivo General del Poder Ejecutivo de Oaxaca, Censos y Padrones, Distrito: Juchitán, 1890, legajo 1, expediente 1.

Census data make clear that the rise of class society did not dissolve caste society in Juchitán, but incorporated it into a bipolar image of society, reflected in the city's spatial grid: new linear streets, lined with houses of brick and adobe stood next to chaotically arranged thatched-roof huts, made of mud and stick; and whiter, educated, Spanish-speaking gente bien were encompassed by the poor, illiterate, Zapotec-speaking masses for whom they were supposed to serve as a social and cultural model. Wealth and whiteness remained in homeostasis, as did poverty and Indianness, not despite, but because of, the consolidation of liberalism as the dominant ideology; or at least the consolidation of a particular, Porfirian version.[56] Justified by positivist social science and informed by the developmentalist vogue, disparity was built into the fabric of the "modern" peripheral city, as modeled by Juchitán: a visually ordered and structurally stable center reflected a growing civil society; a burgeoning educated middle class populated the center and fueled its continued growth; and a poor, uneducated, indigenous population disappeared to the margins, both literally and figuratively. These disparities were not without real political consequences. Rather than encourage slow assimilation, residential segregation compounded overlapping, sublocal identities of class, ethnicity, and simple proximity and implied competing modes of cultural mediation for Juchitán's distinct and divided populations.

A Tale of Two Cities II: The *Partido Rojo* and the *Partido Verde*

Internal distinction and social segregation in Juchitán made possible distinct and competing forms of cultural mediation: the mediation of local "intellectuals," based on solidarity with and the public articulation of the demands of the poor and indigenous majority, and that of regional power brokers, whose prestige and authority stemmed from their influence in political administration and the control of economic resources. While both types of mediators were trapped in the dialectic of concern for local issues and interest in the prestige derived from engaging in broader national and regional debates, local intellectuals articulated community interests and demands in broader political arenas, while those brokers engaged in broader debates tended to function primarily as agents of surveillance and discipline for national and regional power blocs. While local intellectuals drew prestige and legitimacy from local sources, the primary role of the power broker was, according to Florencia Mallon, to enforce "more dominant forms of political culture."[57] In Juchitán, two competing "parties" (really just informal factions), the partido rojo and the partido verde, came to represent the dichotomy between surveillance and solidarity, respectively. Rooted in the punitive expedition of 1882, the differences between the rojos and the verdes were cemented in Juchitán's spatial division: "For a long time the people of Juchitán have been divided into two factions or parties: the party of the barrio de arriba and the party of the barrio de abajo." During the Porfiriato, state patronage favored the rojos, "whose partido," continued Juan Sánchez, "supported by don Rosendo Pineda, has always dominated public affairs," while excluding the partido verde from participation in public politics.[58]

The local prestige of the leaders of the partido rojo depended on their connections to regional and national power blocs, for whom local rojos functioned primarily as surveillance agents—enforcers of the dominant political culture and defenders of the status quo. Specifically, access to political office and economic resources in Juchitán was brokered by Rosendo Pineda and Rosalino Martínez, two sons of Juchitán who had managed to gain entrance into Porfirio Díaz's inner circle. As one Juchiteco noted, "in those days Porfirio Díaz governed together with Rosalino Martínez and Rosendo Pineda, both *tecos*."[59] Pineda and Martínez were beneficiaries of a scholarship program set up by Díaz to reward a select few children from Juchitán with an education in exchange for Juchitán's service against the French.[60]

Rosendo Pineda took advantage of the opportunity by studying law at Oaxaca's prestigious Instituto de Ciencias y Artes del Estado (ICA). Under the tutelage of Porfirio Díaz's brother Félix, Pineda distinguished himself as a poet, public speaker, and lawyer. In 1885 he became the federal deputy for Juchitán, where he would stay for the remainder of the Porfiriato. Shortly after assuming his post, Pineda became the private secretary and "political protégé" of Porfirio Díaz's father-in-law and minister of the interior, Manuel Romero Rubio.[61] Romero Rubio was the patron and mentor of the powerful circle of technocrats and financiers known as the *científicos*, who came to be the nation's dominant political camarilla under Díaz. From Romero Rubio, Pineda not only gained nearly unlimited political power but also "learned political intrigue," a skill he put to frequent use in Juchitán. According to historian Gonzalo Jiménez López, Pineda "was always concerned about having political control on the Isthmus of Tehuantepec, making sure that his friends occupied the government of the state, as unconditional supporters of the dictatorship in Juchitán."[62] After Romero Rubio's sudden death in 1895, Pineda assumed a leadership role among the científicos, becoming the most powerful and influential of Díaz's loyal Oaxacan acolytes.

For his part, Rosalino Martínez used his scholarship to study at the Colegio Militar in Mexico City. Martínez distinguished himself in battle against the Maya in Yucatán, and later in the repression of the textile workers' strike in Río Blanco. As a reward for his service in the latter, in 1907 Martínez was awarded the position of undersecretary of war. Like Pineda, Martínez used his influence to secure offices in Juchitán for his friends and relatives. Most notably, Martínez's brother-in-law, Mariano Saynes, served several terms as Juchitán's jefe político and municipal president.[63] Between Pineda and Martínez, the partido rojo had the political patronage of both powerful subgroups of the Díaz regime, the científicos and the military.

Locally, the partido rojo took advantage of their connections within the Porfirian administration to dominate land, commerce, politics, and the army. At the top of the local hierarchy sat the Maqueo Castellanos family. The Maqueos were wealthy landowners who had presided over the bulk of commercial agricultural development on the Isthmus since 1836, when family patriarch Esteban Maqueo migrated from Milan, Italy, and purchased the extensive Haciendas Marquesanas. Since taking over in 1836, the Maqueos had come into constant conflict with the growing populations of the neighboring villages, becoming the primary target of popular discontent. Throughout the nineteenth century the Maqueo Castellanos family defended its holdings against squatters and insurgents, and during the Porfiriato it used its relationships with Porfirio Díaz and Rosendo Pineda to expand its fortunes and consolidate its regional power. While Matilde Castellanos was the legal owner of the family's haciendas (and the largest landowner in Oaxaca), her two sons, Esteban and José, both baptized godsons of Porfirio Díaz, controlled the family business from Mexico City. Esteban Maqueo Castellanos, the most powerful member of the family, graduated with a law degree from the ICA in 1897 and quickly climbed the political ladder. After spending time as the jefe político of Juchitán, he served as a judge in Sonora and Chihuahua, and within a few years was named to the Supreme Court of Mexico. Maqueo Castellanos was an avowed científico, and his interpretation of Mexican social conditions reflected the influence of social Darwinism on the sociological worldview of many of his positivist colleagues, especially in Oaxaca. In his essay *Algunos problemas nacionales*, Maqueo Castellanos represented the nation's indigenous population as a degraded, inherently backward "obstacle to progress" that could be overcome only by the mass influx of European immigrants. His belief that Indians were good only for "carrying a rifle in war, paying taxes, and sowing someone else's land" provided him and his family with ideological justification for their immense financial success (and for, allegedly, lowballing their farmhands).[64]

Much of the economic power in Juchitán trickled down from the Maqueo Castellanos family through a series of merchants and paid collaborators who, together, comprised the bulk of the expansive camarilla roja. Local merchants connected to the Maqueo Castellanos family and Rosendo Pineda (including Spanish, Norwegian, and French interests) owned estates and irrigation ditches in Juchitán, San Jerónimo, and Tehuantepec, controlled the flow of commerce in the new port of Salina Cruz, and oversaw the negotiation of development plans with the electric company. In this highly politicized economy, the commissioning of contracts for these services was strongly influenced by the Maqueo Castellanos family, who worked through their cousin José W. Maqueo in Juchitán and científico Governor Emilio Pimentel in the state capital. By controlling land and the flow of water, capital, and electricity in the region, the rojos made themselves wealthy. Embezzlement was a standard practice and common knowledge in Juchitán, as was the expansive roster of henchmen who provided the muscle for the partido rojo and worked in the shadows of local politics.[65]

The most important provider of muscle for the rojos was Pancho León. His tenure as jefe político spanned the 1880s, when he made a name for himself as a sturdy and often brutal political leader, capable of ensuring order while overseeing Juchitán's extensive modernization project. León's administration supervised the construction of most of Juchitán's infrastructure, including the massive municipal palace, the central market, most of the roads, and the initial forays in the rail and telegraph service. In the process, León came to embody Porfirian rule in Juchitán: economic growth, urbanization, and political stability, all guided by a firm and unforgiving hand. León vacated the jefatura in 1889, but he continued to influence local politics for the remainder of the Porfiriato. Once respected by the poor and indigenous population, by the turn of the century he was recognized as the axis of the partido rojo and an enduring symbol of the Old Guard in Juchitán. The jefatura política later passed through the hands of a series of notable members of the camarilla roja: Fernando de Gyves, the son of the French consul on the Isthmus, and large landowner; Esteban Maqueo Castellanos; and on the eve of the Mexican Revolution, Mariano and Román Saynes, the jefe político and municipal president, respectively, and in-laws of Rosalino Martínez. The omnipresence of the federal army maintained political stability and ensured the dominance of the partido rojo. The local barracks became the home of the Twenty-Fifth Battalion, while nearby San Jerónimo Ixtepec was converted into the central command for the Ninth Military Zone, one of the largest military garrisons in Mexico.[66]

While the presence of a compliant federal army deterred public manifestations of popular discontent, it did not eliminate them altogether. Social segregation had a different effect on those pushed to the city's margins in the barrio de abajo, among whom developed a separate cultural identity from those of the north as well as a nascent political consciousness based on a shared sense of alienation and the collective awareness of their own marginality. Cut off from access to political and economic resources by the growing power of the camarilla roja, the resentment of Juchitán's poor and indigenous majority simmered just below the surface of social and political life in the city. "The partido rojo hated the gente de abajo, [those] of the south," recalled one Juchiteco, and "that's why the people hated that party."[67] Despite being driven underground, the partido verde increasingly became identified as the "partido de abajo." A prominent local lawyer explained that despite the fact that "the two great party divisions that were bred [in the people] have been quieted with the presence of the army," there remained "much latent desire to rebirth hatreds and bitterness."⁶⁸ These "hatreds and bitterness" remained latent for the duration of the Porfiriato, awaiting the right stimulus to call them forth to manifest. The coming revolution would provide such stimulus.

Conclusion

During the Porfiriato, Juchitán was transformed into a modern peripheral city divided into two separate worlds, reflecting the disparities of Porfirian economic development. The influx of capital to the region, combined with the arrival of effective roads and two railways, made Juchitán an important transportation hub on the Isthmus and a regional economic center. The social impact on the city was dramatic. In line with the developmentalist model in vogue, urban planners reordered the space of Juchitán to reflect socioeconomic and ethnic difference by concentrating the symbols of modernity and wealth in the city center while relegating perceived backwardness and poverty to the peripheries. The stark contrast between the two barrios reflected the contradictions of Porfirian development: separated by a chasm of social and cultural difference, the gente bien of the barrio de arriba modeled modernity—spatial order, technological innovation, education, and whiteness—for their indigenous neighbors in the barrio de abajo. That the city consisted of two separate worlds, inhabited by people with different identities and consciousnesses, was accepted by both; that these two worlds should be so dramatically unequal—that one should so clearly dominate the other—was less accepted.

While Porfirian ideologues heralded the Pax Porfiriana as the transcendental and bloodless end of the anarchic nineteenth century, when political outcomes were determined at the end of a rifle, Porfirian rule was effected, at least in Juchitán, by force without consent. The elite and their middle-class clients controlled the political process in Juchitán through the extensive camarilla roja, but they were completely divorced from public opinion. While camarillas generally constructed political machines by drawing both upward and downward on patron-client networks—using personal connections with high-level agents in the regime to ensure their control of political power and privileged access to economic resources, while exploiting personalist authority or extended social and familial networks to maintain stability among the popular classes—the capacity of the partido rojo to peddle its influence down the political pyramid was questionable. The camarilla roja undoubtedly had some downward ties of patronage to their workforce (itself a form of soft coercion), but the poor and indigenous majority of Juchitán deeply resented the rojos. The inequality between *los de arriba* and *los de abajo*, and the domination of the partido verde by the partido rojo, was maintained by state intervention, not by bonds of affinity or even clientelage. The Pax Porfiriana did not transcend the politics of force, but was its embodiment. In Juchitán the Porfirian peace was enforced at the end of a rifle; or about five hundred rifles, stationed in the local barracks. The raw force of the Díaz regime would be laid bare by the Revolution: when the federal army withdrew from Juchitán in 1911, the elite and their middle-class allies withdrew, too, fearful of being left alone with their poor, indigenous neighbors.

Rather than dissolve the retrograde "corporate spirit" lamented by liberals of the previous generation, the Porfirian (científico) brand of liberalism hardened "premodern" collective identities of class and ethnicity, compounding them into one cultural identity, politicized by the imposition of residential segregation and a shared sense of alienation. Isolation and alienation collapsed class and ethnic identity and created solidarities that would render the consolidation of classic liberal democracy nearly impossible in Juchitán. In 1910, when revolutionary reformers resurrected the old liberal discourse of universal citizenship based on the rational behavior of autonomous individuals, the gente de abajo of Juchitán gravitated toward articulations of democracy and citizenship that reinscribed their corporate identities, and toward leaders who would represent their collective interests in the public sphere. Reflecting their overriding pessimism about the political capacity of the poor, indigenous masses, elite and middle class revolutionary reformers rejected corporate (and especially ethnic) identities and sectoral representation in the public sphere and sought to limit democratic reform by retaining the disciplinary structures of the Porfiriato, particularly the jefatura política and the federal army. Thus, the limits of revolutionary democracy were born in the Porfiriato.

2 "The Rebirth of an Old Political Party"
Liberal Politics and the Rise of the Chegomista Movement

On May 25, 1911, as revolutionary violence engulfed the Mexican countryside, Porfirio Díaz resigned after thirty-five years in power. Two weeks later, Francisco I. Madero, the "Apostle of Democracy," triumphantly arrived in Mexico City, where he was greeted by throngs of jubilant admirers and hailed as the liberal hero of the Revolution. However, the jubilation of Madero's victory march shrouded an undercurrent of growing pessimism. After only five months of violent struggle, critics both within the Maderista movement and without feared that the Revolution had reached its culmination too fast, and too easily, before the lines between revolution and reaction had been clearly drawn, and before the contours of democratic reform could be clearly defined. Madero's call for democratic restoration through armed revolution liberated a multitude of disparate political players who had previously been controlled through the political system, particularly the rural masses, and brought them into the political sphere in distinctly undemocratic terms, through violent direct action. Fearing a descent into anarchy, the revolutionary zeal of liberal politicians gave way to the anxiety of pacification, and the self-congratulatory applause that greeted their ascent was quickly drowned out by the cacophony of unsatisfied demands emanating from the countryside. For many in Mexico's peripheral regions, Porfirio Díaz's resignation signaled the beginning, rather than the end, of the Revolution.

Even the government of Díaz's home state of Oaxaca, renowned for its undying support of the Old Caudillo, responded to the clarion call of democracy and capitulated to the state's liberal opposition. When Oaxaca's liberal stalwart, Heliodoro Díaz Quintas, was named interim governor, the news was greeted with "interminable applause" in the state's Chamber of Deputies and "unusual popular jubilation" in the streets of the state capital. Oaxaca's leading newspaper, *El Avance*, struck a particularly optimistic chord: "Now that the situation has been clearly clarified, the people have obtained their desired end. No more disorders or subversive demonstrations will darken our good name: let us all be democrats!"[1] However, the clarity of the moment was quickly muddied as Díaz Quintas discovered that the amorphous network of popular revolutionary movements that brought down the state government had different, and often conflicting, ideas about how to be democrats. These competing interpretations of the Revolution came into full relief as the new governor appointed interim jefes políticos in the state's districts. As a lightning rod of discontent, the jefatura política had unified middle-class and plebeian opponents of the regime in their mutual desire to eliminate the office, long seen as an instrument of the dictator's authority. However, with popular violence threatening to engulf the nation, Madero relinquished his commitment to abolishing the jefatura at least until the countryside had been stabilized and prepared for democratic renovation. In so doing, the new regime created its first crisis. If the jefatura política had once held together Madero's patchwork coalition in common commitment, it now threatened to tear it apart.

In maintaining the jefes políticos while the nation transitioned to democracy, the new regime faced two challenges. First, the persistence of the jefatura política combined with the principle of popular sovereignty—the cornerstone of liberal revolutionary ideology—to produce a political situation that cultivated personalist authority and rewarded direct action, in contradiction to the new regime's stated goal of institutional, impersonal democracy. The discourse of democracy and citizenship resurrected by liberal revolutionaries located the legitimacy of the state in the sovereign will of the people, and thus, at least in the abstract, empowered "the people" (broadly defined) to authorize leaders and institutions that best defended their interests. In an ideal liberal world, inhabited by "modern" citizens, the authority to represent "the people" to the outside world would be transferred legally by the people (acting as autonomous, rational individuals), through free and popular elections. However, thirty-five years of autocratic rule, embodied locally in the jefatura política, had degraded institutional means of expressing popular opinion and rendered local elections ineffectual. At the same time, the spread of popular violence with the Revolution favored the transfer of political authority and legitimacy through direct action, of which the jefes políticos were the most frequent targets. By May 1911 roughly half of the nation's jefes políticos had been replaced, with Madero's consent, through mass protest.[2] With the May peace treaty Madero called for an end to public shows of force, particularly in those areas that remained outside the control of revolutionary forces. However, these "unliberated" areas proved unwilling to wait for the electoral process to run its course to effect political change, and even then the electoral process did not extend to jefes políticos, who remained under the legal jurisdiction of state governments. In practice this situation fostered the continuation of personalist authority by forcing competing factions to demonstrate their worthiness to the state, often by mobilizing patronage networks and "premodern" corporate groups in mass public demonstrations. For all the new regime's talk of formal institutions and legal universalism, so long as the jefatura política remained unaltered, local authority would still be determined, at least in part, by who had the power to *traer gente* (mobilize people).

Second, by the summer of 1911 the Revolution had introduced to the public sphere a previously marginalized group of political players: the rural masses and their leaders (known as *cabecillas*). Opposition to the Díaz regime began in the realm of formal politics, led by educated men steeped in liberal ideology and culled primarily from the growing middle class. When electoral opposition failed to yield a legal transfer of power, armed revolution submerged formal political opposition, and a new class of armed men took the place of civilian politicians at the forefront of the Revolution. The "new men" of the Revolution, only tenuously connected to Madero, used the smoke of revolution to redress old grievances, leveraging their prestige among the popular classes to mobilize them to bring down the symbols of their oppression—jefes políticos and *hacendados* primarily—while Díaz's middle-class critics observed anxiously. When the treaty of Ciudad Juárez brought an end to the armed revolution, shifting the balance of power back toward formal politics, the "platonic" middle-class revolutionaries staked their claim to the spoils of victory. In so doing they confronted their plebeian "allies," who themselves had a considerable claim to the Revolution's inheritance. Among the most coveted spoils of revolutionary victory was the jefatura política, and the political authority and economic control that came with it. The process of fixing jefes políticos brought the new regime and the civilian middle-class politicos it represented face-to-face with populist cabecillas, and the masses they represented, in a struggle that was as much cultural as it was political.[3]

No region in Mexico more perfectly encapsulated the challenge facing Madero than did Juchitán. With the Revolution a powerful cabecilla, Che Gómez, returned to Juchitán to mobilize the poor, indigenous majority of the barrio de abajo and stake their claim to political representation, and his own to the jefatura política. Passed over by the state government in favor of moderate middle-class reformers, Gómez responded by organizing a popular movement that challenged not only the state's political authority in Juchitán but also the new regime's interpretation of liberal-democratic reform. The Chegomista movement came together in the summer of 1911 to support the candidacy of Che Gómez for the office of jefe político of Juchitán, in the name of popular sovereignty. While the jefatura fell under the legal jurisdiction of the state of Oaxaca, the Chegomistas demanded that the appointment be made in consultation with popular opinion and in accord with the popular will. Anything less, in the words of the Chegomistas, would signify a "return to past imposiciones, contradicting the principles conquered by the popular revolution."[4] As a defense of the sovereignty of the pueblos, the demand for popular sovereignty was more accurately a call for social and ethnic inclusion—an assertion by the poor and indigenous majority of their right to self-determination, and to be governed by one of their own (an *hijo del pueblo*). By embedding their demands in the same language of liberal republicanism that the revolutionary coalition had used to justify the Revolution and mobilize popular support, the Chegomistas presented the revolutionary regime, already uneasy with the presence of the indigenous masses in the public sphere, with the indelible challenge of restricting the public sphere, and returning the popular classes to the margins of political life, without undermining its own liberal-democratic legitimacy.

If the Chegomista movement invested "premodern" social forms of political representation (based on class and ethnicity) with "modern" political discourse, in practice the movement reflected more traditional understandings of political legitimacy that privileged personal prestige and direct action over formal political institutions. In June and July 1911, Che Gómez staked his claim to political legitimacy in Juchitán and demonstrated his prestige by organizing mass public manifestations of his power, ranging from public petitions and peaceful demonstrations to violent lynch mobs. These public shows of force not only provided visual and visceral evidence of his power and popular support but also intimidated his political opponents (especially given the ethnic and class composition of the Chegomistas), inhibiting public political expression and the consolidation of democratic reform. Rather than fight, during the first week of July the local garrison of the federal army evacuated Juchitán, taking with it Gómez's opponents and their families. On July 3 the standing jefe político tendered his resignation and fled, explaining that it would be "ridiculous" to continue in his position, as he could no longer guarantee the safety of his supporters, or even his own, "since the people obey only the president [Gómez]."[5] Che Gómez and his rejuvenated political party had seized control of Juchitán, but the issue of the jefatura remained unresolved, the elephant in the room.

Liberal Opposition I: Madero and the Fall of Porfirio Díaz

Following the turn of the century, opposition to the authoritarian regime of Porfirio Díaz increased in scope and intensity, as Díaz allowed a socially conservative, technocratic ruling class (the científicos) to consolidate its political authority and economic dominance at the expense of the old oligarchy. Sectors of the elite bristled at the new científico hegemony, as liberal opposition spread throughout the country. Liberal clubs formed and rapidly expanded, fueled by a growing middle class that demanded democratic reform and the restoration of municipal power as an antidote to the regime's increasing centralization of authority. While the bulk of the liberal oppositionists shied away from directly challenging Díaz, preferring a peaceful, moderated transformation of political culture, a growing radical faction associated with the Partido Liberal Mexicano (PLM) saw Díaz's ouster as a necessary precondition for Mexico's political resurrection. The Díaz regime responded with intense repression targeting radical liberal factions, driving them from the public sphere and leaving more moderate liberals without a party. Afraid to confront the regime directly, the moderates struggled to formulate a coherent critique of the Porfirian political system, at least until 1909.[6]

In early 1908, in a now-famous interview with an American journalist, James Creelman, Porfirio Díaz declared that he would be open to political competition in the election of 1910, insinuating that after thirty years in power he was ready to step down as president. While the intentions behind Díaz's statements are the subject of much historical debate, in effect the interview energized his relatively dormant opposition, who set about organizing for the upcoming elections. In 1909 two national liberal parties, the Partido Nacional Antirreeleccionista and the Partido Democrático, formed to challenge Díaz's vice-presidential candidate, both drawing the bulk of their following from the massive pool of moderate, middle-class liberals who had been left adrift by the suppression of the radical faction, and disaffected elites whose economic and political interests had been trampled by the científicos. As a result, the strength of the liberal opposition was located in the rising petit bourgeoisie of the newly industrialized cities of the north and the financial support of a significant number of elite anti-científicos. By the beginning of 1910 the Partido Antirreeleccionista had separated itself from other, nominally liberal challengers behind the tireless campaigning of its dynamic leader, Francisco Madero.[7]

The eldest son of one of Mexico's wealthiest and most influential families, Francisco Madero came to the Partido Antirreeleccionista through the growing national network of liberal clubs. For eight years, beginning in his home state of Coahuila, Madero fought against the rubber-stamp elections of the regime's favored candidates, and when Díaz invited political competition in 1908, Madero threw his hat into the ring with his polemic, *The Presidential Succession of 1910*. In his book, Madero argued that the Díaz regime had brought economic prosperity and political stability to Mexico at the expense of the general interest; through corruption, repression, and clientelism, Díaz had sapped the nation of its civic virtue. Madero believed, however, that the public spirit could be recovered through the restoration of classic liberal principles, embodied in Benito Juárez. Demonstrating unusual optimism, Madero believed that once democracy was effectively implemented, new, enlightened politicians would take over and govern in accord with the general interest, and thus heal the nation's social ills. The principles elucidated in *The Presidential Succession of 1910* became the political program around which Madero's presidential campaign was based.[8]

Madero ran a shrewd campaign, picking up momentum through the spring of 1910, but as the elections neared and Madero's popularity reached a crescendo, Díaz ordered Madero arrested and jailed in San Luis Potosí, ending Madero's legal bid for the presidency and setting the table for his transition to armed revolution. In October, Díaz won the election in a predictable landslide. Two days later, Madero escaped from house arrest and fled across the border to San Antonio, Texas. Although Madero and the bulk of his followers were reticent to resort to revolution and abhorred the prospect of mass violence, Díaz's show of force made it clear that revolution would be the only means of dislodging his regime. With the help of his inner circle of *antirreeleccionistas*, Madero drew up the Plan de San Luis. The plan maintained Madero's focus on political—rather than social—reform, denounced Porfirio Díaz and named Francisco Madero as provisional president, and explicitly called for an armed revolution to begin on November 20, 1910.[9]

The call for an armed uprising transformed his coalition of supporters in ways unforeseen by Madero, shifting the locus of political conflict from town to country, and away from his middle-class followers and into the hands of "anonymous" men of the pueblos, with whom Madero had little or no connection. When the urban component of Madero's planned revolution arrived stillborn, disintegrated by the state's preemptive strikes or simply handled by Díaz's army, the thrust of the Revolution was picked up by rural folk. Beginning in the northern state of Chihuahua, local leaders of varying stock led villagers in short, powerful revolts, aimed at taking down the local symbols of Porfirian rule: here a jefe político imposed by the state, there a landowner who had taken village lands. By January, mountain rebels had taken control of a large chunk of the state of Chihuahua, alarming the state's ruling elite, and causing no small discomfort within the regime. Once a *foco* had been established in Chihuahua, revolutionary violence took on its own circular logic (the calculus of force): upheaval and insurrection spawned more upheaval and insurrection, as the discontented of the countryside used the chaos of revolutionary violence to gain redress for their various grievances through armed direct action. As localized and disparate revolts spread throughout the nation, ostensibly bound by their adherence to Madero, they carried out political and social reform as they went, placing their own leaders in power, occupying dispossessed lands, and effecting, in the minds of Porfirians and more than a few Maderistas, a "descent into anarchy." By April 1911 this network of disconnected "jacqueries" had spread to every state in Mexico, causing the regime to waver for the first time in thirty-five years.[10]

As disorder spread throughout the countryside, Díaz capitulated, inviting Madero to negotiate a peaceful end to his presidency. After a series of aborted talks and cease-fires Madero gave in and the two sides came to an agreement, equally eager to end the violence. On

May 21, 1911, in Ciudad Juárez, Madero and his inner circle met with Díaz's principals and signed the treaty that they hoped would not only end thirty-five years of political domination but also stanch the spread of political violence.[11] The Treaty of Ciudad Juárez represented neither unconditional victory for the revolutionaries nor the logical culmination of an organized revolution: it was the response of two politically opposed groups of elites to an armed movement that was beyond their control. While the Porfirians used the treaty to gain a foothold in the new administration, the Maderistas used it to slow down the Revolution, bring an end to the violence, and regain control of a diffuse coalition of forces. As a result, the treaty more closely resembled a "transaction," with the victorious revolutionaries giving as much as they took, despite the abject weakness of the Porfirians. The treaty called for the resignations of Díaz and his vice-president, named a Porfirian functionary the interim president until regular elections could be held, and ordered the end of hostilities and the demobilization of all revolutionary forces, while allocating funds for the latter. Continuity with the Old Regime was built into the treaty, beginning with the interim president himself, Francisco León de la Barra, who was granted the authority to name a new cabinet and fourteen provisional governors in the wake of Díaz's resignation.[12] The sudden end to the Revolution left much to be decided, and as the dust settled, the struggle over who would define the contours of the Revolution had only just begun.

The Liberal Opposition II: Oaxaca

Despite the state's historic loyalty to its native son, Porfirio Díaz, in many ways Oaxaca reflected perfectly the larger, national processes of opposition and revolution in Mexico. In concert with growing liberal movements throughout the nation, an active liberal opposition emerged in Oaxaca, characterized by middle-class participation and deep ideological fissures, and beginning with the founding of the Asociación Juárez in 1901. Established as an homage to the state's favored son, Benito Juárez, in ideology and constituency the Asociación

Juárez was typical of Mexico's liberal clubs: an eclectic mix of Porfirian politicians, wealthy businessmen, and middle-class professionals, dedicated to the restoration of the Juarista principles of democracy, municipal power, and state's rights, as a counterbalance to bloated executive authority. The first major public political act of the asociación was to oppose the reelection of Governor Martín González in 1902. González, who had already served two terms in office, perfectly embodied the fading militarist faction of Díaz's inner circle. An ill-mannered, rugged mestizo, he became the target not only of Oaxaca's established elites but also of the ascendant bourgeoisie. As their candidate, the liberals chose the president's nephew, Félix Díaz, who generated tremendous support among the upper and middle classes and divided Porfirio Díaz's patronage networks in Oaxaca. Rather than choosing one group over the other, Díaz forced both González and his nephew to withdraw from the race and declared Emilio Pimentel the "official" candidate. Pimentel, a founding member of the científico circle, enjoyed very little organic support in Oaxaca but won the election and continued to occupy the governor's chair for the remainder of the Porfiriato. The Oaxacan oligarchy had deep reservations about Pimentel, and the científicos in general, but out of respect for Díaz they fell in line with the new científico governor. The liberal faction would not consent so easily to the new regime, but neither could they come to an agreement on how to express their dissent.[13]

Like liberal movements elsewhere in Mexico, the Asociación Juárez was rife with internal factions, which were brought to the surface by the repressive pressure of the state. From the founding of the asociación to the eve of the Revolution, Oaxaca's liberal coalition was gradually shorn of its fringe membership, ultimately leaving a core of committed but moderate liberal oppositionists. The disintegration of the Asociación Juárez began in 1904, when middle-class members seized positions of leadership and began to steer it in a more openly anti-científico direction. Afraid of being labeled opponents of the regime, the upper classes chose to leave the organization. With the withdrawal of upper class support, middle-class liberals began distributing their own opposition newspaper, publicizing a slightly radicalized political platform. In these years, the Asociación Juárez became a reservoir of middle-class discontent but lacked a coherent ideology, save that of general anti-científico sentiment. In 1905 the ideological disunity of the asociación came to the surface during state elections, and a radical faction broke off, leaving opposition to Pimentel divided. Pimentel cruised to victory, and in the aftermath of the elections, used his mandate to unleash a wave of repression on the radical faction. Those members of the liberal opposition associated with the PLM faced harassment, dismissals, and incarceration, forcing them from public political life. The state's repression left in its wake a formal liberal opposition dominated by a particularly moderate middle class.[14]

Although the repression of the radical faction played a prominent role in moderating Oaxaca's middle-class opposition, other forces were also at work. As Chassen-López has noted, unlike democratic reformers elsewhere, Oaxaca's liberal opposition shied away from challenging the Díaz regime directly. This can be explained in part by the parasitic nature of Oaxaca's liberal politicians. Unlike the North's entrepreneurial bourgeoisie, Oaxaca's middle class was dependent on professional positions provided by the state or the oligarchy. Middle-class liberals enjoyed tremendous professional success under Díaz by participating in the patronage networks that emanated from the capital and permeated political life in the provinces. Social mobility for the Oaxacan middle class depended on access to public employment or private positions opened up in the financial sector, both of which were dictated by elite patronage. While northern politics produced a powerful dissident oligarchy, in Oaxaca the upper class walked in lockstep with Díaz, leaving middle-class reformers structurally vulnerable, with no patriarchs to champion their cause. Moreover, the typical career pattern of Oaxacan politics fostered a degree of social cohesion between elite Porfirian politicians and their bourgeois opposition. Liberal reformers may not have shared the early refinements of their conservative opponents, but most came together at the prestigious Instituto de Ciencias y Artes, where they shared curriculum and social networks. Thus, while we must take into account that the middle-class liberals opposed the regime at great personal peril, their reluctance to repudiate the Porfirian status quo in its entirety should come as no surprise. Professionally, they did well by the custodians of Old Society, and in many economic and cultural respects they were as conservative as their opponents. Ultimately, the moderation of Oaxaca's liberal politicians left more radical liberals in a precarious position. By 1906 the few radicals who did emerge in Oaxaca (mostly rural schoolteachers, far removed from Oaxaca City) bore the brunt of the state's repressive apparatus. Isolated from the moderates and with no one to protect them, the bulk of the radical faction were fired and jailed by the state, leaving only the most pliant and moderate reformers to participate in public politics. As a result, while moderate opposition reemerged to contest the 1910 gubernatorial election, in Oaxaca Madero's bandwagon remained nearly empty until well into 1911.[15]

While Madero's brief campaign stop in 1909 did yield a modest Club Antirreeleccionista in Oaxaca City, most moderate liberals chose to sit out the presidential election, focusing instead on state elections. When Governor Pimentel announced his intention to run for governor again in 1910, the moderates united behind the candidacy of Benito Juárez Maza, eldest son of the *Benemérito* himself. A career diplomat, Juárez Maza did most of his political service abroad before being elected as the first president of the Partido Democrático in 1909. Despite his new political standing, his general goodwill, and his prestigious last name, Juárez Maza did not inspire confidence in his colleagues. High-ranking politicians, including Francisco Madero, questioned Juárez Maza's "scarce political skill," pointing out that his role in the Partido Democrático was largely symbolic. Nonetheless, in April 1910, the leaders of Oaxaca's moderate opposition traveled to Mexico City to ask Juárez Maza to run against Pimentel. Juárez Maza accepted the nomination, and the Centro Antirreeleccionista in Mexico City supported the decision, declaring him "a democrat of the highest standing." Although his presence on the ballot sparked the democratic fervor of committed liberals, Juárez Maza's inexperience showed, as he spent only three days on the campaign trail and was soundly defeated in the June 26 elections. Mirroring national politics, the 1910 elections had raised the hopes of Oaxaca's moderate liberal faction, only to leave them unfulfilled.[16]

Madero's call to arms in 1910 was greeted with indifference by the bulk of Oaxaca's liberal opposition, but as revolutionary upheaval spread the Oaxacan countryside responded. In the first half of 1911, as the Revolution swept across the nation, villages in the western and northern parts of the state mobilized and expelled local officials in short, powerful, nominally Maderista revolts, frequently led by radical supporters of the PLM (Angel Barrios, Sebastian Ortíz, Manuel Oseguera, and Faustino Olivera, to name a few). By April, mass mobilization in the countryside rendered the state of Oaxaca ungovernable, forcing Governor Pimentel's resignation on May 1 and beginning what Francisco José Ruiz Cervantes has dubbed "the Dance of the Governors." While regular elections were scheduled for July, over the next six weeks the state legislature trotted out no less than six interim governors, hoping to slow the spread of popular mobilization and placate the liberal opposition, who, now feeling their revolutionary oats, demanded some influence over the process. Finally, the Old Guard gave in to the inevitable, agreeing to appoint a governor who would represent the ascendant liberal faction and, presumably, the nominally Maderista forces that had swept the Oaxacan countryside.[17]

On June 8, Heliodoro Díaz Quintas, the founder of the Asociación Juárez, was announced as the interim governor of Oaxaca to great public satisfaction. Nobody better represented the emergence and ascent of the petit bourgeoisie than Díaz Quintas. Born into the middle class and educated in law at the ICA, Díaz Quintas enjoyed ample professional success under the Díaz regime, serving as a judge in Etla, a professor at the ICA, and occupying a position on the Oaxacan city council. Nonetheless, he became the stalwart of the moderate liberal opposition movement of Oaxaca as president of the Asociación Juárez and editor of its newspaper, *El Bien Público*. Like most other Oaxacan liberals, despite his opposition to the Oaxacan regime, Díaz Quintas remained loyal to Porfirio Díaz nearly to the end, and at the eleventh hour he converted to Maderismo. As in the nation's capital, through a combination of negotiation, conciliation, and raw power, it was the moderate liberals, represented by their respected leader, who "took the spoils" in Oaxaca, as the radicals and local cabecillas remained on the outside, looking in. As interim governor, Díaz Quintas was charged with one seemingly simple task: maintaining peace and order for the upcoming elections. Fulfilling this charge, it turns out, would be easier said than done.[18]

The Liberal Opposition III: Juchitán

The emergence of a politically active middle class and the evolution of liberal opposition in Juchitán mirrored that of the nation and the state of Oaxaca. Owing to the region's intense economic growth, during the Porfiriato Juchitán developed a sizable middle class. As early as 1890, 4 percent of the working population of Juchitán was classified as "professionals," the bulk of whom were state employees and merchants. Compared with data from the national census of 1895, Juchitán's middle class appears to have been about half the size of the national average but on par with other peripheral urban centers. It should be noted that while 1890 is the last census data available for Juchitán prior to the Revolution, the city's population grew by almost three thousand (about 33 percent) between 1890 and 1910. Given the nature of this growth and the region's economic prosperity, it does not require a massive leap of faith to infer that Juchitán's professional class grew in both size and diversity in the last two decades of the Porfiriato. Residential patterns also suggest, as noted in the previous chapter, that the middle classes were integrated into the gente bien of Juchitán's barrio de arriba. Of the 162 identified professionals in the 1890 census, only 5 lived in the barrio de abajo. Their relative prosperity notwithstanding, Juchitán's middle class did generate ideological opposition to the Díaz regime.[19]

The trajectory of liberal opposition in Juchitán is best illustrated by the divergent political careers of Juchitán's two most prominent liberal leaders, Adolfo Gurrión and Severo Castillejos. Adolfo Gurrión was born to humble parents in the town of El Barrio, in the district of Juchitán, and parlayed his success in primary school into a scholarship to study first at the School of Agriculture in Mexico City and later at the Normal School of Professors in Oaxaca City. Severo Castillejos was born into a well-to-do family in Juchitán, studied law at the ICA, and upon graduation found work in the judicial branch of the state government. The two came together in 1902, joining the opposition to the reelection of Governor Martín González. Castillejos began publishing a liberal newspaper, *El Estandarte*, which supported the candidacy of Félix Díaz, and for which Adolfo Gurrión was a contributor. In 1904, Castillejos ran for criminal court judge in Oaxaca City on the ticket of the Magonista-affiliated Club Liberal Santiago de la Hoz. The following year both Castillejos and Gurrión joined the Asociación Juárez, with Gurrión serving as secretary. Both were active contributors to the Juarista political organ, *El Bien Público*, and members of the PLM.[20] With the dissolution of the asociación in 1905, both returned to Juchitán, where they formed part of "a pernicious little circle" of Magonistas, who, according to the jefe político, went about their "thankless work of upsetting the masses" and distributing copies of the Magonista newspaper, *Regeneración*.[21] However, as the PLM began to radicalize and the liberal opposition began to diverge, so too did the career paths of Gurrión and Castillejos.

When the Asociación Juárez split between radical and moderate factions, Adolfo Gurrión left his position with *El Bien Público* and began publishing his own radical newspaper, *La Semecracia*. While *La Semecracia* maintained a liberal focus on political, rather than social, change, Gurrión did not shy away from open attacks on the Díaz regime. Gurrión's opposition, like that of other Oaxacan radicals, made him the target of state repression. After the publication of the second edition of *La Semecracia* in March 1906, Governor Pimentel ordered the press shut down and jailed Gurrión, without a trial, on the charge of defamation. Despite the protests of his family and the objections of his PLM partisans, Gurrión remained in the infamous La Martinica prison, where he was denied visitation rights and held in solitary confinement, in a humid cell without ventilation, lights, or furniture, for almost a year. Following his release in 1907, Gurrión took up educational positions far away from Juchitán, the last in Baja California, where he remained until 1911.[22]

In contrast, though he left a much slimmer archival trail, Severo Castillejos became a major player in local politics. By 1910 he was the informal leader of a group of educated, middle-class reformers in Juchitán, linked politically to the Asociación Juárez and the PLM, but professionally to the conservative partido rojo of Juchitán. The core of this group consisted of the Matus family (Evaristo, the patriarch, Germán, Herminio, and Vicente, a well-known lawyer who had publicly defended a prominent Magonista from the persecution of Governor Pimentel), Ricardo León (son of Porfirian strongman, Francisco León), Mauro Ortega (a former judge in Tehuantepec, and member of the PLM), Victoriano Rueda (a lawyer and PLM*ista* from Tehuantepec), and Federico Sandoval (the local judge). While it is difficult to discern the precise nature of their political opposition, the evidence suggests that this group represented typical middle-class moderates. First of all, their opposition was aimed squarely at state rather than at national politics. They endorsed the anti-científico, Félix Díaz, as governor against Pimentel, until transferring their support to Juárez Maza in 1910. Moreover, none of this group openly challenged the Díaz regime by supporting Madero's presidential bid: not until after Díaz's resignation (and Madero's victory) did they come together to form a Maderista club. Perhaps more indicative of their tepid opposition, the members of Juchitán's liberal circle were tremendously successful under the Díaz regime: they held prominent public offices, enjoyed financial prosperity, and had close connections to the partido rojo, the elite camarilla that dominated the politicized economy of Juchitán. Castillejos, the Matus family, and Ricardo León were tightly linked to Francisco León, the military strongman who dominated political life in Juchitán under Díaz and came to symbolize Porfirian authority. Castillejos and Evaristo and Vicente Matus formed León's legal team, while also providing legal representation for landed elites, such as the Parragua brothers (majority owners of the region's salt flats). For his part, Castillejos became a prominent landowner during the final years of the Porfiriato, buying up communal lands liberated by Díaz's economic policies. At the very least, Juchitán's middle-class liberals knew their way around elite political networks and undoubtedly considered themselves among the gente bien of Juchitán. With the victory of the liberal faction in state politics, Castillejos, Matus, and their circle of liberal oppositionists saw themselves as the rightful heirs to political power in Juchitán. So when Che Gómez reentered local politics after a long, informal exile, they became his most vocal and virulent opponents.[23]

"'Sr. José,' as They Vulgarly Call Him": The Return of Che Gómez

While moderate liberals were able to ride the wave of social upheaval to political victory in the state and national capitals, corraling the popular response was decidedly more difficult on the periphery, where the stark realities of revolutionary violence left moderate, middle-class politicians face-to-face with their more popular, plebian allies. The spread of disorder to the countryside liberated the rural masses, who by force of arms or simply strength of numbers forced their way into the public sphere, ushering in a new era of egalitarianism to Mexican political life, embodied by the "new men" of the Revolution. Coarse, young men with little education and virtually no connection to Madero now competed with educated professionals, career politicians, and wealthy landowners for access to political power and control of economic resources. Even in those areas left relatively unscathed by revolutionary upheaval a change was apparent, as the plebeian masses began to invade the political and social space previously reserved for the gente bien. Juchitán was one such area. While a garrison of the federal army protected the town from violent revolt, it could not prevent a self-described "humble lawyer" from returning from informal exile to proselytize and organize among the gente de abajo.

José Fructuoso Gómez was a "squat, fat mestizo," born in Juchitán in 1858 to relatively wealthy, landowning parents, Gregorio Gómez and Rosalía López. His uncle Cosme Gómez led the militia of Juchitán against the French army during the intervention, served as the jefe político and military commander of Juchitán, and fought in defense of Porfirio Díaz's Plan de Tuxtepec in 1876. When Cosme Gómez joined Mexu Chele's rebellion against the federal government in 1882, his brother Gregorio accompanied him. When Pancho León ordered the forced relocation of the wives of suspected rebels, one of those exiled to San Miguel Chimalapa was Rosalía López, beginning an enduring feud between the León and Gómez families. However, despite the violent repression of the punitive expedition and the enmity with Pancho León, the Gómez family continued to enjoy considerable power in the region, including favorable contacts in the Díaz regime, and substantial landholdings in the district. For his part, after graduating primary school in Juchitán, José Gómez went on to study law at the ICA in Oaxaca City. Here he was plugged into the vast social network of the dictator's loyal Oaxacan supporters, dubbed "Díaz's Jesuits" by Chassen-López for their missionary zeal in defense of the president, and their far-flung presence throughout Mexico.[24] Like other "Jesuits" from the ICA, upon graduation in 1887 Gómez was rewarded with a comfortable entry-level position, in his case as a judge in Tlacolula, Oaxaca. Unlike most of the dictator's acolytes, however, after a short time away Gómez returned to the fray of local politics in his hometown.[25]

In 1893 "Che" Gómez (as he was known locally) returned to Juchitán to run for the office of municipal president, and in so doing offered his *paisanos* on the Isthmus a preview of events to come. Gómez's candidacy galvanized Juchitán's deep social and ethnic divisions, as he won the support of Juchitán's poor and indigenous majority and reactivated the dormant partido verde, founded in part by his father and uncle. Gómez's success prompted a vigorous response from the partido rojo. The rojos, interpreting Gómez's success as a challenge to their political monopoly, appealed to the governor of Oaxaca and to Díaz himself to remove Gómez from the region. Foreshadowing what would later congeal into a dominant public image, local politicians represented "'Sr. José,' as they vulgarly call him here," as a demagogue who had won the municipal elections by "patronizing groups of indígenas." Specifically, they complained that Gómez had mobilized the "unwitting" indígenas by promising access to privately owned salt flats and the expansion of the communal landholdings of Juchitán at the expense of the state's largest landowning family, the Maqueo Castellanos (and notably not his own family). While he was clearly incapable of complying with such promises, according to his opponents, he had duped the indigenous population ("fools") into believing that he had the support of "people in high places in the government." By "making his clients [patronizados] believe that they have rights that they would probably never think of acquiring," Gómez politicized the masses, creating a situation that "could very easily give way to conflict." Once he had bought the elections (using his father's money), according to the jefe político of Tehuantepec, Gómez would surely call for the separation of the Isthmus of Tehuantepec from the state of Oaxaca. In conjuring the ghost of separatism, local politicians also expressed a calm confidence that Gómez would be removed from office and order would be restored.[26]

In Mexico City the situation drew the attention of Gómez's childhood friend and former ICA schoolmate, Rosendo Pineda. Informed of the trouble in Juchitán, Pineda invited Gómez to Mexico City to meet with President Díaz himself. Though the subject matter of their meeting is not fully known, it appears that they cut some sort of deal in which Gómez would be awarded prestigious political positions far away from the Isthmus so long as he promised not to meddle in the politics of Juchitán. In a letter to Gómez, Pineda hinted at the exchange: "Open your eyes, your mouth, and whatever else you can open and be amazed... the General's promise is complete.... You are the diputado propietario for the State of Guerrero. Admit that you weren't expecting this cushy job [ganga]. Now do not say anything to anybody, and, above all, do not make a show of this." For the next fifteen years Gómez lived far away from Juchitán, accepting positions in Guerrero, Tlaxcala, and Baja California.[27]

Che Gómez does not appear much in the public record between 1894 and 1910, but we know that despite this professional success, Gómez's history before the Revolution had its hardships. Gómez became embroiled in a property dispute with his sisters upon the death of his parents in 1904. For reasons not entirely known, Rosendo Pineda took up the cause of Gómez's sisters, using his influence with the jefe político and circuit judge of Juchitán to ensure José's defeat. Afterward, as a form of punishment, Pineda had Gómez transferred to Baja California to work for the Treasury Department. The demotion left Gómez incapable of supporting his family on his Treasury Department wage, and he began practicing law privately on the side. When Treasury Minister José Yves Limantour found out about Gómez's practice, he demanded that Gómez discontinue, and refused to enter "discussions of any nature" with him.[28]

Gómez becomes more difficult to track after 1905. Though he fits the profile of a stifled, lower-level bureaucrat, what little trace he left in the public record seems to indicate that he remained a man of considerable influence in Juchitán and that his connections with Rosendo Pineda remained intact. When José and one of his sisters fought over who would inherit their parents' landholdings in 1905, Pineda intervened directly, informing Gómez's lawyer (Severo Castillejos) that a resolution should be found as quickly as possible, "for the good of everyone, and especially for José's good name." In 1908, when a fire from the railroad damaged the property of a family friend, Gómez's brother-in-law appealed to José to use his influence with Pineda to win him an indemnity from the railroad company. Though the resolution of the case is unknown, it is clear from the correspondence that Gómez was understood to be a man of some influence and that he and Pineda had an ongoing relationship. Nonetheless, Gómez remained a middling bureaucrat, isolated from his hometown. In 1910, with the winds of revolution beginning to swirl, Che Gómez tired of the bitter caviar of exile and returned to Juchitán.[29]

"Whoever Dares to Sound the Cry of Rebellion":
The Formation of the Chegomista Movement

Che Gómez's return to local politics brought into sharp relief the conflict, built into the Revolution organically, between middle-class, civilian políticos and personalist, populist cabecillas. In this competition between the moderate liberal faction and Che Gómez, both sides had legitimate claims to revolutionary authority. The moderate liberals derived legitimacy from their credentials as ideologically committed opponents of the dictatorship and from their connections to the moderate liberal bourgeoisie—their *partidarios* who had seized control of the state government through popular elections. Their claims to authority were dependent on their influence in political administration in the state capital. Though he resembled them in social and ethnic profile, Che Gómez distinguished himself from the middle-class professionals of the moderate faction with his boldness in appealing directly to the popular classes and his willingness to articulate their interests, values, and demands in the public sphere. His claim to authority was based on his overwhelming popularity among Juchitán's poor, indigenous majority—the gente de abajo—which opened him up to charges of demagoguery and called into question his motivations.

As a mestizo born into the provincial landowning class, educated at the prestigious ICA, and a stifled bureaucrat with no history of political opposition, Gómez fit the profile of a typical cabecilla: a political opportunist who mobilized the masses to advance his self-interest, his desire for political power. Certainly this would become the dominant image of Che Gómez in the press and among his political contemporaries. More recent studies have rejected this interpretation, attempting to rehabilitate Gómez's image and restore the political legitimacy of his movement. In so doing, they have portrayed him as an authentic and sincere revolutionary—in the words of Víctor de la Cruz, "a son of the local landowning bourgeoisie" who "turned his back on his class in order to serve the cause of the Indians."[30] Here, Gómez was bonded to the poor, indigenous population of Juchitán by his "socialist ideology," reflected in his interest "in the recovery for his people of the salt flats ... and the restitution of communal lands."[31] By establishing Gómez as an ideologically committed agrarian reformer, motivated by genuine solidarity with his lower-class followers, this interpretation provides his burgeoning movement with a well-defined aim and a coherent political program. As a result, Che Gómez's poor, indigenous supporters, dismissed as prepolitical dupes by their contemporaries, can be understood as fully class-conscious, revolutionary peasants.

While useful in its insistence on the inherently political nature of Gómez's immense popularity, this image of Gómez and his supporters creates its own set of interpretive problems. First of all, there is little evidence in the public record of Gómez's presumed commitment to agrarian reform. Gómez never mentions land in his correspondence. In fact, the only references made to land redistribution came from his enemies, who used it as evidence of his demagoguery.[32] Second, this interpretation reinscribes colonialist understandings of popular rebellion, which reduce anything short of mature class consciousness—reflected by a clearly defined political program and ideologically committed leadership—to the realm of the primitive (bandity at worst; "social banditry" at best).[33] Ultimately, since it is impossible to either prove or disprove Gómez's sincerity or his radical agrarian agenda (both are asserted without substantiation), it seems prudent to assume that he was motivated, at least to some degree, by self-interest. However, allowing this does not negate the inherently political nature of his movement, nor does it reduce his followers to mere fodder for his political aspirations.[34]

Che Gómez's rise to popularity in Juchitán was not the product of spontaneous political combustion coinciding with his return, nor was it a reflection of his radical agrarian agenda. The resurrection of the partido verde, as Gómez's supporters came to be identified, was an act of ethnic and class resistance decades in the making. Che Gómez's return tapped into the insurgent consciousness of the poor and indigenous of the barrio de abajo—a political consciousness formed by the collective awareness of its inverse, the coercive code of domination that denied them access to political and economic resources, relegated them to the margins of the city, and offered discipline and dependence on "good society" as the only path to redemption. Gómez's arrival offered the gente de abajo an opportunity to turn this code upside down and give vent to their collective resentment.[35] "The revolution of Che Gómez," stated one of his followers, "happened because of party motives": "The partido rojo hated the gente de abajo of the south. The people of the north belonged in their majority to the partido rojo, and it was always them who controlled justice; always them. That is why the people hated that party." Another affirmed that "those of the north of Juchitán, who were Porfiristas," united with the *federales* to oppose Gómez and his burgeoning political party.[36]

The presence of a mass of poor indigenous people, bound by a common ethnic and class identity, networks of sociability and solidarity, and the shared experience of marginalization, facilitated Che Gómez's work of mobilizing and organizing collective action under the banner of the partido verde. However, Gómez did not conjure the partido verde out of thin air: "the party had already formed" before Gómez's arrival, recalled one participant, "and he had the trust of the people, which is why he returned."[37] Gómez's supporters began wearing green branches in their sombreros to distinguish themselves from the partido rojo, a telltale sign that harked back to earlier conflicts, and symbolized for local moderates, "the rebirth of an old political party, the same that made the Istmeña revolution in 1880–1883, and that now called itself the '*partido gomista*.'"[38] Indeed, one Chegomista later remembered that "in this zone of the south [the barrio de abajo]," when Gómez returned, "many men came together, elders of the pueblo who had seen the revolution of 1882; [and] they supported him."[39] If Che Gómez saw the Revolution as an opportunity to stake his claim to political power by mobilizing the gente de abajo, the gente de abajo saw Che Gómez's return as an opportunity to destroy the coercive code of domination that ordered social and political life in Juchitán. This was not a well-defined, radical agrarian movement—the product of a mature and fully realized class consciousness—but a broad, collective demand for class and ethnic inclusion that may or may not have included agrarian reform, but that was fundamentally political.

Given his willingness to appeal directly to the popular classes, Che Gómez's participation in the municipal elections of 1910 set off a firestorm of protest in Juchitán. Responding to widespread rumors that Gómez had been sent to Juchitán at the behest of powerful Maderistas, the jefe político and the municipal president, Mariano and Román Saynes, respectively, complained to the governor that Gómez intended to ignite a seditious movement against the Díaz regime; an accusation echoed by Severo Castillejos in his liberal newspaper, *La Voz del Istmo*. However, the local garrison commander denied having any knowledge tying Gómez to larger opposition groups, and Gómez was allowed to campaign. In December 1910, elections for municipal president pitted a representative of the Saynes brothers and the partido rojo against Gómez's compadre Teófilo Fuentes. Fuentes won the election, but the Saynes brothers successfully petitioned to have the results nullified. New elections were scheduled for April 1911, this time with Che Gómez in the running. With the Revolution now in full force, Gómez won the April election in a landslide, supposedly with 90 percent of the vote. While Juchitán's moderates cried foul and moved to have the results nullified on the grounds that Gómez had used extra-official means to obtain victory, the results were eventually ratified, dealing "a mortal blow to [our] group of young oppositionists," according to Ricardo León.[40]

Given the choice between Gómez and the middle-class professionals of the moderate faction, the overwhelming majority of Juchitán chose Gómez. The moderates simply could not compete with him. Composed of middle-class gente bien, educated in Oaxaca City, and associated through ties of business and family to the partido rojo, the moderate liberals were men of power in Juchitán, but they lacked prestige, despite their commitment to the cause of liberal democracy. Their authority depended on their "enlightened" ideology and the patronage of their partidarios in the state government. Their doctrinaire appeals to a legalistic, universal interpretation of citizenship fell on deaf ears among the popular classes, who gravitated toward familial discourses.[41] Because it was almost wholly dependent on state patronage, the moderates' authority was interpreted locally as a state imposition, a continuation of the authoritarian practices of the Porfiriato. On the other hand, Gómez's undeniable popularity, confirmed by municipal elections, validated his claim to represent the will of the people and legitimated his claim to authority. In the midst of a democratic revolution, steeped in the rhetoric of liberal republicanism, this was not to be easily dismissed. On May 27, 1911, just two days after Díaz's resignation, Che Gómez took office as the municipal president of Juchitán. However, the power of the municipal president meant little without the support of the jefatura política, which remained in the hands of the state government.[42]

Having constructed, or reactivated, a large constituency for local elections, Gómez and the resurrected partido verde now took aim at the jefatura política. In a telegram to the president, Che Gómez explained that the people of Juchitán were "vehemently against" their jefe político, Mariano Saynes. In a bit of foreshadowing, Gómez warned Porfirio Díaz that hostility against the jefe político was such that the people of Juchitán would "side with whoever dares to sound the cry of rebellion."[43] With Díaz's resignation and the victory of one of Gómez's former classmates, Heliodoro Díaz Quintas, in Oaxaca, Gómez undoubtedly entertained the notion that he might be named jefe político in Juchitán. On June 8, Gómez's hopes were sidetracked, when Díaz Quintas appointed Carlos Rodríguez, "a known Juarista," to the position on an interim basis. Rodríguez was an "honorable" man "with a lot of political tact and prudence," but he was also a man of little prestige.[44] His primary function was as a placeholder for the victorious moderates and to serve notice to the burgeoning partido verde that Gómez was not considered a viable candidate for the position. Frozen out of formal power, Gómez and the partido verde began to mobilize the people of Juchitán to demand their share of the spoils of revolutionary victory. This mass mobilization would become known as the Chegomista movement.

"The People Obey Only the President":
The Practice of Popular Politics

In June 1911, with the Revolution seemingly in full bloom, the competing "revolutionary" factions of Juchitán found themselves in the complicated position of staking their respective claims to political authority and democratic legitimacy within a political structure that lacked both democratic institutions and customs. Once the governor appointed Carlos Rodríguez to the position of jefe político, albeit on an interim basis, Che Gómez and his supporters had no institutional or legal means by which to challenge his authority. Local liberals could fall back on their political bona fides, as "true Maderistas," to justify their authority, but they knew well that Gómez enjoyed the support of the overwhelming majority of the population. For their part, with no formal recourse by which to occupy the jefatura, Gómez and his supporters appealed to more traditional, informal means—direct actions, petitions, and mass demonstrations—to demonstrate his capacity to *mandar gente* and his democratic legitimacy as a representative of the popular will. The Chegomistas' shows of force blurred the lines between formal and informal definitions of democracy, but they proved politically expedient. Over a short span of two weeks the Chegomistas used the raw strength of their numbers to seize control of Juchitán's political apparatus.

Tensions between Che Gómez's supporters and the moderate liberal faction existed from the outset, as Gómez strategically expanded his political authority. Invoking his mandate as municipal president, Gómez filled local offices with supporters and family members, naming his half brother *regidor*, his cousin chief of police, and his brother-in-law deputy municipal president. At the same time, Gómez established two Maderista clubs in Juchitán, ostensibly to begin organizing support for Madero in the upcoming presidential election, scheduled for October. While his historical connection to Madero is unclear, his followers perceived themselves as "the first in the South to support Madero in his struggle."[45] Gómez's play to publicly align himself with

Madero drew a spirited response from his liberal opponents, who no doubt saw themselves as Madero's rightful heirs on the Isthmus.[46]

The moderates, who had only recently founded their own Maderista club, countered Gómez's maneuvers by lobbying the state and federal governments, taking advantage of personal contacts to portray Gómez as a *revolucionario de la última hora*. This refrain was not uncommon in 1911 Mexico. Throughout the country, conservative landowners, lifelong Porfirian politicians, apolitical caciques, and known bandits cynically took up the banner of Maderismo to either protect their interests against the tide of revolution or ride it to political power.[47] Fear of counter-revolutionary infiltration had become the source of no small concern in the capital, and the moderates of Juchitán seized the moment to inundate the president, the interior minister, and the governor with information aimed at undermining Gómez's revolutionary credentials, focusing on his specious political past and his belated adhesion to Maderismo. The letters represented Gómez as "an instrument of the Científicos," sent to Juchitán by his close friend, Rosendo Pineda. Now, by launching "two insignificant Maderista Clubs" in the wake of Madero's victory, "Sr. Gómez is wanting to make Sr. Madero believe that he that he is a consummate Maderista and is asking for his support to become Jefe."[48] As an article from the local liberal newspaper asked, "will there be no account of the true Maderistas, or of those enrolled before Sr. Madero's triumph as allies of Díaz, in order to expose the false [Maderistas], or those who try to be [Maderistas] only to preserve a political position and because the revolution has already won? In the concept of the triumphant revolution, and mine, humbly, a man brought to power by Don Porfirio, without a previous accord with Madero, cannot be a Maderista."[49] According to Vicente Matus, the jefe político's secretary, transferring the jefatura to Gómez would contradict "the public interest" and ensure that "true Maderistas are the next to be surpassed by the false."[50]

The political chess match escalated into conflict beginning on June 24, when the jefe político recalled popularly elected officials in two of the district's smaller municipalities. The restitution of pre-revolutionary authorities, no doubt intended to serve notice to Che Gómez, sparked "energetic protests" throughout the district that quickly spread to Juchitán.[51] The following morning Rodríguez was tipped off that Che Gómez had called for mass demonstrations throughout the city, aimed at forcing the new jefe político to resign. According to the rumors, which circulated in Zapotec to safeguard the information from local authorities, if the situation was not resolved by ten o'clock the crowd would use force to compel his resignation. That morning Rodríguez noted "more liveliness" in town than usual and passed the news on to the chief of military operations in San Jerónimo, requesting and receiving a small protective detachment. At eleven o'clock Rodríguez received news from his family that a group of protesters had gathered in front of his house, shouting "vivas" to Madero and Gómez and "mueras" to the jefe político. Fearing for his family's safety, Rodríguez called on Gómez to disperse the crowd. Gómez claimed that when he arrived he found a group of about ten men resting in the shade of a tree. Finding them "perfectly peaceful," he ordered them to disperse anyway, which they did, according to Gómez, with no trouble.[52]

In the wake of the protest, the two sides set about preparing for a seemingly inevitable clash. Once again invoking his authority as municipal president, Gómez organized an auxiliary police force, to be appointed on a volunteer basis. Rodríguez protested the unit's formation as an obvious strong-arm tactic intended to intimidate Gómez's opponents, and denied them access to the municipal armory. "In the absence of firearms," Gómez outfitted the volunteers with machetes.[53] Galled by the prospect of machete-wielding indígenas patrolling the streets, the moderates recognized their need for outside protection and began pooling their resources in a concerted effort to appeal for state intervention. Using the Club Democrático Juchiteco as their headquarters—what Vicente Matus described as "a union of all of the intellectuals of [Juchitán], three lawyers, two engineers, commerce, and the *gente culta*"—the moderates resolved to begin printing their own newspaper, and sent a representative to lobby the governor directly.⁵⁴ "In the name of the club," Severo Castillejos traveled to Oaxaca and Mexico City "to inform the state and federal governments about local political conditions."⁵⁵ While it is difficult to discern the effect of the moderates' lobbying efforts, their pleas apparently resonated with Governor Díaz Quintas, who hatched a plan to roust Pancho León from retirement and install him as the new jefe político. The old strongman acquiesced, and the secretary of war agreed to provide him with a military escort.⁵⁶

News of León's pending return quickly spread to Juchitán, where it was received with intense indignation. Pancho León's legacy in Juchitán was somewhat mixed. On the one hand, it was during his tenure as jefe político that Juchitán became a city, replete with modern architecture, roads, and irrigation. These technological achievements had not been realized without a little coercion, and the prevailing wisdom in the capital was that León was the only person who could restore order to Juchitán. For the poor and indigenous majority, on the other hand, "just the name 'León' provoked repudiation," conjuring memories of press gangs and punitive expeditions.⁵⁷ Learning of the governor's plan, on June 30 the people of Juchitán presented him with a petition signed by 1,084 men and backed by 630 more who could not sign their names. Calling León "a cruel, bloodthirsty coward imposed on us by the despotism of Porfirio Díaz," the petitioners made their opposition clear, in no uncertain terms: "No; this pueblo, all of us, today swear that Francisco León . . . will never exercise public power in this district."⁵⁸ Che Gómez, himself a longtime enemy of León, warned Díaz Quintas that the last time León had served as jefe político the people had forced him from power.⁵⁹ Perhaps impressed by the emotional response, the governor scrapped his plan, assuring the petitioners not only that León would not be installed as jefe político but that it was still the government's intention to abolish the jefaturas altogether.⁶⁰

The following day the escalating tensions of the previous week finally boiled over in an armed standoff between the Club Democrático and the newly formed auxiliary police. Unsurprisingly, the two sides

The Rise of the Chegomista Movement 103

told distinctly different stories regarding the confrontation. On the night of July 1, the Club Democrático convened in the home of Vicente Matus to print the first issue of their official newspaper, *El Demócrata*. The editors, including Matus and Ricardo León, requested special protection, fearing Che Gómez's "elements" would interfere with their work.[61] Despite the obvious conflict of interest, Gómez obliged by ordering extra rounds of the auxiliary police to patrol the area around the press. Around ten o'clock that night, according to Gómez, the patrol picked up two men entering the house through a secret door. Finding one of the men armed, the patrol arrested both. When the two men were seized, the doors to the press slammed shut, and a shot was fired at police from inside the house. Backup arrived shortly thereafter, and the police passed the rest of the night surrounding the house and guarding its exits, to be sure no one escaped. At sunrise, the editors of the newspaper negotiated their exit with authorities and were taken into police custody.[62]

The moderates had a different interpretation of the event, framing it as another example of "Gómez's tenacious and furious persecution of his opponents."[63] For weeks, they explained, they had been posting political propaganda on kiosks throughout the city, only to have them torn down by Gómez's supporters as quickly as they could be hung. To bypass the problem, they decided to begin printing and distributing their own small newspaper, *El Demócrata*, the publication of which Gómez also tried to prevent. However, finding no legal grounds by which to block the newspaper, Gómez opted for an extralegal solution, ordering his men to lay siege to the press and destroy everything, and to kill the editors. Those inside were able to repel the siege that night, but the following day they were thrown in jail, where they feared execution at any moment. They survived the ordeal, "thanks to their strength of character, prudence, and cold blood to ward off danger"—and, no doubt, to their friends in the federal government, who intervened on their behalf.[64] The following day, when the jefe político discovered that those who had been arrested were his partisans, he and Circuit Judge Federico Sandoval (a member of the Club

Democrático) stormed into the weekly session of the ayuntamiento, demanding the release of their beleaguered colleagues. Finding them to be agitated and armed, Che Gómez ordered the two men expelled from the meeting and arrested by municipal police. The two were later released from custody, and copies of *El Demócrata* hit the local newsstands the following day, but relations between the moderates and the Chegomistas had become unbearably volatile.[65]

The fallout from the confrontation was immediate. Carlos Rodríguez tendered his resignation, explaining that it would be "ridiculous" to continue as jefe político, as he was incapable of imposing his authority. "The people obey only the president [Gómez]," he complained, explaining that he could no longer guarantee the safety of his people, or even himself.[66] Another member of the Club Democrático lamented that "at night one can no longer go for a peaceful walk, even in the center of the city, for fear of being humiliated by the police if he does not shout 'Viva el Lic. Gómez.'"[67] Emboldened, Gómez's supporters assumed a more aggressive stance and began gathering large groups of armed men from as far away as Tehuantepec in front of the municipal palace on a nightly basis.[68] If these mobilizations were intended to strike fear in their opponents, they seem to have served their purpose. The moderates bombarded the state and federal governments with requests for outside intervention to resolve the deteriorating situation in Juchitán. They reiterated that, by agitating the masses, Gómez had rendered the city unsafe for his opponents and for otherwise peaceful inhabitants, and they called for "radical measures" to restore peace and security. Judge Sandoval implied that the federal army garrison in Juchitán ought to be allowed to intervene on behalf of local officials, and directly requested that the municipal police be taken from Gómez's control and placed under the jurisdiction of the jefe político.[69] The moderates' complaints again found a receptive ear in Governor Díaz Quintas, who (repeatedly) requested from the interior minister that an auxiliary detachment of soldiers be transferred from the Ninth Military Zone in nearby San Jerónimo.[70] The moderates received their detachment, but it was not exactly what they had in mind.

The minister of the interior, Emilio Vazquez Gómez, responded to calls for intervention by sending to Juchitán a detachment of the insurgent army, rather than the federal army.[71] The Revolution had left behind two antagonistic military forces, the federal army and an insurgent army, about sixty thousand strong. In attempt to stabilize a potentially volatile situation, the Treaty of Ciudad Juárez called for the demobilization of the insurgent army, under the supervision of the interior minister. However, Vázquez Gómez resisted this charge, much to the chagrin of the interim president, who favored a speedy disarmament of the insurgents. In the first days of July, Vázquez Gómez dispatched two hundred insurgent forces from Veracruz to "reestablish order" in Juchitán—a move that deepened the growing wedge between himself and the president and did little to assuage the anxieties of the moderates in Juchitán and Oaxaca.[72] The arrival of General Gabriel Gavira on July 5 actually heightened tensions in Juchitán by drawing the city's federal army garrison into the fray. Fearing an armed clash with Gavira's new arrivals, the commander of the Twenty-Fifth Battalion requested from the secretary of war that the regiment be withdrawn from Juchitán and relocated to nearby San Jerónimo, to be stationed with the Ninth Military Zone.[73] In light of this request, Che Gómez's local opponents and the bulk of Juchitán's elite families prepared for evacuation. Local functionaries, including the jefe político, began requesting leaves of absence from their positions, citing a lack of personal security.[74] On July 9 the Twenty-Fifth Battalion led a mass exodus to San Jerónimo, taking with them more than one hundred families, including "the principal families and all the public employees" of Juchitán.[75]

As the families of the gente bien packed their belongings and prepared for evacuation, Governor Díaz Quintas felt his control of the situation in Juchitán slipping away. Desperate, he played his last card, reactivating his plan to send Pancho León to take control of the situation and, as one Mexico City newspaper put it, "to be the voice of reason."[76] Juchitán's Club Democrático begged the governor to reconsider in light of recent developments—with the federal army relocating they feared for León's safety. Their fears were hardly allayed a day later, when the municipal armory was broken into in the dead of night and its inventory emptied. Unsurprisingly, Che Gómez's inquiries into the missing cache of rifles turned up no suspects. Ignoring the writing on the wall, the governor pushed ahead, boarding Pancho León on a train bound for Juchitán. In anticipation of his arrival, "thousands of armed men" gathered at Juchitán's train station "with the intention of lynching the intruder." One resident later estimated that about 90 percent of the population turned out: "Never in the political history of Juchitán, not then nor now, had so many people come together to receive a person."[77] Luckily for León, the army garrison in San Jerónimo caught wind of the gathering lynch mob and detained him before he could arrive. The massive show of force thwarted the governor's last chance to maintain a political beachhead in Juchitán. In a few, short weeks, the partido verde had taken control of the Juchitán, leaving its opposition to lament, "Gómez has taken advantage of circumstances and for the moment dominates the situation."[78]

"To Be or No to Be": The Discourse of Popular Politics

For decades jefes políticos in Juchitán had been appointed by the state government in consultation with Porfirio Díaz, without the consent of the local population. In uniting behind Che Gómez and his candidacy for the jefatura política, the poor and indigenous majority of the partido verde sought not only to break the cycle of political imposition but also to destroy the prevailing social order that defined the terms of its subordination. Social life in Juchitán during the Porfiriato was articulated through a series of overlapping dichotomies—rich and poor, civilized and uncivilized, central and peripheral, powerful and powerless—that were imagined in gendered and ethnic terms.[79] For those disconnected from the larger fields of politics and commerce (the powerless), Che Gómez represented the opportunity to reclaim their masculine honor, submerged by decades of dependence, and demand ethnic and social inclusion, and to do so with the same language of liberal republicanism that Madero's coalition had used to justify the Revolution. In defense of popular sovereignty—the "republican principle of the dominion of the majority"—the Chegomistas demanded recognition of their right to govern themselves, as a "sovereign pueblo"; or more specifically, to be governed by one of their own (an hijo del pueblo), selected by their own "free will." Anything less, warned Gómez, "would be the same as leaving the revolution unfinished."[80] Ultimately, the defense of popular sovereignty provided the Chegomistas with an accepted political language—a discursive "repertoire of contention"—capable of bridging the gap between popular political practice and high political theory, and legitimizing their demands for political representation and self-determination within the ideological framework of the ongoing Revolution.

In their public protests and correspondence with the government, Che Gómez and his supporters undermined the political and economic justifications that sustained the social hierarchy of Juchitán, emphasizing the "disjuncture between political centrality and social-moral centrality" by representing their opponents as instruments of outside commercial and political forces, "divorced from public opinion" and thus unauthorized to speak on behalf of the majority.[81] For the gente de abajo, the gente bien—both moderates and rojos alike—were men of power but not prestige; their social status derived from the control of natural resources and bureaucratic appointments, both sustained by the federal army. The sitting jefe político was, according to one Chegomista petition, a "useless" lackey whose only authority came from "his aptitude for collecting taxes and unconditionally backing the suggestions" of the local circle of liberal judges and lawyers (Matus, Castillejos, Ortega, and Rueda). For those of the barrio de abajo, to be ruled by a man held in such low public esteem was a "disgrace."[82] Gómez, in particular, recast his opponents' high social status and material wealth as a negative, feminine trait, while embracing the low social standing of his followers as a reflection of his own legitimacy. In his correspondence, Gómez often quipped about his own economic status, referring to his opponents as "notable lawyers" and to himself as a "humble lawyer." "Who could be so lucky, to be so esteemed by his friends that they pay for his trips," he asked sarcastically when explaining his lack of funds to travel to Mexico City: "My friends are poor and cannot help." Rather than respected, however, Gómez represented the "conspicuous citizens and famous lawyers" of the moderate faction as effete, repeatedly and sarcastically describing them as "Ciéntificos," "model citizens," and most markedly "abstainers from alcohol."[83]

The subtle barbs lobbed by Gómez at the masculinity of the official candidates paled in comparison to those aimed by his supporters at Pancho León. For many León was a paragon of masculinity, whose severity and strong-arm paternalism had brought sustainable peace to unruly Juchitán. However, for the gente de abajo León was the epitome of the bad patriarch: one capable of mobilizing force but not consent; of commanding obedience but not respect. Rather than a symbol of masculinity, to them León was a "cruel, bloodthirsty coward." His authority lacked legitimacy because it did not emanate from the people, who "hate him with all of our heart," but also because he was an outsider who needed the support of the federal army to impose his will. To the Chegomistas he was not a war hero but a "colonel without service papers, without any military record"—or, as Gómez called him in a clear double entendre, the "colonel of one hundred battles and a virgin sword." For the gente de abajo, the "promises of the Revolution" would remain unfulfilled until the government appointed an "honorable person, who consults public opinion" to the jefatura.[84]

From the beginning, the defense of popular sovereignty—"the republican principle of the dominion of the majority over the smaller number"—formed the cornerstone of the Chegomistas' public discourse. By demanding recognition of their sovereignty, the Chegomistas asserted their "traditional" rights, as men, to self-governance, but did so within the "modern" legal-rational language of the Revolution itself. Che Gómez articulated his understanding of the revolutionary project and Juchitán's place therein in a June 26 telegram to Díaz Quintas:

> I will consider any movement that restores the sovereignty of the people within the revolutionary movement to be just. I consider this to be the appropriate opportunity to create a strong government supported by sovereign pueblos. If the current government intends to maintain past impositions, then there will definitely be serious difficulties. . . . [I]t would be best for you to respect the people's movement within the system, given the present circumstances to go against the well-directed will of the people today is the same as considering the revolution unfinished.[85]

Whatever the intentions of the revolutionary leaders were, failure to respect the will of the people would signify a "return to past impositions, contradicting the principles conquered by the popular revolution that gives glory to Don Francisco Madero."[86] Local political authority could no longer be passed from one group of elites to another, but would have to respect the will of the people, regardless of socioeconomic or ethnic status. In the plain light of the Revolution, political representatives needed to be legitimate in the eyes of the people—they had to be able to *traer gente* by both consent and force.[87]

On June 30, a group of seventeen hundred petitioners declared, as "free people," that they had already chosen their representative: "We want, we ask to be named Jefe Político Licenciado José F. Gómez, [the] current municipal president elected by our sovereign will."[88] The solidarity between Gómez and Juchitán's poor and indigenous majority had many dimensions, but it was rooted in Gómez's status as an insider, an "hijo del pueblo." In indigenous pueblos such as Juchitán, being an "hijo del pueblo" conveyed a sense of trust, tying the subject to communal networks of reciprocal obligations and privileges. Such status was traditionally prerequisite for holding political office in indigenous pueblos, though one that had been widely disregarded during the Porfiriato. Despite his high socioeconomic class and mestizo identity, Che Gómez was an "*hijo del lugar*, [who] has the complete trust of the people."[89] This sense of trust, according to Gómez, emanated from the "just desire" of his pueblo for a "political authority adequate to their temperament."⁹⁰ Gómez was clearly understood by the gente de abajo as an insider and as someone capable and willing to defend their honor against the advancing interests of outsiders. "The licenciado [Gómez], as he was from our pueblo," explained one Chegomista, "said: 'I will not allow my people to be trampled. [I can stop the] justice that they impose so that in its place the people of my pueblo can govern.' That is why Che Gómez formed the partido verde." Another Juchiteco remembered that "those of the government wanted a stranger [to govern] and Che Gómez asked that it be a person of our pueblo, so that he be of our blood."⁹¹ So tight was the bond between Gómez and the gente de abajo that the term "los de abajo" itself became synonymous with "gomista," and outside of Juchitán he was even thought to prefer "Zapotec, his native language" to Spanish.⁹²

If Che Gómez had the legitimate authority to rule by consent, he also had the capacity to mobilize force. By the end of the nineteenth century, Juchitán had established a place for itself in the national political imagination as "a warrior center of absolute importance," renowned on the one hand for the "Spartan bravery" of its inhabitants and on the other for its "unruly" and "turbulent politicians," known for frequently "enforcing their opinions at the point of a bayonet."⁹³ Rather than distance themselves from this reputation, both Gómez and his supporters made it clear that they could and would mobilize their notorious violence when conflicts sharpened. Through written ultimatums to the state government the Chegomistas repeatedly threatened to violently defend their sovereignty. A June 20 letter warned the governor that "the truth is in the people. We beg you to find an effective way to avoid unrest. False information may bring unfortunate consequences."⁹⁴ Such veiled threats of violence became less oblique in the correspondence of Che Gómez himself. Early on, Gómez warned Díaz Quintas, foreshadowing future events: "I am on the trail of those who prepare for an encounter with the people . . . if tolerance for the jefe continues, for my own conservation I will take the necessary steps to hit the target." He later warned the governor to avoid indecision, for it is "synonymous with failure. . . . [T]he people know the source of indecision and believe they are being tricked. You should not play with fire."[95]

The interplay of competing notions of masculine honor and legitimacy made its way into the private correspondence between Gómez and the Oaxacan governor. In long letters, Gómez lobbied Díaz Quintas for the jefatura, constructing his legitimacy—his authority to represent public opinion—by locating himself outside the legal realm of formal politics, in a more authentic realm of informal action. In his work on Tepoztlán, Claudio Lomnitz has identified this type of discourse, based on the rejection of professional politics, as part of a strategy of integration articulated by intellectuals in peripheral communities. This strategic discourse rejects politics as a necessarily "dirty" activity in juxtaposition with the harmonious work of peasant agriculture. While agriculture fulfills a cycle of production, politics produces and capitalizes on conflict and is inherently destructive. Thus, "political speech is to be systematically distrusted because it is always masking the politician's interest."[96] This distinction was clear in Che Gómez's correspondence with Díaz Quintas. Gómez drew a clear dichotomy between the domains of action and political speech, representing action as masculine—concrete and authentic (honest in its irreversibility)—and speech as effeminate—ephemeral and dishonest (open to dissimulation). In his letters to the governor, Gómez repeatedly begged forgiveness for his "frankness," but "that is my character": "I am spirited in action; I like solid foundations so that the building will be solid too." The same could not be said for his enemies, whose only "grand elements" were meaningless signatures, and "gossip, gossip, and always the gossip in all forms imaginable." Rather than represent the interests of their "poor paisanos," they wanted to deceive them, to tell them what their best interests were ("les quiere dar atole con el dedo"). However, Gómez warned Díaz Quintas not to trust the "false tinsel" of the "notable lawyers" of Juchitán. When issuing the governor an ultimatum between himself and his moderate opponents, Gómez wrote, "Now we will see if the fictive is worth more than the real and effective; if an IOU for one hundred pesos is worth more than one hundred pesos in the pocket." The implication was clear: Gómez and his followers were authentic, and with them the governor knew what he was getting; the same could not be said for their opponents, who trucked in rumor and innuendo, the least trustworthy forms of speech. "My vouchers are solid," Gómez concluded, "not wet papers."[97]

In his letters to Díaz Quintas, Gómez sought to relocate their relationship from the "dirty" (destructive) domain of politics to the "clean" (productive) domain of friendship. He repeatedly swore his loyalty to and eternal amity for the governor, explaining that "between true friends there should always be honesty, is my way of thinking. If honesty does not exist, all else is superfluous." Gómez's insistence on honesty and friendship saturated his letters to Díaz Quintas, which often assumed the tone of a jilted lover. "As I am like a woman who loves," he wrote, "I need to be loved too ... if I am to be your friend in politics I need all your trust and all your support, in order for action to be effective, energetic, and to produce the desired effects." Gómez fretted, "with pain I see ... that you do not trust me, as you tell me nothing concrete. ... I can see in your words ... that you are preparing my spirits to receive the stick." Gómez repeatedly warned the governor against indecision: "I see in your words that you want to contemplate everything, which is not possible in this treacherous world."[98] Like an anxious lover, Gómez fills his letters with ultimatums to Díaz Quintas: "There are no half measures: either you sacrifice me, or the jefe and his [people]." Fittingly, Gómez concludes his final letter to Díaz Quintas, "I am hurt by the vacillations and vagaries with which you treat me," ending, in broken English, on a Shakespearean note: "To be or no to be."[99] Unfortunately for Che Gómez, it was *no* to be.

Conclusion

By demanding their right, as a "sovereign pueblo," to be governed by one of their own and in accord with popular will, the Chegomistas laid bare the contradictions between hegemonic paradigms of marginality, which portrayed Mexico's poor and indigenous population as pre-political, and emergent revolutionary discourses of universal citizenship and liberal democracy. By using the same language of popular sovereignty used to justify the Revolution, Che Gómez and his supporters challenged elite liberal revolutionaries to deny Juchitán's poor and indigenous majority access to the spoils of revolutionary victory without undermining their own political principles. Moreover, while the Chegomistas' claim to represent the popular will was subversive, in that it implied the inversion of the local social (and cultural) order, their demands for social and ethnic inclusion did not explicitly threaten the rights of property owners or call for a fundamental transformation of the structures of rural society. Thus, unlike more radical agrarian movements like the Zapatistas, the Chegomistas' demands could feasibly be accommodated within the framework of liberal republicanism, as they did not threaten the status quo outside of Juchitán.

At the same time, however, the Chegomistas' use of informal means by which to manifest the will of the people—the only means at their disposal—undermined their larger claims to revolutionary legitimacy. Large crowds of crudely armed, poor indígenas shouting "mueras" to the jefe político, obstructing the instruments of civil society, and publicly threatening the gente bien resurrected the specter of the anarchic nineteenth century, when personalist caciques carried the day, armed force was an accepted tool for achieving political goals, and the nation disintegrated under the weight of civil war. Certainly, this was not what Madero and his followers had in mind when they called for the restoration of the liberal principles of the nineteenth century. Nor was this the democracy Madero had in mind when he reluctantly issued his call to arms in October 1910. This was, however, exactly the image of democracy Mexico's conservatives had in mind when they warned Madero that he was conniving at anarchy, or when Porfirio Díaz famously remarked, "Madero has unleashed a tiger. Now let us see if he can control it." Faced with such a daunting task, Madero and his coterie of like-minded reformers began to lean more heavily on the Old Guard for their political survival.

In a letter to President de la Barra, written on the eve of the federal army's withdrawal from Juchitán, Vicente Matus warned that those who approved the evacuation "have forgotten the historical reason why Juchitán has always been guarded by two or three battalions." He explained:

> The plaza of Juchitán has been well protected since '82 as a result of the rebellions of Melendez, el Chele, Binu Gada, and other cabecillas who ... obligated on the Isthmus the mobilization of 11,000 federal soldiers apart from volunteers from the pueblos. The two great party divisions that were bred [in the people] have been quieted with the presence of the army; but currently ... there is much latent desire to rebirth hatreds and bitterness.[100]

Matus's letter exposed the dilemma facing Mexico's liberal reformers, and recalled the nineteenth-century concept of *la república posible*: so long as society continued to be defined by nineteenth-century collective identities and loyalties ("old parties" and their "hatreds and bitterness"), authoritarian political institutions and a strong, repressive apparatus were needed in order to avoid the pitfalls that doomed nineteenth-century democracy to chronic instability and national disintegration ("the rebellions of Melendez, el Chele, Binu Gada, and other cabecillas"). Democracy remained the ideal, but until Mexico developed an educated citizenry capable of eschewing the bonds of corporate and personalist loyalties, political liberties would necessarily be restricted to a small, enlightened minority and protected by the federal army. "It would be better to guard Juchitán with one thousand men who up to this point have not had the need to fire one shot to ensure peace," rationalized Matus, "than to run the risk of the government having to mobilize 11,000 federales as in 1882."[101] Faced with the stark realities of constructing a "modern" democratic society on a "premodern" population, Juchitán's liberal reformers began their retreat, literally and figuratively, into the arms of the federal army.

3 "They Imagined That the Horse and the Rider Were One"

The Chegomista Rebellion

On October 29, 1911, Enrique León arrived in Juchitán at the head of four hundred federal soldiers, charged by the governor with relieving Che Gómez of his office and assuming the jefatura política. A throng of protesters greeted them at the train station, demanding that the president either "comply with the promise of suppressing the jefaturas políticas" or "maintain the current jefe político [Gómez]." While the protesters were unarmed and dispersed peacefully, arriving soldiers noticed that the walls of the buildings surrounding the local barracks had been crenellated, the holes barely hidden by a thin coat of lime. The gun slits in the walls were telling: beneath their peaceful pleas to "humanity, Justice, and democracy," Che Gómez and his followers were prepared for a battle; they knew well that "the state government, ignoring its proclaimed principles, [was] dead set on imposing another jefe." To them this was the struggle that would define the Revolution—a clash "of the principle of authority against the principle of popular sovereignty." By sending the federal army to "purposefully sustain an imposition," Gómez protested, the "tyrannical" government of the state sought to "provoke a revolution," knowing that the people were "disposed to once again conquer their liberties" and that "if I turn over the jefatura política, the people will declare themselves in complete rebellion." Resigned to the inevitable, Gómez concluded plainly, "The [state] government itself will be responsible before the nation [and the] civilized world for all spilling of Mexican blood."[1]

The state government met the Chegomistas' resolve with intransigence. Two days after the arrival of the federal army, Governor

Benito Juárez Maza convened an extraordinary session of the state legislature to debate the merits of armed confrontation. One after another, deputies of all political stripes took the floor of the assembly to support the governor's chosen course of action, but none captured the spirit of the delegation more dramatically than Herminio Acevedo. A lifetime Porfirian and poet from the Sierra Mixteca, Acevedo called on his fellow deputies to "reject out of hand these silly requests in which we see nothing but the bastard intentions of... a small group of individuals who fight desperately, by reprobate means, for the realization of a desire that satisfies their particular interests," and exhorted them to "put a stop to those demonstrations that poorly dressed in the clothing of false popularity... want the administration to follow their whim, without considering that the aspirations of the people are already represented in the government, legitimately selected in the past elections." He ended with an impassioned plea to let the "bandits" of Juchitán know "not to threaten us with the spilling of blood": "It's blood they want? Blood they'll get!" The deputies offered no rebuttal, and on October 31 the state congress voted unanimously to use the federal army to install a new jefe político in Juchitán.[2]

The state government's hard-line stance toward the Chegomistas reflected the Revolution's "conservative turn" as it transitioned from military victory to electoral consolidation. The historiography of the Revolution has generally pointed the finger at the interim regime of Francisco León de la Barra and the provisions of the Treaty of Ciudad Juárez for steering the Revolution in a more conservative direction. Specifically, the argument goes, the interim de la Barra regime, conservative in composition from the outset (per the "transaction" in Ciudad Juárez), allowed advocates of the Old Regime to retrench even before the Revolution had finished. By controlling the legislative and judicial branches of the federal government, many state governments, and much of the national press, these Porfirian holdovers exercised tremendous influence over the interim regime. Most importantly, the Treaty of Ciudad Juárez called for the demobilization of revolutionary forces but left the federal army intact. The interim administration doggedly pursued an uncompromising policy toward demobilization, either to protect elite interests (especially property) or to reduce the crippling effects of the swollen military budget on the national treasury, at the expense of tremendous bloodletting in the countryside and the alienation of the revolutionary coalition's more radical elements. Francisco Madero, for his part, does not escape this interpretation unscathed: caught between the powerful interests of the Old Regime and the inflated demands and expectations of popular revolutionaries, Madero proved unwilling to intervene in the internal politics of the interim regime, and thereby allowed for the "conservative turn" of the Revolution before even entering office.

The case of Juchitán, however, suggests that the critical division of the first interregnum of the Revolution was an internal split within the revolutionary coalition, between moderate civilian reformers and more radical popular revolutionaries, and that the so-called conservative "counter-revolution" was implemented not by advocates of the Old Regime but by moderate liberal revolutionaries. Despite the Chegomistas' valid claim to popular democratic legitimacy (once recognized by revolutionary leaders), the persistence of popular violence throughout the country and the continued participation of the masses in public politics drove moderate, middle-class reformers of the New Regime into the arms of the Old Regime. With the Revolution the popular classes had entered the domain of the political not as autonomous individuals but collectively, through old-style networks of personal loyalty, and advanced their collective interests through direct action (public demonstrations and petitions) rather than formal, legal channels (elections). As such, despite its conformity to the broad principles of the Revolution, the assertion of self-determination through informal practices represented an obstacle to the consolidation of representative democracy. As a result, liberal revolutionaries and representatives of the Old Regime conspired to drive the popular classes from the public sphere, violently suppressing expressions of popular sovereignty in the name of national sovereignty, embodied in the state and the Constitution (which, notably, protected states' rights).

However, the prospect of restoring peace and centralized authority on the periphery forced the New Regime to turn to the unreformed disciplinary structures of the Old Regime, driving a wedge between moderate liberal revolutionaries and their more radical allies.

On a national level, the division between the moderate and radical factions of the revolutionary coalition was most clearly embodied in the split between the coalition's nominal leaders, Francisco Madero and the Vázquez Gómez brothers, Francisco and Emilio. The relationship between Madero and the Vázquez Gómez brothers had always been strained, but it reached a breaking point in July over the decommissioning of insurgent forces and Madero's selection of a vice-presidential running mate. As Madero moved to marginalize the Vázquez Gómez brothers, they abandoned their previous caution regarding popular revolution, and in an attempt to drum up popular support for Francisco's vice-presidential bid, Emilio (the interior minister) resisted pressure from de la Barra to demobilize popular revolutionary forces. The impact of this decision on the situation in Juchitán was indelible. Emilio Vázquez Gómez entered into an illicit pact with Che Gómez, in which Gómez promised to deliver Juchitán for Francisco Vazquez Gómez in the vice-presidential elections in exchange for logistical and financial support and the assurance that his political authority would be officially recognized upon the Vazquistas' victory. Buttressed by money, arms, and a contingent of the insurgent army, Che Gómez firmed his grip on local politics, while his supporters took retribution against the gente bien. The short-term effects of the alliance favored the political fortunes of the Chegomistas, but when Francisco Vázquez Gómez lost the vice-presidential elections in October (despite carrying Juchitán), the Chegomistas were locked into a confrontation with the increasingly hostile state government. Led by newly elected Governor Benito Juárez Maza (who had made no bones about his intentions to remove Gómez), the state government worked with de la Barra to resolve the situation in Juchitán before the more conciliatory administration of Francisco Madero could take office. Working quickly, in late October Juárez Maza appointed a new, unknown jefe político to Juchitán and secured the backing of the federal army for his installation. Without a patron to protect them, the Chegomistas were forced to decide between "humbly submitting themselves ... or launching a rebellion."[3] They chose the latter.

A brief interpretive note is necessary. In the historiography of the Chegomista Rebellion, Gómez's association with the Vazquistas is either completely ignored or dismissed as the false product of rumors propagated by his numerous enemies.[4] What is agreed upon is that in early July, Emilio Vázquez Gómez sent a company of two hundred insurgent soldiers to Juchitán, at a time when he was supposed to be decommissioning the insurgent army. Shortly thereafter, Che Gómez met privately with Vázquez Gómez, while he was still minister of the interior. The precise subject matter of their meeting is unknown, and neither would ever publicly acknowledge an agreement, but there is an abundance of circumstantial evidence, gleaned from private correspondence, newspaper accounts, and official reports by government officials (both Mexican and U.S.), to suggest that an alliance between the two did exist. Without going into details here (the evidence is embedded in the following narrative), my reasoning is based on six factors. First, while rumors circulated linking the Chegomistas to myriad political figures and movements, the volume, persistence, and matter-of-fact nature of the rumors and testimonies connecting Gómez to the Vázquez Gómez brothers are overwhelming. Quite simply, Gómez was assumed by nearly all of his contemporaries to be aligned with the Vazquistas. Second, multiple soldiers and officers in the corps of insurgent forces sent to Juchitán by Vázquez Gómez went on to play crucial roles in the rebellion. Third, during the summer of 1911 the Chegomistas were receiving arms from somewhere. While no secondary sources have interrogated from where, contemporary accounts nearly all point the finger at Vázquez Gómez. Fourth, Juchitán was the only district in the state of Oaxaca to register a disturbance during vice-presidential elections. Specifically, electors charged Che Gómez with attempting to manipulate the vote in favor of Francisco Vázquez Gómez. Fifth, the Chegomista Rebellion began two days after the Vazquistas' Plan de Tacubaya called for an armed revolution. And finally, the alliance simply made sense for both sides. The Vázquez Gómez brothers, outflanked in the political arena, were desperate for support to maintain their tenuous hold on political power, and Che Gómez must have understood that his movement could not survive without a patron in national politics to protect him. Both were right, and when Francisco Vázquez Gómez lost the vice-presidential elections, both his and Che Gómez's political days were numbered.

"A Half-Measures Revolution": The Dissolution of the Revolutionary Coalition

Beginning in July 1911, Francisco Madero's revolutionary coalition began to unravel in earnest, splitting between what can broadly be called a "radical" faction and a "moderate" faction. In the short term, two critical issues divided the coalition, both of which stemmed directly from the Treaty of Ciudad Juárez: the discharge of revolutionary forces, and the upcoming vice-presidential elections. The split that emerged from the debate over these issues centered around the radicalizing faction of the Vázquez Gómez brothers and the conservatizing interim regime of Francisco León de la Barra. Polarization in the high politics of the nation's ruling coalition had a profound impact on ground-level politics in Juchitán, as it provided the Chegomistas an opportunity to take control of Juchitán by garnering the protection and patronage of the radical faction of the Vázquez Gómez brothers and the insurgent army (under the control of the interior minister, Emilio Vázquez Gómez).

Although the political behavior of Francisco and Emilio Vázquez Gómez during the summer of 1911 embodied what Stanley Ross once characterized as "the essence of radicalism," their emergence as the leaders of the revolutionary coalition's radical faction was, as Alan Knight has pointed out, more likely the product of opportunism and political preservation than any sort of ideological transformation.[5] The Vázquez Gómez brothers entered politics shortly after the Creelman interview, as fairly typical elite anti-científicos. Francisco, the older of the two, was a prestigious physician and the personal doctor to Porfirio Díaz, in addition to being a landowner and a railroad concessionaire. Despite their professional success, in early 1909 both brothers joined the opposition to Porfirio Díaz. Francisco was elected the first president of the Popular Sovereignty Club in Mexico City, while Emilio published a critique of Porfirian politics, called *La reelección indefinida*. In late 1909 the brothers joined the Partido Antirreeleccionista and hitched their political fortunes to its rising star, Francisco Madero. Madero actively recruited the Vázquez Gómez brothers to his party for a number of reasons. The brothers, particularly Francisco, were prestigious public intellectuals with connections to the Díaz regime. In converting them to the anti-reelectionist cause, Madero hoped that they could serve as political mediators between the opposition and the regime, while bringing with them an air of respectability, and more elite, anti-científico converts. By drawing defecting elites to Madero's coalition, the Vázquez Gómez brothers protected the Partido Antirreeleccionista from government repression, but also raised suspicions among the rank and file, who regarded the brothers as too conservative. Despite these suspicions, the Vázquez Gómez brothers gave Madero's political campaign a boost of momentum, and on April 5, 1910, the Antirreeleccionista convention elected Francisco Vázquez Gómez as Madero's vice-presidential running mate in the 1910 elections.[6]

Tensions began to emerge between Madero and his presumptive vice-president once their political campaign began to feel the brunt of repression. In June 1910, while Francisco Madero languished in prison in San Luis Potosí, Francisco Vázquez Gómez entered negotiations with the Díaz regime to forge a political compromise. Madero rejected Vázquez Gómez's political meddling, done without his consent, as "unbecoming and undesirable."[7] Tensions between the two mounted in the coming months, as Madero began to seriously consider the possibilities of revolution. Both brothers warned Madero against radicalizing the opposition. "If our campaign began inside the law," Francisco Vázquez Gómez advised Madero, "so it ought to end next month in order to give proof of our capacity as a party of government." Emilio Vázquez Gómez echoed his brother's sentiment, warning that revolution "would be a useless, sterile sacrifice" that "we ought to avoid at all costs."[8] Madero, however, did not heed their warnings, and upon escaping to San Antonio in October he began making plans for a revolution.

The Vázquez Gómez brothers joined Madero's revolutionary coalition reluctantly, and even then only after victory seemed in the offing. In February 1911, Francisco Vázquez Gómez began lobbying the U.S. government on Madero's behalf, and in the coming months he served as one of the lead negotiators between the revolutionaries and the teetering Díaz regime. The Treaty of Ciudad Juárez prominently bore Francisco's fingerprints: he was instrumental in negotiating Díaz's resignation, the interim appointment of Francisco León de la Barra, and positions for both himself and his brother in the new cabinet. Ironically, applying the provisions of the treaty brought the relationship between the Vázquez Gómez brothers and Madero to its breaking point.[9]

Signed in May 1911, the Treaty of Ciudad Juárez made provisions to address the two most pressing concerns for the incoming provisional government: the demobilization of armed revolutionary forces and the arrangement of democratic elections, particularly for the president and vice-president. Most of those involved in the negotiation of the "transaction" in Ciudad Juárez agreed that disarming popular revolutionaries was the only way to establish peace and prepare the ground for free elections, but they could not agree on a suitable timetable. By midsummer armed revolutionaries continued to control large swaths of the countryside and even a few important cities, creating a crisis for the new interim regime. The presence of nearly sixty thousand active, armed revolutionaries on the government payroll drained the national budget and represented a constant threat to public order. The existence of antagonistic, parallel military forces occupying the same space led to tensions that, despite the May armistice, occasionally spilled over into open hostilities, causing great alarm about the nation's continuing instability. Nowhere was the concern greater than in those regions under the control of popular revolutionaries, where "peaceful citizens" (the gente bien) complained that the revolutionaries' lack of discipline and reprobate nature had fostered a climate of lawlessness and insecurity. The dull hum of low-intensity violence emanating from those myriad areas—like Juchitán—where popular revolutionaries took control, and now took retribution, made clear to both Interim President de la Barra and Madero that free, democratic elections would not be possible so long as so much of the country continued to be controlled by popular revolutionaries.[10]

The more radical elements of the revolutionary coalition balked at the prospect of leaving the Revolution in the hands of an unreconstructed federal army, and Interior Minister Emilio Vázquez Gómez actively obstructed the regime's pacification program. Claiming that the presence of armed popular revolutionaries provided a much-needed counterbalance to federal forces, Vázquez Gómez encouraged revolutionary soldiers to avoid demobilization, continued to allocate funds to revolutionaries for arms, cash, and supplies, and converted massive numbers of armed revolutionaries into federal rural police (the rurales, still under the interior minister's authority), rather than demobilizing them altogether. Vázquez Gómez's strategic foot-dragging brought him into direct conflict with the interim president, who favored immediate and even forcible disarmament.[11] The conflict came to a head on July 12 in Puebla, where a shootout between popular revolutionaries and the federal army left forty-six dead in the heart of the city. The incident forced Madero's hand. The following day, Madero, who happened to be visiting Puebla, made clear publicly that he supported the immediate disarmament of popular revolutionaries and considered the federal army the only legitimate military force in Mexico.[12] While Madero may have seized on the issue as an opportunity to begin marginalizing the Vázquez Gómez brothers, his stance was not inconsistent with his previously stated ideology. The same could not be said for the Vázquez Gómez brothers, for whom advocating the continued mobilization of the armed masses represented an about-face from their previous caution. Perhaps sensing the coming break with Madero, they adopted a sort of radical *realpolitik*, aimed at winning the support of the insurgents. If this were the case, their gambit yielded limited success, but their political intuition proved to be quite keen.

On July 9, Madero announced the end of the Partido Antirreeleccionista and appointed a committee to organize a new revolutionary organization called the Partido Constitucional Progresista (PCP). Madero's announcement was met with disapproval from the Partido Antirreeleccionista, and especially from Francisco Vázquez Gómez, who read the maneuver as a blunt attempt to remove him from the Madero Vázquez Gómez electoral ticket. Madero assured his running mate that if the convention of the new PCP selected other candidates for either the presidency or vice-presidency, they could reject the convention. Unsatisfied with Madero's reassurances, a few days later, following Madero's speech in Puebla, Emilio Vázquez Gómez suggested during a cabinet meeting that de la Barra be removed from office and that Madero assume presidential powers effective immediately. The suggestion, which would have forced Madero to keep Francisco Vázquez Gómez as his vice-president had it been taken, was the last straw for Madero and de la Barra. Citing Emilio Vázquez Gómez's "lack of tact in handling delicate matters" and inability to work within the administration, they agreed that he should resign from the Ministry of the Interior, effective at the end of the month. In light of these developments, the Centro Antirreeleccionista withdrew its support of Madero and named Francisco Vázquez Gómez as the new head of the party. While the split cost Madero purchase among popular revolutionaries and conservatives alike, for the Vázquez Gómez brothers it signaled the beginning of the end of their careers in formal politics.[13]

"Vine, vi, vencí": Navigating the Revolution in Juchitán

The split between Madero and the Vázquez Gómez brothers had a profound impact in Juchitán, where Che Gómez and his supporters used the division to consolidate their control of local politics. As the growing strength of the Chegomistas forced the resignation of the standing jefe político on July 3, the local liberal faction pestered Governor Heliodoro Díaz Quintas and President de la Barra to intervene to protect their lives and property and to stem the rising tide of Chegomismo. Rather than transferring a detachment of the federal army from the nearby Ninth Military Zone, unbeknownst to President de la Barra, Interior Minister Emilio Vázquez Gómez responded by sending to Juchitán a contingent of the insurgent army from the state of Veracruz. On July 5, General Gabriel Gavira arrived in Juchitán at the head of about two hundred insurgent soldiers, with express orders from Vazquez Gómez to "reestablish order," assess the situation, and make an official recommendation. The choice of Gavira was not an accident. Gavira, a carpenter from Orizaba, was a dedicated revolutionary who had been imprisoned for his support of Madero, and joined him in exile in San Antonio. He earned his stripes in the fires of revolutionary combat in Veracruz, and in May 1911 he took the city of Córdoba at the head of five hundred men, for which Madero appointed him chief of the insurgent army in Veracruz. However, in the wake of revolutionary victory he began to look askance at the conservative policies being pursued by the interim regime, particularly the deauthorization of the insurgent army.[14]

Gavira's arrival did little to placate the demands or assuage the fears of civilian politicians in Juchitán and the state capital. Governor Díaz Quintas bristled at the insurgents' arrival, immediately requesting that Gavira be placed under the authority of the state of Oaxaca, while reminding the jefe político, Carlos Rodríguez, in no uncertain terms that he was to answer to the governor, not General Gavira.[15] The arrival of the insurgent army also created tension with the federal garrison stationed in Juchitán. Anticipating conflict, the commander of Juchitán's Twenty-Fifth Battalion requested from the secretary of war that the regiment be withdrawn from Juchitán and transferred to the more mestizo town of San Jerónimo, where they would be accompanied by the rest of the Ninth Military Zone. Much to the chagrin of Che Gómez's enemies, the garrison commander's request was satisfied. Fearing being left alone without federal protection, the *gente bien* of Juchitán began preparing for evacuation. Local functionaries requested leaves of absence from their positions, citing a lack of personal security in Juchitán, and on July 9 more than one hundred of Juchitán's most respected families joined the Twenty-Fifth Battalion in a mass exodus to San Jerónimo.[16]

In the absence of the federal army, the Chegomistas and Gavira's regiment of insurgent forces forged an alliance. After a few days surveying the political landscape, Gavira concluded that Che Gómez had the support of "an immense majority of the population, which is who we should satisfy." He officially recommended that the governor accept the jefe político's resignation and either leave the position vacant or appoint Gómez, adding that "any other resolution [was] destined to produce disorder."[17] The recommendation did not sit well with Gómez's opponents, who claimed that Gómez had unfairly influenced Gavira by treating him to "banquets and other flatteries" while taking "great pains to parade his popularity" for the insurgent commander.[18] Governor Díaz Quintas rejected the recommendation outright and urged Vázquez Gómez to conduct further research toward "a firm resolution that reconciles popular interests and the political interests of Señor Madero ... in the work of pacifying the country."[19] Ultimately these complaints fell on deaf ears, and Gavira's recommendation carried the day: Che Gómez's brother-in-law Julio González was named jefe político on an interim basis; and when Gavira returned to Veracruz on July 13 he left behind about one hundred insurgent soldiers under the command of Guadalupe Ochoa, another committed revolutionary from Veracruz who shared his commander's dissatisfaction with the regime's conservatism. In the coming weeks, Vázquez Gómez decommissioned Ochoa's forces and officially licensed them as rurales.[20] "The licensing of the *gavirista* soldiers," complained an editorial in *El Avance*, combined with the evacuation of the federal army, left "Gómez and his men *dueños del campo*, without fear of anyone or anything, as it left there no other force or authority capable of standing up to them."[21]

Meanwhile, the interior minister called Che Gómez to the capital to meet with him personally on July 15. At the time of the meeting the Vázquez Gómez brothers' political fortunes had just been dealt a crushing blow: the interim president (with Madero's support) had just dismissed Emilio as interior minister, and Francisco's clear path to the vice-presidency had just been blocked by the unexpected formation of the PCP. Emilio was, however, still the interior minister until the end of the month, and Francisco remained a viable, if outside, candidate for the vice-presidency. While the subject matter of the July 15 meeting remains unknown, it seems that Emilio Vázquez Gómez sought to enlist Che Gómez's support for his brother's vice-presidential bid by offering, at least, to officially recognize Gómez's authority in Juchitán upon his brother's victory. Documents recovered by *El Imparcial* in December revealed that the Vázquez Gómez brothers had offered much more: that parts of Oaxaca, Chiapas, and Veracruz would separate and form a new territory, known as the Isthmus, to be officially recognized by the federal government, contingent on Francisco's successful candidacy. Supposedly, these documents (which *El Imparcial* did not reprint) did not specify Che Gómez's proposed role in this new federal territory.[22] While the specter of separatism hovered over all political conflicts on the Isthmus, making it difficult to separate fact from paranoia, it was generally understood on the Isthmus that Gómez had struck a deal with Vázquez Gómez. Gómez himself, according to a local liberal newspaper, bragged publicly that Vázquez Gómez had given him fifty thousand pesos "to distribute among the *chusma* that has been acting on his orders," and promised to send four more battalions of the insurgent army. "Putting four battalions in the hands of Don José," the editorial lamented, "is like putting the Church in the hands of Lucifer."[23] A story in the Maderista newspaper *Diario del Hogar* later claimed that after his meeting with the interior minister, Che Gómez telegrammed his brother: "Vine, ví, vencí" ("I came, I saw, I conquered").[24] While the newspaper's story smacked of hyperbole, one could forgive Gómez for feeling a little like Caesar when a massive crowd of supporters greeted his return to Juchitán by marching him under the triumphal arch of Juchitán as the municipal band played the national anthem.[25]

Whatever the relationship between Gómez and the interior minister, on the ground in Juchitán the Chegomistas were, indeed, *dueños del campo*, and they exploited their advantage by carrying out reprisals against their opponents. These reprisals ran the gamut from highly coordinated demonstrations specifically intended to intimidate their enemies (shows of force) to more individualized acts of violence that bore the marks of retribution and resentment (pelting houses with stones, public beatings, and even homicide).[26] By controlling the legal apparatus, particularly the local and federal police, the Chegomistas operated with impunity, occupying the social space formerly reserved for the gente bien and creating a climate of fear and insecurity that drove their opponents from the public sphere. "At night," complained a prominent, self-proclaimed Maderista, "one cannot walk peacefully *even downtown* without the danger of being humiliated by the police if they do not shout 'Viva el Lic. Gómez.'"[27] This particular form of intimidation seemed especially prevalent. Vicente Matus reported that many had been injured and that no fewer than five "peaceful citizens" had been killed "for not wanting to shout 'Viva Che Gómez.'"[28] Others reported having their doors kicked in by "armed Gomistas," who ransacked their houses, threatened their families with violence, and took strong-arm bribes to leave them alone.[29] Those left in Juchitán, "living among savages devoted to Gómez," complained that they were not allowed to leave, while those who escaped to San Jerónimo "could not return to their homes without being harassed to death." Those targeted had no hope of legal recourse, because "nobody dared testify against a gomista."[30]

The Chegomistas also mobilized more organized, less violent shows of force for their more powerful enemies, intended to visually demonstrate their strength and show that no level of status could guarantee safety. Esteban Maqueo Castellanos, the owner of Oaxaca's largest estates and the most powerful man on the Isthmus, complained to President de la Barra that "a party of Maderistas" under Ochoa had visited his hacienda three times, mistreating his manager (who even Governor Díaz Quintas admitted ran his properties like a "Spanish viceroy"), inspecting the account books, demanding a list of all the workers on the hacienda, and threatening to occupy and redistribute his land. Maqueo Castellanos urged the president to order the insurgent forces to withdraw from his property, but to no avail.[31] Severo Castillejos, Gómez's most vocal critic, reported that while passing time at a friend's house a group of nearly two hundred armed men gathered in front of the house, responding to a series of bugle calls (for "assembly," "enemy in front," and "fire"). The "mob" quickly grew to nearly two thousand and began threatening to break down the doors and kill Castillejos. Gómez's people dispersed the crowd before anyone was hurt, but the "panic was terrible among the families who lived close to the threatened house."[32] This latter incident encapsulated perfectly the sort of extralegal intimidation that became a staple of the Chegomista repertoire of contention.

Gómez's supporters dismissed the allegations against them as exaggerations of a small group of derogated elites who had lost political control and now aimed to discredit their opponents. "Public peace has not been altered in the least," reported interim jefe político Julio González, "not by the residents themselves, much less by the Maderista forces, whose jefes, in my mind, are very courteous people." He attributed reports to the contrary to "the simple need of misinformed people to paint Lic. Gómez in dark colors."[33] Guadalupe Ochoa added, "those who had abandoned [Juchitán] were the minority who had tried to win over the Indians to support their candidacies."[34] While there was a kernel of truth in this defense—Gómez's enemies were prone to hyperbole, and undoubtedly exaggerated their claims—the sheer volume of complaints against the Chegomistas painted a picture of political life in Juchitán that was wholly incommensurate with liberal notions of democracy. Physical assault, corruption of the legal system, and shows of force not only limited political expression in the public sphere, thus circumventing formal political processes, but opened up the Chegomistas to charges of wanton and uncontrollable violence.

Cut off from formal channels through which to express their dissent, and subjected to violent reprisals, the gente bien of Juchitán recognized that nothing short of the return of the Twenty-Fifth Battalion would bring back the old social order. Sidelined in San Jerónimo, these families resigned themselves to bombard federal authorities with letters and telegrams begging for the return of the federal army. Their requests found a sympathetic ear in the interim governor, but until official elections could be held in the state there was scarcely anything he could do.[35]

"The Government Does Not Treat with Rebels": A Change of Course

While Che Gómez and his supporters had worked the fragmentation of the revolutionary coalition in their favor during the first half of the summer of 1911, navigating the turbulent waters of revolutionary politics proved to be tricky business. Between August and October of 1911 the tide turned against the Chegomistas, setting them on a collision course with the federal army. Specifically, the election of a new governor in Oaxaca, the appointment of a new, conservative interior minister, and the defeat of Francisco Vázquez Gómez in the vice-presidential elections all left the Chegomistas vulnerable and lacking federal protection as the interim government moved to pacify the Revolution. With both federal and state governments committed to restoring order and bringing popular revolutionaries to heel—and pushing to do so before Francisco Madero could be sworn in as president—the Chegomistas were caught between a rock and a hard place.

The 1911 campaign for governor in Oaxaca was a contest between two lackluster candidates with illustrious names: Benito Juárez Maza and Félix Díaz. "El Chato" Díaz, Porfirio's nephew, had served a variety of functions in his uncle's administration and had run for governor unsuccessfully in 1904 as an anti-científico. However, in 1911 his support scarcely went beyond a small group of the Oaxacan oligarchy, as he lacked any revolutionary bona fides to offset his allegiance to his uncle's regime. For his part, Benito Juárez Maza, known affectionately as Don Beno, was widely perceived as a figurehead for the liberal opposition. Though he had been elected the first president of the Partido Democrático in 1909, it was often remarked that his best political skill was being his father's son. Madero, for his part, disliked both candidates and even toyed with the idea of postponing the elections until a suitable candidate emerged. Despite Madero's disapproval, however, Juárez Maza did have strong support among Oaxaca's moderate liberal faction, and especially with the interim governor, Heliodoro Díaz Quintas. With Díaz Quintas's support, Juárez Maza rode the wave of liberal opposition into the governor's chair, defeating Díaz soundly in the July 30 elections.[36]

Upon taking power, Juárez Maza's first order of business was designating jefes políticos in the districts. While the new governor's politics were relatively unknown at the time of his election (he was neither active nor ambitious), during a campaign speech in Oaxaca City he explained that his first priority would be the suppression of the jefes políticos, "that is, all the pueblos will have direct communication with the capital and will not be subject to secondary superiors."[37] Once in office, however, Juárez Maza found the situation to be more complicated. On July 12, with ten of the state's districts under the control of insurgent forces, who almost invariably replaced incumbent local officials with their own men, interim governor Díaz Quintas passed a law recognizing all sitting jefes políticos. Once in power, Juárez Maza moved to reverse his predecessor's stopgap measure, complaining that "those appointments of jefes políticos made by the interim government of the state in favor of revolutionary chiefs ... have been ineffective.... [T]hose chiefs have brought to the pueblos a group of well-armed people, which is a threat to the villages, and weakens the authority of the government."[38] As governor, Juárez Maza recognized the need to subordinate the revolutionary chiefs, and the utility of the jefatura política in so doing.[39]

The gubernatorial elections were not the only state elections to have an impact on the local politics of Juchitán. On August 14 the state held elections for deputies in the state legislature, and the results from the twelve recognized districts (those not controlled by insurgents) demonstrated that in Oaxaca, as Chassen López has noted, "the radicals had won the battles, but the moderates took the spoils."[40] Moderate liberals with political roots in the Asociación Juárez and *El Bien Público* won the elections in six districts, while Porfiristas held on in three districts and radicals took three, including Juchitán. Of the three victorious radicals, neither Che Gómez nor Angel Barrios, a Magonista from Cuicatlán, ever participated in the general assembly, leaving only one active representative of the radical faction in the state congress. The rapid turnover in the state legislature reflected the fragility of the Porfirian political system in Oaxaca, but it did not represent a dramatic reversal of public policy. In regard to the situation in Juchitán, both the moderate liberals and the Porfiristas complied with the governor and his plan to bring the popular revolution to an end.[41]

At the national level, Alberto García Granados replaced Emilio Vázquez Gómez as the interior minister on August 3, dramatically changing the interim regime's orientation toward the remaining revolutionary chiefs. A founding member of the Partido Democrático, García Granados was a genuine opponent of the Díaz regime, but he was also an avowed hard-liner against popular revolution, who "despised the rebels who had done the fighting," according to John Womack. The new interior minister, "intent on sabotaging the policy of conciliation," quickly made a name for himself by assuming total intransigence with persistent revolutionaries.[42] While de la Barra pushed to have all remaining insurgent forces classified as bandits, García Granados made it clear that "the government does not treat with bandits." Within a few short days of taking office, García Granados had sent the federal army into Celaya, Guadalajara, and Morelos to forcibly disarm remaining revolutionaries. He saved his worst for Morelos, where, freed from the drag of Vázquez Gómez's resistance (and despite Madero's careful obduracy), he unleashed the federal army of Victoriano Huerta against the Zapatistas, who refused to disarm, transforming Morelos into a violent war zone. Although the situation in Juchitán did not at the moment demand such measures, certainly Governor Juárez Maza had found in García Granados a more receptive collaborator for his plans to suppress the growing Chegomista movement.⁴³

Emilio Vázquez Gómez's resignation left no doubt about the inevitability of the coming split between Madero and Francisco Vázquez Gómez, rendering moribund the latter's vice-presidential aspirations. Francisco, along with a few vocal insurgent chiefs, protested the forced resignation of his brother, contending that it would leave the true revolutionaries underrepresented in the increasingly conservative cabinet. He asked that, at least, his brother's resignation be postponed until the Madero Vázquez Gómez electoral formula could be solidified. Madero's intractability on the matter no doubt sent a signal to Vázquez Gómez. The newly formed PCP called for a convention on August 27 to define its political program and to choose its candidates for president and vice-president in the upcoming elections, scheduled for October 1 and 15, respectively. Although the fifteen hundred delegates at the convention adopted a new political program and nominated Madero as their presidential candidate without much debate, the selection of a vice-presidential nominee was much more contentious. Madero made explicit his preference for the relatively unknown governor of Yucatán, José María Pino Suárez, but urged the delegates to vote freely. On August 31 the PCP officially elected Pino Suárez as its vice-presidential candidate, to the outrage of the Vazquista contingent, for whom the entire process smacked of Porfirian political maneuvering. In choosing Pino Suárez over Vázquez Gómez, Madero squandered much of his political capital, and in the coming weeks he worked tirelessly to make amends with disgruntled Vazquistas. As the revolutionary coalition tore at the seams, Francisco Vázquez Gómez resigned from his cabinet position and announced his plan to run against Pino Suárez in the October elections as the candidate of Partido Antirreeleccionista.⁴⁴

While Francisco Madero's election as president was a foregone conclusion, the vice-presidential election promised to be a more competitive and exciting affair. Surprisingly, however, October 15 came and went without much ado—the elections "were among the cleanest, most enthusiastic, and most democratic elections in Mexican history." Pino Suárez won the nomination handily, carrying 53 percent of the vote, to 29 and 17 percent for de la Barra and Vázquez Gómez, respectively. More shocking was the fact that throughout most of Mexico "the election was a quiet affair." In Oaxaca the vice-presidential elections went off without a hitch, with the exception of one district. In Juchitán, where Pino Suárez won a shockingly low two electoral votes, electors charged that the municipal president had unfairly influenced the voting.[45]

In accordance with electoral law, each pueblo voted in primary elections for electors, one for every five hundred inhabitants, and on election day the electors traveled to the district cabecera (Juchitán) to cast their vote for their choice of the vice-presidential candidates. Electors from Rincón Antonio, Petapa, El Barrio, and Palomares—all pueblos controlled by the Maqueo Castellanos family—complained that on election day Che Gómez changed their votes from Pino Suárez to Vázquez Gómez and then, when they protested, threatened to have them arrested. One elector from Rincón Antonio later claimed that Gómez even wanted to have them executed. Fearing for their lives, the electors fled Juchitán "to escape the Gomistas' violence." Their protests sparked an investigation, after which the votes in question were returned to Pino Suárez, but Vázquez Gómez still carried the district by a count of 65 to 39. Che Gómez had upheld his end of the deal but lost his *patrón* in the capital. The Vázquez Gómez brothers challenged the results to no avail, before considering other, less formal avenues to political power.[46]

With their protection in Mexico City crumbling, Che Gómez and his supporters began preparing for a confrontation with the federal army. General Telésforo Merodio, the chief of the Ninth Military Zone in San Jerónimo, reported that the federal army "had knowledge" that in September and October, "Gómez had received in various shipments, boxes of arms and ammunition." According to prominent rumors, these arms shipments had been smuggled into Juchitán through the swamps that ran up against the city's southern edge. One source reported that Gómez scheduled a large fiesta to serve as subterfuge and that during the fiesta he received a large cache of arms from "little canoes" that arrived from the Laguna Menor. Speaking with *El Imparcial*, the source noted that afterward the rebels seemed to be very well armed, though the newspaper would later put the consignment at only fifty rifles.[47] The United States' consular agent in Tapachula, Chiapas, also verified that it was "generally understood" that Gómez and his people "had received consignments by way of the '*esteros*.'"[48] While the source of these arms shipments was unknown, it was widely assumed that they were coming from the Vázquez Gómez brothers, an assumption that was later "confirmed" by *El Imparcial*. General Merodio also noted that at this time Nicolás López, a first sergeant formerly under Gavira's command, "began giving military instruction to a large group of Gómez's partisans."[49] The general could not confirm this beyond rumors, but many of Gómez's supporters later recalled that along the banks of the Río de los Perros, Nicu Dada (as López was called in Zapotec) and Guadalupe Ochoa "taught us how to fight."[50] Meanwhile, on October 17 his brother-in-law's tenure as jefe político had run out, and Gómez himself assumed the position on an interim basis, hopeful that the new governor would recognize his office. Such recognition was not forthcoming.

The Chegomistas found themselves at a crossroads. They had hitched their dreams of autonomy to the seemingly stable political patronage of the Vázquez Gómez brothers. They had taken control of Juchitán from those who had dominated it for years, and carried out retribution, with the understanding that they had support at the higher levels of government. But as the political fortunes of the Vazquistas diminished, so too did Che Gómez's protection. Left vulnerable, he had to choose between submission and resistance. In an interview conducted with *El Imparcial* in the wake of the coming rebellion, Gómez made clear that the decision to fight was not his: "I have not rebelled; the people, obeying their own impulses, have protested in this manner against the imposition of authority, designating me as their jefe. It was impossible for me to refuse them, and I complied with my duty, respecting the popular will."[51]

"It's Blood They Want? Blood They'll Get!": Prelude to a Rebellion

On October 25, Juárez Maza named Enrique León the permanent jefe político of Juchitán. León was a moderate liberal and loyal supporter of the new governor, described by one of his partidarios as "a wise man, a perfect gentleman of flawless antecedents."[52] He was, however, completely unknown in Juchitán. Though he was not, in fact, related to Pancho León (a point the latter made publicly in the Oaxacan daily newspapers), one Chegomista recalled that "just the name 'León' provoked the repudiation of the Juchiteco people."[53] Essentially, Enrique León was a blunt instrument with which to force the Chegomistas' hand—he had no prior experience in the region, and his arrival was sure to provoke a strong popular response in Juchitán. Prepared for conflict, Juárez Maza secured approval from García Granados and General Merodio to send a contingent of the Twenty-Fifth Battalion to accompany León from San Jerónimo. Juárez Maza indicated in correspondence with high government officials that the soldiers were being sent to quell an uprising, warning that "fatal consequences" could result.[54]

In the coming months, Benito Juárez Maza's hard-line stance against the Chegomistas, characterized by his intractable will to impose an unpopular jefe político in Juchitán, drew fire from some of his liberal-minded colleagues in the federal government as a "capricious" reflection of his overbearing pride, running counter to the spirit of democracy. Indeed, Juárez Maza's intransigence toward Che Gómez and his supporters does beg some historical interpretation. In his own words, Juárez Maza provided three justifications for his actions: "to make them respect the principle of authority and cut off intrigues and destroy caciquismo." On the first count, as the newly elected governor of Oaxaca, Benito Juárez Maza sought first and foremost to establish order and impose his authority in the state, in particular by making revolutionary groups obey the constitutional authority of the democratically elected regime. According to the Constitution, the governor had the right to appoint jefes políticos by fiat, and the duty to protect the lives and property of the state's citizens. Citing Article 116 of the Constitution, Juárez Maza defended his right, if his appointments were not respected, to use the federal army to make them respected.[55]

Second, the governor defended his actions as a "radical measure" taken to thwart a "seditious movement against the General Government." On October 31, the Vázquez Gómez brothers launched the Plan de Tacubaya, calling for the nullification of the presidential and vice-presidential elections, and the elevation of Emilio Vázquez Gómez to the presidency. The plan repudiated Madero's authority on the basis that he had abandoned "those who fought" and "reneged on [the] promises" of the Revolution, by "excluding the revolutionary chiefs," and declaring them bandits. The plan made direct reference to an armed uprising in support of Vázquez Gómez's presidential bid, and authorities throughout Mexico braced for a violent response.[56] "According to reports," Juárez Maza informed the president, "Licenciado José F. Gómez proposes to launch a movement in Juchitán in favor of Vázquez Gómez." Despite Gómez's insistence that the conflict was a "purely local affair," the "persistent rumors" about a "seditious" uprising in support of the Plan de Tacubaya undoubtedly weighed heavily on the governor's decision to send the federal army to Juchitán in advance of the new jefe político.[57]

Third, Juárez Maza claimed that his hard-line stance toward Gómez was aimed at reducing the influence of persistent caciquismo and personalist authority in Oaxaca. While the elimination of personalism and "premodern" networks of patronage were both in line with liberal ideology, this pretext rings hollow—after all, the governor tolerated and even patronized personalist caciques elsewhere in the state. Juárez Maza's intransigence toward Che Gómez was rooted in the historical relationship between Juchitán and the Valley of Oaxaca. Dating back to the rebellions of Gregorio Meléndez in the 1850s, Juchitán had a long history as the flag bearer of istmeño separatism. While talk of the separation of the Isthmus from the state of Oaxaca had been silenced during the Pax Porfiriana, the stunning economic growth of the region did little to quell suspicions in the state capital. With the arrival of the railroads the value of the Isthmus's economic resources had grown to compete with those of the Central Valley, as had the population (the combined cities of Juchitán and Tehuantepec had nearly 25,000 inhabitants, compared to the 38,000 in Oaxaca City).[58] Moreover, despite the growth of the state's infrastructure, no road or rail line connected Oaxaca City directly to the Isthmus, allowing the Isthmus tremendous economic independence from the state capital. This situation engendered jealousy and suspicion in both places: while politicians in Oaxaca City regarded the growth of another industrial area in the state as potential competition, on the Isthmus, political leaders (and would-be leaders) resented their lack of political autonomy, despite the fact that "their contributions to the expense of the state form a considerable part of its total revenue."[59] As a result, the fear of separatism cast a long shadow over the state government's interpretation of the Chegomista movement. "Gómez's desire is to establish caciquismo and absolute domination in that region," Juárez Maza wrote to President de la Barra, "to the point of thinking of its separation, segregating it from this state."[60] The governor was not alone in his fears. As the Chegomista movement progressed, the specter of separatism, whether real or imagined, was resurrected time and time again by politicians and the press and projected onto the movement.[61]

For Juárez Maza, the timing of his appointment of the new jefe político was critical. With Madero due to be sworn in on November 6, de la Barra and García Granados's days in office were numbered. Behind the scenes, many within the interim administration felt Madero was too soft on the remaining revolutionaries and feared that, once in power, he would seek reconciliation. Reading the lay of the political landscape, the governor took advantage of the last days of the interim regime to act decisively in Juchitán with the full support of the federal government. Enrique León arrived in Juchitán on the afternoon of October 29, accompanied by about 150 federal soldiers, who joined the 250 who had arrived a few days before. The massive protest that greeted their arrival was, by all accounts, peaceful, though similar protests "in the name of the sovereignty of the pueblo juchiteco" were repeated every night upon León's arrival.[62] In what was their first and last face-to-face meeting, León requested that Gómez turn over the jefatura or, noting the "numerous groups of armed people" throughout the city, at least calm them down. Gómez refused. For the next three days, León and the federal army remained in the barracks, while Gómez organized massive demonstrations in front of his house and on nearby streets, and personally appealed to Colonel Manuel Zozaya, the commander of the Thirtieth Battalion and an old friend, to withdraw his troops. Zozaya rebuked his appeals, and for three days neither side budged.[63]

With the arrival of the federal army, local authorities in Juchitán snapped into action to express their dissatisfaction with the state's actions and to defend Che Gómez in the name of popular sovereignty. The municipal president, the ayuntamiento, and a prominent association of merchants appealed directly to President de la Barra, demanding that Gómez be left in power, in accordance with the will of the people. All testified to Gómez's overwhelming popularity among the people and his good standing in the community. "In the district everyone respects him, esteems him, and loves him," explained one petition, while another ensured, "the people trust him completely." Notably, all petitions clearly expressed their desire that someone from Juchitán—an hijo del lugar—occupy the jefatura. As an hijo del lugar, they reasoned, Gómez was disposed to "procure [the community's] well-being in all aspects," because he understood the "temperament and demands" of the people.[64]

For his part, Gómez remained obstinate in his defense of popular sovereignty, and in so doing absolved himself of personal responsibility for any blood that may be shed. In refusing to turn over the jefatura, Gómez told both the new jefe político and the president, "the current attitude of the people is not driven by me, but rather by their spontaneity." Thus, to turn over power to an unpopular leader would go against "the imperative will of the people." "In view of such circumstances," he explained to León, "it would be an unpardonable imprudence, on my part, to go against, for the moment, an irresistible will, exposing your person and mine to popular irritation. And what's more, by the popular attitude, at this moment it would give way to a conflict of grave consequences that the entire nation would lament." The accumulation of federal forces had caused "great agitation" in Juchitán, but Gómez insisted that it would not, in itself, spark a "public disturbance." He promised the president that "we will only defend ourselves if they attack us," but he also warned that "if the superior government proposes to sustain the jefe político [León] it had better send a few [more] battalions for reinforcement. I deem the existing force inadequate for such a proposal." Gómez guaranteed "total order" in Juchitán so long as the government "respected the popular will," but any "breach of public peace here will owe itself to the government of the state which instead of satisfying the just demands of a people, provokes it to rebellion."[65]

In Oaxaca City, as we saw, the state legislature voted unanimously to dismiss the petitions from Juchitán. Citing the state's rights as indicated in the Constitution, the lack of formal infrastructure by which to gauge "popular will," and the Chegomistas' failure to use legal political channels to seek redress for their grievances, the state congress gave Governor Juárez Maza the green light to forcibly impose a new jefe político in Juchitán.[66] At the eleventh hour, the governor himself proposed a "radical measure" to resolve the impasse. Stealing a page from Porfirio Díaz's playbook, Juárez Maza proposed to de la Barra, "it may be convenient to call on Gómez, giving him a Treasury job in some faraway state," and even suggested a few potential referees.[67] However, it was too late for such enticements. By the first of November, both sides had dug in too deeply, and on the second, the irresistible force met the immovable object.

"The Crowd Flung Itself on the Barracks": The Chegomista Rebellion

On the morning of November 2, Juchitán awoke in an agitated mood. In an early-morning telegram, Che Gómez gave the president one last chance to avoid bloodshed: "I respectfully urge you to resolve the pending conflict today. The people are extremely worked up. I judge that it will be impossible for me to calm their excitement for another day." The message was no doubt interpreted as an ultimatum. De la Barra did not take the bait, instead urging Gómez to reach a peaceful, legal agreement and to "calm the over-excited over whom you have enough power to make submit to constituted authorities." Enrique León echoed the president's sentiments, asking Gómez if he was "willing to obey superior orders" by turning over the jefatura, and requesting that in the name of "peace and proper order" Gómez "command the diverse groups of armed people to disperse." Gómez struck a familiar refrain in response: "as the current attitude of the people is not driven by me . . . I consider myself incapable of ordering the diverse groups that you refer to in your note." He added that the people "are not disposed to consent to imposition of authorities that do not match their interests and rights," and thus to turn over the jefatura, "given the popular attitude, is very dangerous." In his final line, Gómez transferred blame to the state government, because, he explained, "what is happening does not respect the will of the people." This would be the last communication between Gómez and León.[68]

That morning, from inside the barracks Colonel Zozaya noticed "a large number of armed men" in the streets and the plaza, "heating up" for battle. Around noon the excitement gave way to an ominous silence, as the plaza cleared out for the first time since León's arrival. León later testified that he knew something was amiss when the street vendors did not come to the barracks to sell the soldiers their daily lunch. According to the correspondent for *Diario del Hogar* and General Merodio (neither of whom was actually there), at about 1:30 Gómez gathered the armed masses in front of the municipal palace, took to the balcony, and "directed a violent speech at the people, urging them to spill up to the last drop of blood before giving up their autonomy." Shortly thereafter, "roused to fury by Gómez's seditious words, the crowd flung itself upon the barracks."[69] Conflicting narratives of the events of the following five days were told in the press, in congressional meetings, and in correspondence, and were later remembered and retold as the Chegomista Rebellion assumed a central place in the collective memory of Juchitán, making it nearly impossible to parse fact from fiction. What follows is an attempt to establish the most basic narrative of the federal's army's siege of Juchitán.

Predictably, federal commanders and rebels gave conflicting testimony as to who fired the first shot, each blaming the other for the commencement of hostilities. Regardless of who shot first, all accounts agree that the shooting started around 2:00 and was furious in its opening hours. The federal army hunkered down in the barracks and the adjacent church, while the Chegomistas laid siege, occupying the surrounding buildings and peppering the barracks with bullets, stones, hunting spears, and dynamite, "in the midst of [hurling] the lowest and most obscene insults." The Thirtieth Battalion, for its part, had seized the strategic high ground in the towers of the church, from where they unleashed a "rain of bullets" on the Chegomistas that "left a lot of dead bodies in the streets." Notably, all popular accounts of the siege attribute the federal army's capture of the church towers to the deviousness of Colonel Zozaya, who convinced his close friend, Che Gómez, that his men were prepared to withdraw peacefully. When Gómez ordered his people to stand down, federal soldiers occupied the church towers and opened fire on the rebels. By hook or by crook, the first day of combat established the pattern for the coming days: the outnumbered federal forces using defensive high ground to take advantage of their superior arms, and the Chegomistas launching a relentless siege on the barracks, taking advantage of their seemingly endless supply of reserves.[70]

According to the flood of refugees that poured into Salina Cruz in the evening, between two and three hundred had been killed in the first hour of combat, mostly rebels. Estimates varied tremendously regarding the number of combatants, especially rebels. Reports put the Chegomistas anywhere between three and six thousand strong, and the federal army somewhere between 250 and 500 soldiers. The quality of arms made up for the difference in numbers. The vast majority of the rebels did not have rifles, and those who did carried old Mausers ("de esperame tantito"), allowing the federal army to keep the siege at bay. On the first night, the fighting lasted for about four hours. By nightfall the Chegomistas had cut Juchitán off from the outside world, severing telegraph lines, digging up railroad tracks, and blocking the roads. Reinforcements for the federal army had been sent but did not arrive—they were attacked and repelled in a pueblo outside of town. The refugees who arrived in Salina Cruz that evening would be the last civilians in or out of Juchitán for about a week. The federal army did score one important victory, though: a team of government spies arrested Guadalupe Ochoa (reportedly with a satchel full of money) attempting to blow up the Tehuantepec Bridge. Though both Gómez and Ochoa would insist repeatedly that Ochoa had nothing to do with the rebellion, it was widely assumed at the time that the federal army had captured Gómez's primary co-conspirator.[71]

For the next two days the two sides remained deadlocked, with the Chegomistas laying near-constant siege to the barracks while the federal army defended. Federal soldiers commanded most of the center of town from their positions in the church towers, while the Chegomistas settled in for a war of attrition. By cutting off the army from food, water, and reinforcements, the rebels wanted to wear the soldiers down and starve them into submission, a strategy made possible by the rebels' massive numerical advantage. Reports indicated that on November 4 the situation seemed to favor the Chegomistas. By all accounts, the rebels were taking very heavy casualties but showed no sign of stopping. Meanwhile, the federal army had resorted to eating their horses "without condiments." That day, the rebels took the Hotel Central, one of the city's only multi-level buildings, located on the central plaza. The hotel had been a refuge for notables from

Juchitán and foreigners who had failed to escape on the first day of fighting. The refugees had managed to hold off the Chegomistas for the first two days, but on November 4 the rebels broke through using a massive charge of dynamite. The attack left nearly everyone inside the hotel dead, including members of the elite Vera family, the local judge, an American, and a Spaniard. The assault on the Hotel Central would become a touchstone topic in coming weeks.[72]

On the afternoon of November 5, the arrival of about three hundred reinforcements with heavy artillery completely changed the complexion of the battle. After a few failed attempts, Colonel José Manzano's Fifteenth Battalion arrived in Juchitán via the road to nearby Espinal, bringing with them two 75-millimeter cannons. From their position in the road, the soldiers began strafing enemy positions. Creating a "thunder like no one had ever heard," the cannon fire dislodged the rebels, causing them to flee "in the midst of a horrible panic" and allowing the reinforcements to cut a path to the barracks. The barrage lasted for another four hours, during which the bulk of the rebels abandoned the city. The colonial aspect of the federal army's "conquest" of Juchitán was not lost on one Chegomista participant, who made the analogy that the cannon was "unknown to [the Juchitecos] until now ... as the horse was unknown to the valiant soldiers of Moctezuma when the army of Hernán Cortés appeared, for they imagined that the horse and rider were one."[73] By nightfall, the federal army had seized the entire city center, while the Chegomistas took to the countryside to regroup. Che Gómez himself took refuge on a family ranch about twenty miles south of town.[74]

On the morning of November 6, about 150 soldiers pushed out from the barracks with both pieces of heavy artillery, with the intention of finishing off the rebels and finding food. What they found was startling: the city had been almost completely abandoned, the main buildings in the central plaza almost completely destroyed, bullet holes riddled everything, and "over one thousand unburied cadavers were strewn about the entire city" in various stages of decomposition. The soldiers found the food stand of "a couple Chinese," where they ran into a handful of local notables who had been afraid to leave their houses during the firefight. They later encountered a few small pockets of rebel resistance in the barrio de abajo and "on the other side of the river," but easily set them to flight. In the afternoon, as buzzards circled overhead, federal forces occupied the municipal palace and set themselves to the tasks at hand: securing provisions, attending to the wounded, putting out fires, and burning the bodies of the dead.[75] The smoke from the burning bodies could be seen "day and night" from more than twenty miles away, in Salina Cruz.[76] Nowhere in Mexico cut a more somber image of the faded hope of revolution than Juchitán. Meanwhile, hundreds of miles away, Francisco Madero, "the apostle of democracy," was being sworn in as the new president of Mexico.

Conclusion

On Madero's first day in office, news of the bloody events in Juchitán was making its way into national newspapers. In the coming weeks, as events in Juchitán began to dominate the national press, the Chegomista Rebellion became the Madero regime's first national crisis—a symbol of the failure of the interim regime and a reminder that the Revolution was not yet over. Historian Stanley Ross has argued that upon assuming office, Madero was trapped between "two great forces" that threatened "to engulf the new executive": advocates of the Old Regime, who had been allowed to regroup under de la Barra and who now controlled the legislature, the judiciary, and the army; and the elements of revolution, who "were expecting and demanding far-reaching social and economic changes."[77] However, the story told by the Chegomista Rebellion was not so simple. Madero was, indeed, trapped between the demands of pacification and revolution, but most of the advocates of pacification were not representatives of the Old Regime, nor were the demands of the revolutionaries, in their majority, so "far-reaching." With prominent exceptions, most notably the Zapatistas in Morelos, popular revolutionaries did not call for wide-ranging, structural changes but rather for political reform—specifically, respect for popular sovereignty—that clearly fell under the ideological umbrella of the Revolution. The new regime's failure to pacify the Revolution resulted not from its "abandonment" of radical socioeconomic reforms (which it never endorsed in the first place) but rather from its exclusion of popular revolutionaries from political office. The monopolization of public office by middle-class civilians was not inevitable, nor did it necessarily work in favor of the efficient and expedient pacification of the countryside. It was the result of decisions made by representatives of the new regime, itself constrained by the pressure of revolution.

The "orgy of political patronage" unleashed by the fall of the Porfirio Díaz complicated the practice of designating jefes políticos. After decades of being frozen out from political office, middle-class opponents of the Díaz regime lined up to demand rewards and positions from the new administration, while politicians in the national and provincial capitals consolidated their authority by building vast networks of political patronage that undergirded the electoral artifice of their "modern" liberal regime. As an appointed office, not legally subject to federal supervision or public opinion, the jefatura política was the perfect instrument by which state governors could build their patronage networks. The fixing of jefes políticos gave moderate, Maderista governors the opportunity to reward their fellow civilian oppositionists while freezing out more popular aspirants. On this score Juchitán was more the norm than the exception. As a burgeoning peripheral city, Juchitán did not lack for worthy middle-class candidates. Local professionals and politicians like Severo Castillejos and Vicente Matus had supported the liberal cause for years preceding the Revolution (while climbing the professional ranks), and clearly expected one of their own, or at least someone aligned with their interests, to be promoted to the jefatura. However, the availability of "middle-class worthies" put Juárez Maza in a bit of a bind, familiar to other "revolutionary" governors of the moment: while he owed his supporters political patronage, "platonic," middle-class professionals simply lacked the local prestige to impose their authority, particularly in those districts where more-popular leaders competed for political power.

Such was the case in Juchitán, where the necessities of maintaining networks of political patronage were simply incommensurate with the necessities of maintaining order.[78]

Shackled by the demands of political patronage, as the Chegomista Rebellion took the national stage in November 1911, Benito Juárez Maza cloaked his hard-line stance toward Juchitán in a (somewhat imaginary) Oaxacan political tradition: the federalist defense of state sovereignty. Specifically, Juárez Maza resurrected the specter of istmeño separatism and virulently defended the sovereign right of the states to appoint jefes políticos, free from federal oversight. Regardless of the sincerity of this justification, picking up the torch of state sovereignty in a proud state such as Oaxaca proved to be a political boon for Juárez Maza, generating support in the streets of Oaxaca City and in the state legislature. By taking an unyielding stance toward Che Gómez, Don Beno transformed himself from a political figurehead to a respectable (if conservative) revolutionary governor. Juárez Maza's metamorphosis symbolized the political ascendance of the Revolution's moderate liberals, who consolidated their political authority by restraining the popular revolution that brought them to power.

4 "It Is Not Possible with the Stroke of a Pen to Suppress the Jefaturas"

State Sovereignty and the Peace Process in Juchitán

On November 19, 1911, after several days of negotiations between Che Gómez and a federal peace commission, representatives from Juchitán's eighteen municipalities arrived in the cabecera to take part in a plebiscite to name a new provisional jefe político. Under the watchful eye of the federal army, the plebiscite went off without "the slightest disagreeable incident," and the people overwhelmingly approved the nomination of Cándido Aguilar, a revolutionary chief from Veracruz, whose candidacy had been agreed upon by Gómez and the peace commission. As a result, peace in the region seemed imminent: the Chegomista rebels, now encamped in the interior of the district, "put down their arms and prepared to return to their homes and dedicate themselves to work"; Che Gómez, having renounced his claim to the jefatura, waited at the train station for President Madero's invitation to meet with him in the capital; and even the standing jefe político, Enrique León, admitted that peace seemed to be in the offing. The fledgling Madero regime had seemingly averted its first major political crisis, pending the ratification of the governor of Oaxaca, Benito Juárez Maza. While the governor had shown himself resistant to the process, Gabriel Gavira, the peace commission's lead negotiator, remained optimistic that "once Governor Juárez understands the real situation in Juchitán and the agreed upon demands of the rebels, he ... will accept the accords, facilitating the efforts of the commission." The optimism in Juchitán, however, was met with a deafening silence in the state capital.[1]

After a few days of expectant silence, instead of ratifying the results of the plebiscite, Governor Juárez Maza publicly repudiated the referendum as a violation of sovereignty of the state of Oaxaca. According to the governor, not only had the federally sponsored peace commission violated the state's political jurisdiction by negotiating directly with the rebels (and freezing the state out of the process), but the selection of the jefe político by plebiscite directly contravened the governor's right to appoint jefes políticos at his own discretion, free from federal supervision, as clearly stated in the Constitution. In an extraordinary session of the state congress, the Oaxacan legislature called on the federal government to fulfill its constitutional obligation to put the federal army at the disposal of Governor Juárez Maza in order to suppress an "internal disturbance." When the federal government refused, declaring the issue a "purely local" problem, Oaxaca City erupted in protest. In defense of the sovereignty of the state, throngs of protesters took to the streets of the state capital shouting "Death to Madero," hundreds of armed young men poured in from the surrounding sierra to volunteer their services to the state government, and Governor Juárez Maza, addressing the crowd from the government palace, asked those who supported him in peace to now "support him in war." Exhorted by Deputy Alberto Vargas to join him in "rebellion against tyranny and absolutism," the state government of Oaxaca resolved to withdraw its recognition from the federal government and resume its sovereignty. Only a few days after peace had seemed so imminent, the conflict in Juchitán now brought the Madero regime to the brink of national disintegration.[2]

The negotiation of the jefatura política in the wake of the Chegomista Rebellion resurrected the overlapping and competing sovereignties that had long been at the root of the nation's instability. Ironically perhaps, both Madero and Juárez Maza had publicly called for the suppression of the jefatura política during their respective campaigns, and now, faced with a massive popular insurrection in Juchitán, the struggle for control of the jefatura in Juchitán threatened to embroil them both in "a wicked civil war."[3] Acknowledging in his executive report of November 24 that "it is not possible with the stroke of a pen to suppress the Jefaturas," Madero sought nonetheless to introduce a measure of democracy into local politics, outlining a general prescription for the transformation of the jefatura política in Mexico. Rather than seeking to amend the Constitution, Madero's report explicitly recognized the states' right to appoint jefes políticos independent of public opinion or federal influence, but called on all state governors, and Juárez Maza in particular, to temper their constitutional authority and name jefes políticos in informal consultation with public opinion and in conformity with the popular will. Thus, rather than changing the letter of the law, the revolutionary regime's model of local democracy sought to amend its spirit, recalling the social contractual relationship that characterized the informal "pacts" of the nineteenth century, in which the pueblos exchanged loyalty to the government and conformity to the general will for a degree of local autonomy. However, in so doing the federal government found itself handcuffed by the formal constraints of the Constitution and trapped between respect for the sovereignty of the states and the need to impose democratic rule in the nation's disgruntled peripheral districts. In choosing the latter, the Madero regime ran up against the recalcitrance of the state governments, most notably that of Oaxaca.[4]

The federal government's attempt to negotiate a compromise solution to the problem of the jefatura política in Juchitán transformed the situation from a regional conflict into a national political debate. The peace negotiations in Juchitán came at a critical time for the Revolution. After four months of the interim regime's increasing conservatism had left the revolutionary coalition in tatters, Madero sought to restore unity and pacify remaining revolutionaries by resurrecting the principle of popular sovereignty and replacing repression with reform, at least in those cases that did not require massive social restructuring. Madero's attempt at pacification through reform provoked a fervid response from his increasingly vocal critics, who began to publicly question his capacity to maintain order. For these critics, eager to see the president apply the *mano dura* (iron fist), the conflict in Juchitán represented the perfect test of the new president's mettle. By negotiating with the rebels and constraining the governor's use of the federal army, they argued, Madero had snatched defeat from the jaws of military victory, allowing the rebels to regroup and lending an air of legitimacy to a clearly seditious movement. Other critics of the regime, particularly those in Oaxaca, saw traces of the Old Caudillo in Madero's intervention. They decried the work of the federal peace commission as a transparent attempt by the "midget dictator" to expand the authority of the executive at the expense of the states, and picked up the defense of state sovereignty as a counterbalance to the new regime's centralizing tendencies. All of these different strands of opposition came together to defend the Oaxacan government's right to autonomously appoint jefes políticos and to use the force of the federal army to submit the Chegomista Rebellion to legally constituted authorities.

Faced with mounting pressure in the streets, the press, the Oaxacan legislature, and the national Senate, the Madero regime capitulated to the state government of Oaxaca. On November 29 the national Chamber of Deputies voted overwhelmingly to turn the federal army over to the state government of Oaxaca, reversing its vote of five days previous. A new accord, negotiated privately by Madero and the president of the Oaxacan state legislature, gave Governor Benito Juárez Maza total autonomy over federal forces stationed in Juchitán and the appointment of a new jefe político, while approving amnesty for the rebels and a guarantee of safe passage to Che Gómez to meet with the president in Mexico City.[5] The Madero regime abandoned its commitment to limited democratic reform in Juchitán in the name of restoring peace and order, and within days the federal army swept unimpeded through the rugged interior of Juchitán. On December 4, his movement crumbling around him, a somber Che Gómez boarded a train to Mexico City to meet President Madero and decide his fate.

"A Theater of Dreadful Carnage": The Aftermath of Rebellion

News of the Chegomista Rebellion occupied the headlines of all of the Mexico City newspapers during the first days of Madero's presidency, bringing into the national imagination the rebellion in all of its gory detail and transforming the situation in Juchitán into a national political crisis. Early reports from Juchitán stole national headlines by sensationalizing the carnage in Juchitán, repeating a few basic themes. Prevented by continued light combat from entering the city, news correspondents were forced to get their information from the same pool of refugees arriving in nearby Salina Cruz, fleeing "the horrors of war." According to recent arrivals, the entire city was burning and would soon be reduced to rubble. The dim glow of Juchitán could be seen "day and night" in Salina Cruz, over twenty miles away. The White Cross was stuck in nearby San Jerónimo, alongside press correspondents, awaiting federal reinforcements to open up the road to Juchitán. Until they arrived, the injured could receive neither medical attention nor food or water. Even the animals in Juchitán were dying of hunger and thirst, and the federal soldiers now stranded in Juchitán were forced, again, to eat the horses of the reinforcements of the Fifteenth Battalion, while parceling out bits to the wounded.[6]

On the evening of November 7, federal reinforcements secured the road into Juchitán. The following day, as news of a possible peace commission circulated in the region, the federal army and the rebels called a tenuous truce. As correspondents flooded into the city, they reported that Juchitán "continues to be a theater of dreadful carnage," reduced to "nothing but a mountain of human ruins." They were now firsthand witnesses to the destruction of the central plaza, the stacks of unburied bodies, and the untended wounded. The description of Leopoldo Zea, the correspondent from *El Imparcial*, encapsulated early press accounts: "The streets of the town are strewn with cadavers, piled up and exposed to the elements. Many streets' entrances are completely blocked by heaps of unburied bodies, drenched in foul-smelling blood, which already gives off a nasty odor. The picture is horrendous as flocks of hungry and fierce birds contemplate in the sky, awaiting the opportunity to swoop down and fix their beaks on their prey." This image, including circling vultures, was repeated in other newspapers. The picture was even grimmer for the surviving injured, "who, abandoned, without medical attention, go dying slowly, killed by thirst and desperation." The White Cross and the army's medical brigade immediately set about their work, tending to the wounded and burning the bodies of the dead to prevent the spread of disease. Their work of was slow going, however, as days of neglect had left the wounded infected and in need of complex medical procedures. Understaffed and lacking the proper equipment, the medics went about their work without gas or disinfectant. Burning the bodies of the dead continued daily for over a week. Fearing the spread of "mephitic gasses," the White Cross moved the bodies from the streets and began storing them in designated houses, while burning an estimated eighty-five bodies per day. The lack of food continued to be a problem for newly arriving soldiers, as Juchitán remained isolated. Those who did manage to smuggle food into Juchitán sold it at exorbitant prices. The city itself continued to smolder, with ashes burning and filling the air with black smoke even a week after the fighting had ceased. Much of the smoke may have emanated from the city's barrio de abajo, which, according to reports, the federal army burned to the ground in the wake the rebels' evacuation, "with a view to furnish a warning and as a punishment." While reports varied widely in their attempts to establish a body count, after a week of sorting through the damage the White Cross set the official count at five hundred federal army casualties, including ninety deaths, and about one thousand rebel casualties, with four hundred dead.[7]

As federal reinforcements arrived, relocated from the battlefields of Morelos, they slowly began to expand the federal army's field of operations. Facing light resistance despite an informal truce, the federal army secured the road from San Jerónimo to Juchitán, but the rest of the district belonged to the Chegomistas. Despite the presence of five army battalions, the Chegomistas controlled traffic in and out of the interior by cutting off transportation and communication, digging up rail lines, cutting telegraph cables, and taking up "magnificent positions" along the roads. On November 13, Gómez personally telegrammed the White Cross to assure them that his men would "respect the insignia" and allow them free and safe movement as they tended to the rebel wounded. Reports varied on the number of active rebels, generally settling on five or six thousand. According to the *vox populi* in Juchitán, entire pueblos were draining into rebel camps, to the extent that Gómez and his cabecillas were forced to turn them away due to a lack of arms, ammunition, and horses. Gómez's clandestine fortress near Unión Hidalgo reportedly housed about three thousand rebels alone, organized into eight divisions.[8]

Stuck in Juchitán, newspaper correspondents were forced to depend on the local rumor mill for information, particularly regarding the rebellion's elusive leader. Rumors swirled in the immediate wake of the rebellion about the source of the Chegomistas' armaments and their broader political affiliations. Reports surfaced, were refuted, and resurfaced connecting the Chegomistas to all kinds of larger political movements, both revolutionary and counter-revolutionary, but always anti-Maderista. The majority of the political gossip in Juchitán focused on the status and location of the rebel leader himself. Rarely did a day go by that Gómez was not reported either dead or captured, or having disappeared or escaped to Chiapas. Perhaps most indicative of the public imagination of Gómez was the portrait painted of his political camp in the November 7 edition of *El Demócrata Mexicano*. Based solely on interviews conducted in Salina Cruz, the correspondent reported that Che Gómez had set up headquarters in a straw hut decorated with the sign "Peace and Popular Sovereignty," from whence he declared himself the General in Chief of the Liberating Army and named a primary school teacher from Chihuitán his secretary of war. According to this front-page article, Gómez had further decreed Juchitán an independent "Republic," going so far as to conduct interviews for the position of president of Juchitán.[9]

On November 11, from his secret encampment Gómez arranged formal interviews with a pair of national reporters, hoping to dispel rumors and clarify for a national audience the true nature of his movement. Aldo Baroni of *El Demócrata Mexicano* and Leopoldo Zea of *El Imparcial* both made the long and arduous trip through Juchitán's rugged interior, led by an escort of armed rebels. As they passed through ramshackle camps along the way, they estimated rebel forces to be between three and five thousand in number, "poorly armed," and all "wearing a green twig in their hats, which is the gomista badge." Zea noted that the rebels greeted them with spirited rounds of "Viva Madero," but upon questioning did "not even know that *señor* Madero is the President of the Republic." Both correspondents related that Gómez, for his part, was eager to talk to them about politics and everything else. When asked why he had rebelled, Gómez responded, "I have not rebelled; the people, obeying their own impulses, have protested in that manner against the imposition of authority, designating me as their jefe. It was impossible for me to refuse them, and I complied with my duty to respect the popular will." He denied that he had any personal interest in the jefatura, "a post that seems insignificant to me, given my social and pecuniary position," or that he was a Vazquista: "I have not chosen any political flag; if I were Vazquista do you think that we would not be alone, that the entire Isthmus and the State of Chiapas and other towns would second our movement?" To this end he added that if he had been part of a vast conspiracy, he would not have allowed all of his personal belongings, including photos of his dead children, to be destroyed in the fighting. "The matter is entirely local," he reiterated.[10]

In the interviews, Gómez made clear that he was open to peace negotiations so long as certain preconditions were met. His demands included general amnesty and indemnities for his supporters and the resignation of Enrique León as jefe político. He explained that he had already proposed that the next jefe político be named through a popular plebiscite, and even offered to withdraw his name from consideration. Gómez insisted that a plebiscite would work to pacify the region if the government "named a commission made up of honorable and impartial people to oversee the election and make respected the popular will." While he denied knowing any good candidates, he suggested that the new jefe político should not have any connections to the federal army, as "my paisanos reject all that which militarism signifies." Reflecting his distrust, Gómez made it clear that he would not negotiate with the federal army or the Oaxacan government. Throughout the peace process, Gómez actively pursued a personal meeting with President Madero, with a few conditions: he wanted two days before leaving for Mexico City to explain his absence to his men, so they did not fear that he was abandoning them; he insisted on a federal writ of safe-conduct (a *salvoconducto*) for himself and twelve of his men, to ensure their safety en route to the capital; and he wanted guarantees that if negotiations broke down he would be allowed to return to Juchitán to reunite with his men. For many, particularly within the state government, Gómez's conditions seemed exorbitantly steep, but the rebel leader remained confident that they would be met.[11]

"Jealously Guarding the Good Name of the State": The Rise and Fall of the Peace Process in Juchitán

As hostilities in Juchitán slowly grinded to a halt, the peace process proceeded in fits and starts. The first peace commission, composed of volunteers, never got off the ground. Paralyzed by disagreements over membership and the federal army's refusal to provide security, the commission that had formed on November 7 folded before a single conference could be convened. Hoping to avoid the factionalism that doomed the first commission, on November 14 Interior Minister Abraham González appointed a new peace commission to Juchitán, bestowed with the authority to negotiate officially on behalf of the federal government. González, the popular former governor of Chihuahua, put the commission under the charge of Gabriel Gavira, the former chief of the insurgent army in Veracruz who had brokered an uneasy peace in Juchitán only months before. González expressed his hope that Gavira's presence would restore Gómez's faith in the peace process and help "avoid the senseless spilling of blood," as it had in an "analogous" situation in July. To accompany him, Gavira chose the twenty-two-year-old Cándido Aguilar, a Magonista who had made a name for himself fighting under Gavira in Veracruz. Gavira himself sounded optimistic, telling *El País*, "I have total confidence that I will achieve great success in my pacification efforts," noting, "I have some influence among the citizens of Juchitán."[12]

The federal government's direct intervention in the matter, and especially the inclusion of Gavira on the commission, did not sit well with either the state government in Oaxaca City or Gómez's enemies on the Isthmus. In the state capital, many feared that the influence of "Gómez's friend" would be "adverse to legitimate juchiteco interests and favorable to Gómez's *cacicazgo*," and was destined to produce "illegality, tyranny, and disorder." News that Gavira boarded the train for Juchitán with Gómez's son, Chechito, did little to assuage anxiety in Oaxaca. The peace commission also encountered stiff resistance from hard-liners, especially in the federal army, who rejected any negotiation with the rebels. Since being ordered to suspend military operations, the federal army groused that negotiations would "sully their victory, won at the cost of so much sacrifice." They feared that the Chegomistas, "already defeated," would take advantage of negotiations to steal a political victory. The *jefe de armas* in charge of operations on the Isthmus, Telésforo Merodio, refused to offer protection to peace commissioners because, he explained, "the problem had already been resolved by force of arms." One of the commissioners remarked that Merodio, a longtime enemy of Che Gómez, believed all the rebels "should be exterminated."[13] He was not alone on the Isthmus. Two hundred people in Rincón Antonio signed a petition to the governor, protesting any negotiations with the "bandit" Gómez.[14]

Despite these objections, the second peace commission arrived in Juchitán on November 15 and in short order had worked out a peace accord with the rebels. The following day, Gavira and Aguilar sat down with Che Gómez and his cabecillas at one of the Gómez family's ranches in nearby Xapa and worked out the terms of a peace treaty: Gómez would turn over the jefatura to his brother Félix (who had served as municipal president prior to the rebellion), and representatives from all of the district's eighteen municipalities would come together to select a new jefe político by plebiscite; Gómez and the standing jefe político, Enrique León, would withdraw their names from the contest; Gómez would go to the capital with a writ of safe-conduct for himself and twelve of his men to meet with President Madero; the rebels would fix all of the telegraph lines and railroad tracks destroyed in the conflict; general amnesty would be extended to the rebels' rank and file; and Gómez and his men would be granted indemnities for damages incurred by the federal army. The commission shelved questions about rebel disarmament and the withdrawal of federal forces until after a new jefe político had been selected. When asked about disarming the Chegomistas, Gavira responded that he "considered [the time] inopportune and dangerous, as the rebels maybe would refuse, or even hide their arms." He assured them that "once the motive for the uprising is removed, all difficulties will cease." An anonymous official in Mexico City echoed Gavira's sentiments, telling *El País* that "the Juchitecos will not put down their arms until they 'have seen with their own eyes' that their ideals are not [being] deceived." Gómez refused to surrender to military authorities, preferring to wait for his passport to turn himself in directly to Madero. As a show of good faith, the Pan American railroad resumed its services.[15]

On November 19, as recounted at the beginning of this chapter, the people of Juchitán carried out a perfectly peaceful plebiscite. Delegates from all of the district's municipalities came together in Juchitán and, "without manifestations of hostility," selected Aguilar as the provisional jefe político. Optimism abounded as rebels prepared to disarm and return to their homes, trumpeting "the announcement of a period of calm and prosperity in this region." *El País* reported that Governor Juárez Maza was expected to ratify the results of the plebiscite "today or tomorrow . . . and then calm will be completely reborn." The following day, with the announcement that they would be allowed to return to their homes, groups of rebels gathered on the outskirts of town. In an interview with *El Imparcial*, Gavira promised that federal forces would not withdraw from the Isthmus until they had achieved total pacification, but "as soon as [Aguilar] takes possession of his post, the rebels will put down their arms to peacefully return to Juchitán. . . . [A]fter a tremendous struggle . . . they are eager to return to their homes and make peace." He ended the interview expressing his confidence that the governor would ratify the popular selection of Aguilar in short order. With peace in the air, all of the major newspapers, with the exception of *El Imparcial*, withdrew their correspondents from the Isthmus.[16]

While the press went silent regarding the situation in Juchitán, Governor Juárez Maza worked behind the scenes to dismantle the peace accord and prepare the legal framework for a confrontation with the federal government. Since the announcement of the second peace commission, Juárez Maza had been trying to block negotiations. He warned Enrique León, the jefe político in Juchitán, that Gavira "did not have any power" in the matter but would "try to meddle in affairs that do not correspond to him," and he reminded León that "for no reason are you to turn over the jefatura to anybody without an express order signed by me." Juárez Maza further urged the jefe político to "prevent" the plebiscite, explaining, "this is not the way to appoint [someone] to this office and it attacks the powers of the government."[17] However, there was little the jefe político could do: he was not consulted in the negotiations, and Gavira answered directly to General Merodio. On November 20, Juárez Maza waffled, asking León to resign the jefatura but to remain in Juchitán until further instructed. With the public pining for peace in Juchitán, Juárez Maza feared his intransigence would be interpreted in a negative light. He confided to a friend, "I hope with all of my faith that the sensible people of the nation will do me justice."[18] The governor was not about to give up, however, and after a couple of days of silence he unveiled a new political gambit.

With the results of the plebiscite still awaiting ratification, Madero grew impatient with the Oaxacan governor, advising General Merodio on November 23 that if the situation was not clarified within forty-eight hours, he should resolve matters himself, "without waiting for a decision from the [Oaxacan] government."[19] Juárez Maza took immediate action upon learning of the president's orders. With Gómez in Juchitán awaiting word from the capital, and the Chegomistas gathered around the town's outskirts, Juárez Maza ordered General Merodio to mobilize federal forces in Juchitán to go after Gómez and his men. Merodio responded that so long as the rebels were "not committing outrages against lives or property," he had been commanded not to act without direct orders from the secretary of war. Juárez Maza accused Merodio of "trying to resolve matters with relation to Juchitán that only this government can decide," and vowed to "sustain the sovereignty of the state."[20] Merodio responded, "I have neither wanted nor attempted to meddle in affairs [of] Juchitán. I am a soldier and not a politician." Catching wind of Juárez Maza's intentions, the Chegomistas withdrew back into the interior, and Gómez returned to his camp near Unión Hidalgo. Peace, which seemed imminent only a few days before, had slipped away. Merodio doubled the military patrols in and around Juchitán, León received orders from the governor not to resign the jefatura without his orders, and Juárez Maza called on the state's Commission on Constitutional Points to prepare a statement to be rendered to the state's Chamber of Deputies the following day.[21]

On November 24 the state legislature convened an extraordinary session to discuss the proper course of action in Juchitán. After a brief review of the telegrams between Merodio and Juárez Maza, the Commission on Constitutional Points read its dictum: "The revolutionary disturbances in the District of Juchitán . . . have reached the point of producing the complete rupture of the state's relations with the federal government, because [the federal government] has ordered the jefe de armas in the district to lend assistance to the authorities of the state only under expressed orders of the secretary of war." By refusing to turn the federal army over to the governor, the president not only put the state of Oaxaca "at great risk" but violated Article 116 of the Constitution. According to Article 116, "the powers of the Union have the duty to protect the states against any invasion or exterior violence. In the case of a revolt or an interior disturbance they will lend equal protection, always to be raised by the legislature of the state or by its executive, if the other is not in session." While the terms of the law were vague about what constituted "a revolt or an interior disturbance," the commission concluded that the situation in Juchitán fell under the umbrella of Article 116, recommending that the state legislature invoke the "Supreme Law" and appeal to the national congress to "protect the state with the forces at its disposal, to the end of repressing the interior disturbances occasioned by the uprising of the vecinos of the District of Juchitán."[22] The recommendation was then put to a vote.

The commission's recommendation, made in the name of "jealously guarding the good name of the state and its sovereignty," tapped into Oaxaca's deeply rooted tradition of federalism and sparked a fervent response from the deputies of the state assembly. After a second reading of the dictum, Alberto Vargas, a well-known poet and orator, launched into an impassioned plea, calling on his fellow deputies to defend the sovereignty of the state against the tyranny of the federal government, even to the point of rebellion: "I believe, Señores Diputados, that rare will be the occasion in which I am presented with an opportunity like this to represent so exactly, so dignified, the sixty thousand inhabitants that have given me their vote to occupy this space. Because the patria has spoken, because our dearest interests have been harmed and because before all we should sacrifice ourselves to the death if it is precisely in order to guard the sovereignty of the state safe, respected, and honorable. How sad it is, Señores, that ... in this august place of law we must raise the call of rebellion against tyranny and absolutism."[23] Vargas's emotional defense of Oaxaca's sovereignty captured perfectly (if poetically) the sense of propriety within the state government regarding its internal affairs as well as the sense of provincial pride and growing dissatisfaction with the president felt on the streets of the state capital. The speech yielded neither rebuttal nor affirmation; the deputies voted unanimously to pass the proposal on to the federal government.

"Sovereignty Has Its Limits": The Executive Report

The state's proposal arrived in the capital via telegram at three in the afternoon, interrupting a session of the Chamber of Deputies.

Lacking sufficient information to put the case to an immediate vote, the chamber transmitted the proposal to President Madero with the idea that the executive would put together a report about the matter, to be presented to the deputies before being put to a vote. Based on their extensive files on Juchitán, Madero and the secretary of external affairs, Manuel Calero, quickly compiled an official report, and Calero presented it on the floor of the chamber. In the report, the executive rejected the Oaxacan legislature's interpretation of Article 116 of the Constitution and refused its request for federal intervention. In so doing, the executive report outlined the limits of state sovereignty while proposing a more social contractual approach to the appointment of jefes políticos that accounted for the principle of popular sovereignty. Although the findings of the executive were clearly intended to be general, they were directed specifically at the state government of Oaxaca, as they pertained to the case of Juchitán. By denying the state government access to the federal army in its attempts to repress the Chegomistas, Madero sought to walk back the interim regime's hardline stance toward popular revolutionaries and appease the growing discontent of the popular sector by reconciling with popular political (if not social) interests and reviving the spirit of popular sovereignty.

The executive report of November 24 was both a detailed account of the executive's role in the rebellion in Juchitán and a general prescription for peace in Mexico, focusing on the appointment of jefes políticos. Using confidentially obtained information "about the true motives of the uprising" and "consulting the opinion of the inhabitants" of Juchitán, the report established the basic framework of the regime's official interpretation of the Chegomista Rebellion. The report determined that the rebellion was "totally local in character," "prompted by the naming of an unpopular jefe político," and that, according to a confidential informant, "it was possible, by withdrawing the jefe político designated by the governor, to placate the spirits immediately and get the rebels to put down their arms." Based on this information, the report explained, Madero "then made friendly and private suggestions to the governor of the state . . . to sacrifice a little of his official pride [amor propio] and consent to the withdrawal of that jefe político," in the name of restoring peace. Specifically, the president recommended that one of his own emissaries, Cándido Aguilar, be selected to occupy the position, as he "would be accepted as jefe político by the inhabitants of Juchitán." While Aguilar was unknown to the region, the president gave a "moral guarantee" of his character and suggested that he would, at least, represent "a transitory solution, a measure of political order that met the exigencies of the moment." Governor Juárez Maza, however, remained unswayed, preferring to "stand by his classic theory of the principle of authority, by virtue of which the governor is sovereign and his actions inscrutable."[24]

The executive report went on to explain why the conditions in Juchitán did not meet the criteria for federal intervention established by Article 116. In late October, explained the report, the state government called on the federal government to "assist local authorities" in the installation of a new (unpopular) jefe político, in the face of growing opposition. "In view of the state's impotence to repress the movement," the federal government sent an auxiliary contingent of the federal army to "take up arms against the insurrectionaries." "Unfortunately," read Calero, "the uprising took on a serious character" and the federal forces had "to make a formal engagement with the rebels," which resulted in "the loss of considerable lives." While thousands of rebels remained encamped in the rugged countryside, with the exception of a few minor skirmishes on the outskirts of town, the rebels in Juchitán had observed an informal armistice since November 8, effecting what the report dubbed a *paz rebelde*. The executive "firmly maintains its position that public peace has not been altered, and at this moment there is no combat, blood is not spilling." "In this situation," Calero explained, "[the president] has said to the jefe de armas simply: 'If they attack you, defend yourself; but if they do not attack, if they do not commit outrages against lives and property, if peace remains unaltered, even when it is a ... paz rebelde, permit me to use the expression, you are to simply wait peacefully for orders from the secretary of war, who will give them to you when comes the time when it is essential to spill blood to save the principle of order.'" As more federal forces gathered in Juchitán, the federal government "kept them at the ready" to maintain stability while it negotiated a peaceful resolution to the conflict, "as is humane, as is logical, and as is democratic."[25]

If the state government wanted to break the paz rebelde, or complained that the jefe político was incapable of imposing his authority, then the executive report made it clear that it was the responsibility of the state government—not the federal government—to clean up the mess of its own making. "If [the governor] has the elements to sustain [the jefe político]," read the report, "he should sustain him, as [the uprising] has to do with local authority, and it is up to local authorities to make an effort to make themselves respected by means of its own elements.... [If the people] do not obey the jefe político, the governor of the state can call his police, he can call on the means of coercion that the laws give him to make that jefe político obeyed ... and if public peace is disturbed and the Governor cannot reestablish it, then the federal forces are there to help." The establishment of peace was of paramount importance, and federal force was not to be used proactively, to "make respected" a jefe político appointed autonomously by the state government. "The President of the Republic does not care if the jefe político be Pedro or Juan," Calero explained. "What he wants is peace, that there are guarantees, and he believes that if by the whim of one governor four hundred lives have been sacrificed, he should not thereafter lend a single soldier, nor a single Mauser!" Or as he clarified later in the report, "The executive should intervene only when the state is impotent; but when it crosses its arms, the federation does not have the duty to assume a protective attitude."[26]

The report warned that obligating the federal army to become the protector of otherwise obstinate governors would transform the military into a blunt tool of the states—an impractical and potentially dangerous outcome given the state of disorder that prevailed in the nation. "If the government of the state refuses to accept the suggestions of the President of the Republic," asked Calero, "and lacks at the same time elements to sustain the jefe político, is it possible to consent to federal forces being converted into an instrument of the state government to impose a jefe político by means of bloodlettings? If we admit this principle, citizen deputies, then the federal government will be at the whim of the governors of the states, having to send brigades throughout the Republic when the governors want to impose jefes políticos that are rejected by popular opinion." As Calero stated flatly, "sovereignty has its limits," and a strict adherence to the principle of state sovereignty during such turbulent times was impractical—it would spread the federal army thinly across the country, while doing nothing to address the source of discontent.[27]

Most importantly, the executive report called for the broad reformation of the jefatura política by incorporating into its selection process the principle of popular sovereignty. In the report the executive recognized that the Constitution granted governors the exclusive right to appoint jefes políticos, free from federal interference and without consulting public opinion, but also suggested that "the harmony that the Constitution assumes between the voting public" and the executive power had been broken during the Porfiriato. Under Díaz the jefatura política had become an intensely unpopular institution, losing its legitimacy and causing widespread discontent. However, "since it is not possible with the stroke of a pen to suppress the Jefaturas," the report recommended that governors "temper a little" their zeal in applying their constitutional rights, "accommodating the exigencies of the democratic movement." In the interest of harmony between governors and governed, the report continued, "Governors of States could try to respect popular will and choose individuals that would have a chance to be designated in a popular election for the position in question," thereby "accommodating the dominant sentiment in the region in which those functionaries have to exercise their authority." In lieu of more efficient democratic institutions, if governors applied the Constitution in spirit rather than letter, they would then appoint jefes políticos who did not require the intervention of the federal army to make their authority respected locally, and peace would prevail without the necessity of violating the sovereignty of the states.[28]

The secretary of external affairs made clear for the assembly how this prescription for peace in the Republic applied to the case of Juchitán. "The executive power does not want blood spilled in the district of Juchitán," he read, "but neither does it want the rights of the inhabitants of the state to be trampled by an arbitrary jefe político." Calero also noted "an entirely special circumstance" in regard to Oaxaca. As the president of the Partido Democrático, of which Calero was a member, Governor Juárez Maza had endorsed the party's program, which explicitly stated the suppression of the jefes políticos as its primary political goal. While acknowledging that Juárez Maza was not, as governor, in a position to change the Constitution, had he applied this principle "in its essence" the situation in Juchitán would have yielded better results. Given the governor's political background, "it is easy to resolve this conflict" so long as the "governor of the state understands that before the rigid precepts of the Constitution stands the principle that is the savior of democratic people, that of respect for the will of citizens, that of defense of the popular will."[29]

Che Gómez was conspicuously absent from the executive report, save one oblique reference: "It seems that the jefe político was received unwillingly by the inhabitants of this region and, agitated by men more or less ambitious and with intentions more or less debatable, they rose up in arms against the local authorities." This brief passage seems to imply that, according to the findings of the executive, Gómez's political motives were questionable (and unclear) but ultimately of secondary importance. Regardless of Gómez's intentions, the passage implies, the situation in Juchitán could have been avoided had the state government not named an unpopular jefe político, or would have been resolved had the jefe político been removed. In not addressing Gómez directly, the executive report undercut (or attempted to) all interpretations of the rebellion that focused on the character of its leader.[30]

While Calero's reading of the report drew impassioned rebuttals from a few conservative deputies, the mood in the Chamber of Deputies was overwhelmingly in favor of the executive's findings. Opposing voices feared passing any dictum that circumvented constitutional law, contested the executive's interpretation of the rebellion and its causes, and lamented having to vote on an issue about which they had so little information. Most of the deputies had no knowledge of the rebellion beyond that described in the executive report, yet the urgency of the matter called for an immediate vote. Despite these grumblings, as the session neared midnight the chamber overwhelmingly approved the findings of the executive report—by a count of 116 to 16—"that the moment has not arrived to take the measures referred to in Article 116 of the Constitution." The results were then forwarded to the state government of Oaxaca.[31]

The executive report of November 24 represented the Madero regime's prescription for pacification through reform rather than repression. After the brief interlude of the de la Barra regime, Madero sought to revitalize the principle of popular sovereignty to restore unity to his disparate coalition of followers. By abrogating the law regarding jefes políticos, in spirit if not letter, Madero sought to undercut popular discontent with compromise and goodwill. In this regard, the jefaturas políticas seemed to offer the new regime an opportunity to reconcile with popular interests without having to take on major social restructuring. By simply sacrificing "a little of its official pride" and naming jefes políticos in consultation with popular will, the government could get persistent rebels to put down their arms without addressing stickier social problems like land reform. In areas such as Morelos, however, where acute agrarian grievances provided a constant wellspring for discontent, such conciliation from Madero was not forthcoming. Despite his immediate attempts to compromise with the Zapatistas, Madero quickly backtracked, refusing to negotiate with Zapata, demanding nothing short of unconditional surrender, and allowing the federal army to take up offensive positions in Morelos, in anticipation of armed conflict. In late November, with peace talks at a standstill, the Zapatistas declared themselves in open, violent rebellion against the Madero government. The contrast between Juchitán and Morelos is illuminating: by targeting for reform only the most obvious political cases, Madero failed to win over more radical revolutionaries; and by violating the sovereignty of the state of Oaxaca he gave his moderate-to-conservative critics an opportunity to band together in common cause and undermine his efforts. News of the increasingly grave situation in Morelos would soon eclipse the Chegomistas, but for the time being the public's attention remained fixed on the grave situation in Oaxaca, and the trouble in Juchitán.

"Before Imposition, They Would Prefer Revolution": The State Responds

If Madero thought he could pacify the Revolution by championing the cause of popular sovereignty at the expense of state sovereignty, in the coming days he would realize how mistaken he was. The president's attempt at reconciliation sparked a furious response from the state of Oaxaca. Only hours after the publication of the executive report, Governor Juárez Maza ended negotiations in Juchitán, indicating to General Merodio his refusal to recognize any arrangements made by him as well as his "firm resolution to maintain at all costs the sovereignty of the State."[32] As the peace commission disassembled and prepared to withdraw from the Isthmus, the state legislature convened to officially reject the findings of the executive report, and the governor himself publicly severed all ties to the federal government. Protestors took to the streets of the state capital to show their support of the governor, while the state government began recruiting and arming volunteers, ostensibly to help extinguish the rebellion in Juchitán (in lieu of federal assistance). In light of the growing state militia, the national press fanned the flames of discontent, piquing public fears of a coming split with the state of Oaxaca.

Support for the Oaxacan government and Governor Juárez Maza was decisive in the state capital. A special one-page edition of *El Avance* rushed to declared itself "the first in recognizing and applauding as good the attitude of the state government.... [W]e will resume the sovereignty of the state, disowning, in consequence, the government or any authorities that try to violate it." *El Avance* was especially complimentary to the governor: "If this works, C. Benito Juárez will remind all oaxaqueños of . . . the Benemérito of the Americas, his father, when he ruled the destiny of the state." In Oaxaca (or Mexico, for that matter) one could hardly receive a more flattering compliment, but such flattery seemed to be the order of the day. Governors, political clubs, and interested citizens from around the nation inundated Juárez Maza with congratulations, gratitude, and votes of confidence, all sounding a refrain similar to that of a group of "Juchiteco citizens": "[We] applaud your patriotic attitude as defender of the sovereignty and Constitution of the state, revealing you as the worthy son of the Great Juárez." Mexico City's sizable Oaxacan contingent, the Colonia Oaxaqueña—which counted among its members a generous proportion of the national congress—cosigned an expression of gratitude to Juárez Maza and pledged, "in any case," to be "on the side of your very dignified attitude." While letters of support overwhelmed the government palace in Oaxaca City, the governor's supporters flooded the national palace with petitions of protest. Most notably, a large contingent of the "pueblo oaxaqueño" closed a public rally with a telegram to Madero, registering its "disgust" with "the attacks on its sovereignty" and asking the president "to leave in complete liberty the state government," which the people "support unconditionally." The telegram warned Madero, "You will be responsible [for any] spilling of blood."[33]

More galling to the federal government, no doubt, were the throngs that took to the streets of Oaxaca City. On the night of November 24, under close police surveillance, a "compact multitude" of protesters marched through the streets of the capital, shouting "¡Viva la libertad! ¡Abajo la tiranía! ¡Muera Madero!" before finally settling in front of the government palace. A round of speakers addressed the governor, assuring him they were "resolved to defend the sovereignty of Oaxaca. Also letting him know that before imposition, they would prefer revolution." Juárez Maza later took the stage, promising the gathered masses that "even at the cost of his life he will sustain the dignified attitude he has adopted." He expressed his hope that those "who supported him in peace would support him in war." The protest concluded with the reading of a telegram drafted by its organizers and signed by the people, warning President Madero "to respect the sovereignty of the state of Oaxaca, or the people will defend it by means of arms." Similar protests followed for the next three nights, with "the entire population, without distinction of sex or class" offering the governor "their holy fire of anger" as a demonstration of their support. Party divisions disappeared, and "all came together as Oaxacans to defend the sovereignty of the state," making for "a very agitated" mood on the streets of Oaxaca.[34]

Juárez Maza's call to arms did little to quell unrest in the state, as the ranks of the state militia swelled. As early as mid-November, with the federal army observing the informal armistice in Juchitán, the governor began recruiting volunteers for the state militia in his paternal homeland in the Sierra Juárez. About three hundred volunteers offered their services to Governor Juárez Maza in exchange for pay, arms, training, and quarters in Oaxaca City.[35] On November 25, to the great fanfare of the crowd of protesters gathered in the *zócalo*, the Batallón Sierra Juárez arrived at the government palace to defend the sovereignty of the state, led by regional cacique Pedro León. Juárez Maza later made public his intentions to "put himself at the front of the serranos to fight the juchiteco rebels." While the people of Juchitán braced themselves for the arrival of the state militia, the fervor of provincial pride spread, and volunteers began lining up in "the majority of the districts" of the state. One federal deputy from Oaxaca estimated that Juárez Maza had at his disposal "fifteen hundred perfectly armed men who will know how to repel the charge of the rebels." In some districts the recruitment of volunteers created tensions, as new recruits threatened to clash with rebel sympathizers. Although these confrontations dissipated without recourse to open violence, the agitation was palpable throughout the state.[36]

The volatile rhetoric of state sovereignty and the buildup of armed forces in Oaxaca conjured images of civil war in the press, which transformed the conflict between Oaxaca and the federal government into a national political sensation. "In these days full of popular agitations that have stirred up a frenzy," read the November 29 edition of *El Ahuizote*, "the conflict in Juchitán has been the principal topic." With the state government of Oaxaca "resuming its sovereignty, and initiating an open break with the federal government," *El Imparcial* commented that it would not be difficult to imagine the worsening situation in Oaxaca "taking on truly frightening proportions." More than one commentator in Mexico City disapproved of the intransigence of both the federal and state governments, fearing that the situation, which began as "a small and sterile fight of pueblo against pueblo," would be transformed into "a battle of caprice against caprice, person against person, passion against passion, vanity against vanity." Such a stalemate could produce "a lamentable split, winding the nation up in a wicked civil war." Whether real threat or hyperbole, the perceived possibility of civil war pushed the president's handling of the situation to the center of public discourse.[37]

"Demagoguery Has Now Been Enthroned in the Executive": The Nation Responds

The escalating conflict with Oaxaca provided Madero's opponents a pretext to attack his regime on a variety of scores. Critics of all political stripes used the new president's mishandling of the situation in Juchitán, and particularly his refusal to use the federal army to subjugate the Chegomistas, to illustrate his incapacity as head of state. On the one hand, they argued that by negotiating with the rebels and accepting a peaceful stalemate, the president's reluctance to apply the mano dura to the rebels had handcuffed the federal army and allowed the rebels to win, thereby undermining the security necessary for the establishment of democratic rule, and potentially transforming a simple local conflict into a prolonged guerrilla war, or worse. On the other hand, the president's critics interpreted his call to reconsider the appointment of jefes políticos as a naked attempt to expand executive authority at the expense of state sovereignty, and in direct contradiction of constitutional law. Taken together, the response to the executive report in the court of public opinion, or at least in the opinion-producing industry, was overwhelmingly unfavorable, ultimately representing a sort of public referendum against the regime.

Since the arrival of the peace commission, Madero's opponents had criticized the federal government's strategy of negotiation, claiming that by restricting the army it had snatched defeat from the jaws of victory, denigrated the valiant efforts of federal soldiers, and given undue legitimacy to the rebel forces. It was no secret on the Isthmus that federal soldiers, not least of all General Merodio, were loath to lay down their arms for peace negotiations. For the federal army, "and a great number of the distinguished people of good standing," the cessation of combat made no sense, coming as it did when the federal army had taken clear control of the field of battle, with the rebels "just about reduced to impotence." Inviting the Chegomistas to negotiate peace provoked "profound disgust and general protest among the 'sensible inhabitants'" of Oaxaca, because it "shows weakness and an admission of defeat, when the real situation is precisely the contrary, as the federal force is the more powerful, having beaten the rebels in every single fight." *El Avance* declared the negotiations "absurd," not only because they "implied the recognition in [the rebels] of a belligerence that they did not deserve, because they are not, properly speaking revolutionaries," but also because "it denies [the government's] triumph and demands peace conditions from the defeated." Peace negotiations gave the rebels the opportunity to win at the negotiating table "that which they would have never thought to win in battle," and exposed the fundamental weakness of the Madero regime. "This weakness," opined the radical *Regeneración*, "revealed itself in the panic sown in official spheres by the uprising in Juchitán; panic so great that it has made the federal government forget its vain boasts and threats of force and forced it to send four of its delegates to go before the rebels and beg them to put down their arms." In allowing the rebels to dictate the terms of their surrender, added *El*

Correo del Sur, "the latent spirit of rebellion and rancor will remain in the region . . . and *tutti contenti*, Gómez [has] won."³⁸

In a well attended and widely publicized conference of Mexico's "confederated parties"—the three nominally liberal parties that had been frozen out of Madero's regime—"Porfirista luminary" Jorge Vera Estañol argued that by negotiating with the rebels, Madero had set a dangerous precedent in Juchitán that could have important repercussions for the establishment of democracy in Mexico. Specifically, he argued that by responding favorably to "the noisy apparatus of the masses" and contradicting the decisions of elected officials, Madero's politics favored those "who have the audacity to rise up in arms" over "peaceful men, men of order," and rendered useless formal, rational means of gauging public opinion. As a result, Madero encouraged the expansion, not the contraction, of the informal, popular political forms that overwhelmed more valid democratic practice. Vera Estañol argued that this would ensure that "popular will will be personified only in the chusmas [rabble]," and "from this moment the nation will no longer manifest the will of its people in constitutional forms . . . but rather through convulsive forms and with the spasmodic jolting of rebellions, revolts, and uprisings." According to Vera Estañol, Madero's handling of the situation in Juchitán directly counteracted the goals of pacification by encouraging popular groups to pursue informal and illegal means of political redress, rather than teaching them how to participate peacefully in democratic institutions and procedures. Ultimately, the president's actions in Juchitán threatened to establish a precedent for other disgruntled groups that would lead the nation down the path of "anarchy, ruin, and desolation."³⁹

Vera Estañol also took aim at the president's interpretation of "paz rebelde," as spelled out in the executive report. By "giving to an uprising sustained with arms in hand" the "specious and suggestive name of 'paz rebelde,'" Vera Estañol argued, Madero offered "metaphysical support" to the rebels, while "neglecting the most elemental obligation of the executive power, that of avoiding the spilling of blood." Specifically, by articulating and publicizing in the executive report the army's preventative stance toward the rebels, Madero emboldened operating rebels, who now, with "wind in their sails," threatened the security of peaceful citizens on the Isthmus. Once articulated by Vera Español, this criticism picked up traction in the conservative press, which began reporting daily on rebel activity in Juchitán. According to correspondents for *El País* and *El Imparcial*, the situation in Juchitán was worsening by the day. The rebels, previously worn down, now cut the power to Juchitán and marauded with impunity on the town's outskirts, looting abandoned houses under the cover of darkness and disrupting the flow of commerce and traffic. Local merchants complained to *El País* that "roaming bands of Gomistas" harassed the railroads on a daily basis, committing "infinite robberies" of the trains, attacking rail stations, and making a "provisional camp" of five hundred rebels along the Panamerican line. When the people requested more road patrols from General Merodio, *El Imparcial* reported, the general refused. To make matters worse, the withdrawal of Cándido Aguilar from Juchitán piqued fears that, with talks adjourned, the Chegomistas would break the unofficial armistice and rise up again. These daily missives painted a picture of insecurity in Juchitán, where the federal army stood by and waited "for the insurgents to enter the [city] by fire and sword" before taking action.[40]

Madero's critics further argued that his restriction of the federal army in Juchitán had created a potential crisis of national security. Before the president intervened to restrain the federal army, the rebels had been on the verge of total defeat, but Madero's interference had allowed them to melt away into the interior, where they threatened to transform "a simple local disturbance" into "a threatening and uncontrollable anarchy throughout the country." Even as federal forces shored up their control in Juchitán, *El País* noted that "the indígenas ... fled to the sierra, where it will be very difficult to defeat them, because of the ruggedness of the terrain." *El Ahuizote* added, "Juchitán is a warrior center of absolute importance; the people are restless by nature and once the first shot is fired, not even ten thousand of the best soldiers can stop them, as nobody knows the terrain like they do, they fight down to the last women and children, poison the water, have vast space, impenetrable forests, immense deserts, and assisted by the horrible climate, they are unbeatable." If drawn into a guerrilla war, the newspaper estimated, "ten thousand federales with cannons and machine guns will not submit Juchitán. The race is valiant, to the point of heroic. . . . [W]hen twenty die forty come to replace them immediately, and they all fight without rest, singing and shouting to the death. . . . [T]hey will be able to mobilize more than 20,000 men for war." Ultimately, *El Ahuizote* considered the Chegomistas a bigger problem for the army than the Zapatistas, whose valor in combat could not compare to "the brave race" of Juchitán.[41]

At the same time, by handcuffing the federal army at such a critical moment, the president's policy gave the rebels time to recover, regroup, and plot their next move. The fear in the state capital, according to *El Avance*, was that "paz rebelde" would be interpreted as a "moral triumph" for the rebels, who would then "propagate the spirit of revolt" in surrounding districts, particularly Tehuantepec. In the nation's capital, critics feared that Juchitán would become "the spark that lights up the whole countryside" by exposing the federal government's softness toward insurgents or providing potential insurgents with a massive force of armed and organized allies on the Isthmus. The problem with the idea of paz rebelde, concluded Vera Estañol, was that "if it were correct, it would be necessary to wait for the entire conspiracy to explode before being able to repress it, instead of aborting it from its embryonic stages of formation." By adopting a reactive, rather than a proactive, stance toward the remaining rebels, Madero had made a difficult situation in Juchitán immeasurably worse.[42]

The executive report's prescriptive measures also prompted an intensely negative response from the regime's critics, who interpreted the report's suggestion to temper the application of constitutional rights as an affront to the principle of state sovereignty. Madero's critics came together in defense of a "classic" or "strict" interpretation of constitutional law, which understood the codification of states' rights in the Constitution to represent a safeguard against the arbitrary expansion of executive authority. Essentially, the Constitution provided the states with a stable, sovereign domain in which they could exercise political authority, free from the intervention of the federal government. From this perspective, the federal government's intervention in Juchitán represented a clear breach by the executive of the state of Oaxaca's political domain, and an attempt by the executive to bend the Constitution to its wishes. Specifically, imposing a federal peace commission to negotiate with rebel forces, then installing one of its members as jefe político, against the will of the popularly elected governor, represented a clear abuse of executive power. Sonoran deputy Francisco de Paula Morales, a political holdover from the Porfiriato, argued that such an imposition would have critical "import for the entire nation." Specifically, he asked, "how are we to sanction the conduct of an executive that enters into communications, treaties, and negotiations to impose a jefe político? How, now that so much blood has been spilled, is the chamber going to submit itself to a personal politics that tries to impose Aguilar?" If the national legislature "left a constitutional governor without support," Morales argued, the executive would be free to impose local authorities to its liking throughout the countryside, returning the nation to the days of Díaz.[43]

This point resonated in the national press, where many represented Madero's imposition of Aguilar as a naked attempt to expand his dictatorial authority. *El Ahuizote* attacked Madero for using his authority to dole out political rewards and offices to his "true and false supporters and the relatives of his supporters," empowering a new class of personalist revolutionary chiefs, tied to the president through links of patronage, rather than democratically elected authorities. According to the editorial, Aguilar, "the hero of the outrages in Jalapa," embodied perfectly the "new *caudillismo* of Madero." While acknowledging the political difficulties facing Madero, especially the "Gordian knot" represented by fixing the jefatura política, an editorial in *El Mañana* nonetheless criticized the president for attempting "to cut the Gordian knot with the sword of a Maderista chief, imposed by himself." This sentiment echoed through national press coverage, as newspapers in the capital increasingly drew on interviews with "notable" Oaxacans to form opinion on the matter. Without fail, the Oaxacans interviewed—generally members of the national congress—represented Madero's interest in appointing Aguilar as the primary sticking point in peace negotiations. Constantino Chapital, the most frequent commentator, explained to the Maderista newspaper *El Diario* that the government of Oaxaca did not care who the jefe político was, but rejected Aguilar because the federal government wanted to impose him, and he was "supported by Che Gómez and his henchmen." The governor himself reiterated this interpretation in a published telegram to the municipal president of Juchitán, in which he blamed the failure to resolve the conflict in Juchitán on the federal government's insistence on appointing Aguilar, "something that I have not allowed because I know [the power] the law gives me and the form in which questions concerning the internal politics of the state should be resolved."[44]

During the November 25 meeting of the confederated parties, Amado Ostos, speaking on behalf of the Partido Popular Evolucionista, exhorted the congregation of thousands: "If we believe that the executive has exceeded his facilities, if we believe he has trampled or tried to trample the sovereignty of a state, we have an obligation of taking it to a higher court that than of the chambers; to the court of public opinion. In this manner we can make the executive see that he has committed an error, and at the same time motivate him to retrace his steps." Despite the support of a few Maderista newspapers and the national assembly, in the days following the reading of the executive report Madero lost the battle in the court of public opinion, or at least in the press. Besides the specific criticisms outlined above, the tenor of press coverage of the conflict with Oaxaca was generally dismissive of the president, portraying him as incompetent at best, and dictatorial at worst. Or both, in the case of *Regeneración*, which opined that under Madero's brief custodianship the "Mexican government" had deteriorated into "an institution as ridiculous as the nervous and chattering figure of the midget dictator." Madero's presumed failures in Juchitán could be mobilized to illustrate either of these interpretations, perhaps accounting for the enormous popularity of the Chegomista Rebellion as a topic of debate. From the precipice of political reformation, as the court of public opinion turned against him, the president rapidly began retracing his steps.[45]

"A Sterile Standoff": Reconciliation or Capitulation?

Against the backdrop of unrest and mounting unfavorable public opinion, the federal government negotiated a compromise with the state government of Oaxaca that placed the resolution of the Chegomista Rebellion firmly in the state's hands. Specifically, in concert with the state government of Oaxaca, the national congress appointed a special joint commission to open a new investigation into the rebellion, aimed at deconstructing the executive report, while Madero sent a representative to Oaxaca City to negotiate directly with the governor and the state legislature. After a few days, the two sides reached an accord that reflected more of a capitulation by the federal government than a compromise, based on three agreed-upon provisions: that Article 116 would be applied to the situation in Juchitán, and the federal army would be placed at the disposal of Governor Juárez Maza; that rebels found guilty of "political crimes" would receive amnesty; and that the governor would travel to Juchitán and render a decision regarding the jefe político after consulting with the people of the Isthmus. While the language and the enforcement of the accord's provisions remained vague, it was clear that defining them would be at the discretion of the state government, with one exception: the federal government offered Che Gómez a writ of safe-conduct to meet with Madero in Mexico City, where he would face punishment for his crimes. Gómez's fate notwithstanding, the agreement marked a victory for the state of Oaxaca and its defense of state sovereignty, while sounding the death knell for the Chegomista Rebellion and its defense of popular sovereignty.

From the beginning, the state legislature of Oaxaca vehemently rejected the findings of the executive report as a form of political "subterfuge" based on "arguments of questionable force" that were in "flagrant contradiction with the facts."[46] *El Avance* defended the intentions of the federal government as "sound and patriotic," but "its acts, its proceedings, are erroneous and misdirected, because of its lack of precise information about the causes and the producing elements of the conflict."[47] These complaints found common cause in the national Senate, led by its large contingent of native Oaxacans, Porfirian incumbents committed to not repeating the mistake of the Chamber of Deputies. Senator Aurelio Valdivieso, a native of Juchitán and a convinced Porfirista (he had been the director of Oaxaca's prestigious Instituto de Ciencias y Artes multiple times under Díaz), rejected the vote of the Chamber of Deputies, arguing that it had been conducted too hastily, forcing the deputies to depend on the insufficient information of the executive report before casting their votes. To remedy the problem, Valdivieso proposed that the Senate name a joint commission of Interior and Constitutional Points to carry out a more thorough investigation of the rebellion in Juchitán. Two other conservative members of the Oaxacan delegation in the Senate, Miguel Bolaños Cacho and Esteban Maqueo Castellanos, stood up to defend Valdivieso's proposal. After a brief debate, the Senate moved to reopen the investigation into the Chegomista Rebellion under the jurisdiction of the joint commission and to reconsider the vote of the Chamber of Deputies upon review of its findings.[48]

The joint commission's investigation of the Chegomista Rebellion clearly favored the perspective of the state government by privileging information provided by legally constituted political authorities in Juchitán and Oaxaca (and not rebels). In the aftermath of the rebellion in early November, the jefe político, the municipal president, and the entire ayuntamiento of Juchitán fled to the interior with the rebels, leaving all local offices in the hands of the conservative partido rojo, led by Pablo Pineda, who was appointed to the municipal presidency. Now, Governor Juárez Maza and his deputies turned to these same authorities in compiling a file on the rebellion, to be made available to the newly formed joint commission. The file provided by state and local officials established the need for armed federal intervention, the legality and popularity of Enrique León as jefe político, and Che Gómez's guilt for provoking the conflict. Telegrams from Pablo Pineda and the state legislature concluded that the vote against offering federal military assistance had "revived the spirits" of the rebels, who "finding themselves unpunished and with the knowledge that the state is abandoned by federal forces consider themselves to have the most complete liberty to continue in their [current] attitude."[49] Telegrams from the ayuntamiento of Juchitán and Governor Juárez Maza contradicted the executive report's assertion that Enrique León was an unpopular jefe político. The governor even suggested, "Now that [the people of Juchitán] have seen his work, they ask that [León] remain in his post." All correspondence from Oaxaca, including that submitted by the "honorable, sensible, and hardworking people of Juchitán"—a veritable who's who of the local partido rojo—made clear that Che Gómez was the sole cause of disorder in the region and begged that he not be offered amnesty "for the numerous crimes committed by him and his partidarios." On the strength of this new information, the joint commission recommended that Article 116 of the Constitution be applied to the case of Oaxaca and that the federal army be placed at the governor's disposal.[50]

Acting on the recommendation of the joint commission, on November 29 the federal Chamber of Deputies reversed its previous decision, voting to apply Article 116 of the Constitution to the conflict in Oaxaca. Based on "more reliable sources of information," the joint commission proposed a new law, declaring simply that the president would lend the assistance of the federal army to the governor of Oaxaca "until the complete pacification of that federal entity." In the following debate, the stream of arguments in favor of the law underscored the exclusive role of state governments in assessing "disturbances" on their own soil, and privileged the "disinterested" information provided by the state legislature. Deputy Emilio Velasco expressed his opinion that "state governors, whom this clause tries to protect, are the ones charged with maintaining peace and security, they are the judges of the adequate means to achieve these ends, and to them is conceded, as a result, the right to determine if federal protection is necessary for the pursuit of these objectives." Francisco Modesto Ramirez, a native Oaxacan, supported the findings of the joint commission, because they were based on information gleaned from both private and public sources, unlike the executive report. Specifically, he reasoned, the telegrams from the ayuntamiento "deserve complete faith, because they have in their support . . . the true, terrible reports that were given by the representatives from Oaxaca and that deserve complete credit." Another deputy echoed this opinion, expressing that the information rendered by the state legislature was particularly credible, because it "had no interest in the naming of Candido Aguilar or in any other aspect of the district of Juchitán." Overall, the mood of the debate overwhelmingly favored passing the new law and represented a mea culpa on behalf of the Chamber of Deputies, who excused their previous vote as being limited by restricted access to "reliable information." By a vote of 102 to 31—nearly a complete reversal of the previous vote—the chamber passed the law, putting the federal army at the disposal of the Oaxacan governor.[51]

Meanwhile, the president set into motion his own plan to peacefully resolve the conflict with Oaxaca. On November 27 he sent Carlos Trejo y Lerdo de Tejada to Oaxaca to meet with the governor and the president of the state's Chamber of Deputies, Carlos María Gil, "to sort out their difficulties" as the executive's plenipotentiary. In anticipation of Trejo's arrival, a conservative Oaxacan newspaper circulated flyers throughout the city, urging the citizens of Oaxaca to greet the president's representative "as he deserves." The following day, an angry crowd of protesters greeted Trejo at the train station with shouts of "'We don't need your services!' 'You're a *turiferario*!' and 'Leave!'"[52] The crowd followed Trejo's carriage, hurling insults and at least one rock, as federal forces stood at the ready. As the president's representative met with the governor, the protesters surrounded the government palace, "never ceasing their hostile demonstrations." Finally, Governor Juárez Maza took to the balcony to calm the crowd, calling Trejo a "friend of Oaxaca." He was followed by Trejo himself, who, despite being frequently interrupted by "mueras" to Madero and personal insults, assured the crowd that he was not working "on behalf of Mexico, but on behalf of Oaxaca," which won him reluctant applause. The protest continued into the night, characterized by "enthusiastic *vivas* to the ex-president, señor Díaz, and shouts against the current president, señor Madero."[53]

Despite the icy reception, negotiations between Trejo and Deputy Gil moved apace, and after a day of talks they left for the capital to propose a new accord to President Madero. On the morning of November 29, Mexico City awoke to the following telegram, from Trejo and Gil to Benito Juárez Maza, reprinted on the front page of all the daily newspapers:

> We hurry to communicate to you that the difficulties stemming from the events in Juchitán have been resolved definitively and in a manner so decorous and satisfactory as to honor and prestige both governments and confirms the federal government's invariable criteria of not impairing the sovereignty of the state. We sincerely congratulate the heroic Oaxacan people and their worthy magistrate.[54]

The accord, reached between Trejo, Gil, and Madero on the evening of November 28, guaranteed that the federal army would remain in Juchitán until the rebellion had been completely pacified; called for the "more equitable" selection of a jefe político in Juchitán, to be made in consultation with public opinion; and granted amnesty to rebels found guilty of "political crimes." While the details of the accord and the enforcement of its provisions remained vague, it was widely regarded as an unmitigated victory for the state of Oaxaca, as it was clear that the work of defining its terms and enacting its provisions would fall to Juárez Maza, under his constitutional authority as state governor.[55]

The governor wasted little time in applying the provisions of the new accord. Immediately upon receiving the results of the congressional re-vote, he ordered the federal army stationed in Juchitán to take down rebel camps on the interior, while offering amnesty to those who surrendered. Within hours, a column of four hundred federal soldiers occupied the rebel stronghold of Unión Hidalgo without a fight.[56] Led by General Augustín Valdés, who only months before had defeated Maderista forces at Casas Grandes, the federal detachment found the rebel encampments completely abandoned as it moved through the interior. Fearing armed combat with the federal army, the Chegomistas flooded in from the countryside to turn themselves in to the jefe de armas and to the more than one thousand federal soldiers stationed in Juchitán, hoping to partake in the government's promise of amnesty. The agreement struck between the state and federal governments distinguished between "political crimes" and "crimes of common order" in its criteria for amnesty. While "political crimes" were broadly defined as crimes carried out in pursuit of an ideological objective, and were not subject to criminal prosecution, "crimes of common order" were those crimes included in the existing penal code. Essentially, the distinction was made in order to extend amnesty to the Chegomista rank and file while subjecting the leaders to punishment to the full extent of the law. Upon receiving the rebels' arms, General Merodio "assured them that nothing would happen to them, and recommended at the same time, that they invite their compañeros to return to their homes, to enjoy the guarantees that will now be given to all peaceful citizens." A few days later, his forces rapidly dwindling, Che Gómez urged his remaining supporters to return to Juchitán and accept the federal government's offer of amnesty. While some remained armed and entrenched, "many carriages arrived in Juchitán, bringing families and the rest of the rebels."[57]

For his part, Che Gómez remained in the interior, as the movement that bore his name crumbled around him. If he was "worried and beaten" by the sudden turn of events, he remained unbowed. In an angry telegram reprinted in *El País*, Gómez railed against the Chamber of Deputies for reversing its original vote, and especially for taking into account information obtained from his clear enemies, without even requesting to hear his side of the story. "How could the information of the ayuntamiento be taken seriously," he asked, being that it had been "created by the current Jefe Político, señor Enrique León, [and] when it is public and noted, that the entire pueblo juchiteco [wants to] sustain its sovereignty and the right to have authorities that agree with their interests?" Gómez remained resolute and determined to fight the charges against him upon arriving in Mexico City. "Accused, I have the right to be heard," declared Gómez as he prepared for his trip to the capital. "I beg the national representation to not be surprised by false reports [about me], which are a prized instrument of the enemies of the juchiteco people."[58]

Meanwhile, Governor Juárez Maza made final preparations to travel to Juchitán to assess public opinion and "resolve the conflict personally."[59] While the interior minister, Abraham González, admitted that the specifics of the accord regarding the jefatura remained "vague," Juárez Maza made it clear that the decision was his alone to make, according to his constitutional rights. His charge, according to the agreement with the federal government, was "to go to the district [of Juchitán] and resolve the matter in the manner he believes most equitable, [and] in view of the circumstances and listening to public opinion, name a jefe político that satisfies the needs of the district itself, with absolute liberty, without the Executive of the Union getting mixed up in the affair."[60] While the press speculated that the jefe político would be selected by plebiscite, Miguel Bolaños Cacho, speaking on behalf of the governor, clarified that Juárez Maza, "in conformity with his rights," would appoint "a jefe político in the district of Juchitán that he finds suitable, after checking public opinion."[61] If the accord between the federal and state governments clearly carried the explicit provision of consulting public opinion in the naming of the jefatura, it was equally clear that "the pulse of public opinion" was to be taken by the governor himself, and his reading was not subject to federal supervision.

Conclusion

On December 4, 1911, Benito Juárez Maza and Che Gómez crossed paths at the train station in San Jerónimo, going in opposite directions, both literally and figuratively. Juárez Maza, once considered an innocuous political figurehead, was now the toast of Oaxaca and a hero throughout the nation to proponents of state sovereignty and opponents of the federal regime. By stubbornly defending the sovereignty of the state, he had parlayed the conflict in Juchitán into a personal political boon—his offices in Oaxaca City flooded with telegrams and letters of support from around the nation, while visitors lined up to congratulate him in person.[62] The state government collected its files relative to the conflict and ordered them to be printed and distributed throughout the state as a permanent record and a proud symbol of its victory against the federal government.[63] In Mexico City, the governor was feted in absentia at lavish banquets, organized by prominent members of the capital's Oaxacan community. The Oaxacan Fraternal Society, which included the majority of the state's most powerful political figures, agreed to draw up an official memorial and "vote of confidence" to the governor. Jorge Vera Estañol praised Juárez Maza for his "spirit of intransigence" and lauded the state government for its "firmness in defense of the sovereignty of the state." Vera Estañol saved some of his praise for the president, who, in "reconsidering the dangerous precedents that he himself established with his attitude" and by "retracing his steps and agreeing with the state Oaxaca," had proved himself worthy of (albeit smug) applause.[64]

With the unflagging confidence of his most important constituents, Juárez Maza traveled to Juchitán, "to bring peace and order to that region so that the strays can return to their homes and my followers can reaffirm even more their affection for me."[65] Only a scant few days before, the governor had vowed to travel to the Isthmus "at the head" of three hundred armed serranos, but now he brought only his wife and, as he repeated numerous times, his "goodwill." As he explained to Miguel Bolaños Cacho, the only arms he needed were "peace, harmony, and fraternity, which are the best arms when the conscience is clear." As his train pulled in to San Jerónimo, where "most of the streets [were] decorated and triumphal arches ... risen over the streets," a large crowd gathered to greet the governor with "enthusiastic vivas." Over the course of the day, a steady stream of official commissions from the surrounding pueblos and a military procession led by General Merodio lined up to pay their respects to Juárez Maza, "greeting him as he deserves." Only hours before, Che Gómez had arrived at the same train station in San Jerónimo, but to no such fanfare.[66]

If Benito Juárez Maza's arrival in San Jerónimo was a coronation, Che Gómez's was a condemnation. "He who for one day was the idol of the Juchitecos" had been defeated, first in battle, then in politics, and now began his journey to the capital, where punishment—quite possibly capital punishment—awaited him.[67] He did not go without resistance. On December 3 his writ of safe-conduct finally arrived, delivered to his "secret" camp by a contingent of Mexico's rural police led by the twenty-three-year-old "Indian General," Gabriel Hernández. Hernández had risen from campesino to general during the Revolution, before being converted into the chief of the rurales in the state of Hidalgo, and was now charged with convincing Che Gómez to turn himself in to authorities. Over the course of a long conversation, "Hernández made [Gómez] see the senselessness of continuing in his attitude, all the more [considering that the government] had resolved to pursue him until he was eliminated." Gómez, "impressed by what he heard," agreed to travel to the capital, so long as Hernández escorted him. With a writ of safe-conduct signed by President Madero himself, Gómez and twelve of his closest men rode to San Jerónimo with an escort of six rurales, where they would all board the next train to Mexico City. Despite the safety of the president's signature and the comfort of Hernández's presence, Gómez feared he would never make it to the capital.[68]

As Juárez Maza and Gómez crossed paths as symbols of the diverging fortunes of the different revolutionary factions, the setting for their chance encounter, Juchitán, provided a grim reminder of the real sacrifices made by the popular classes in defense of the principles of the Revolution, as well as the emptiness of these principles in a "half measures revolution." In one month, hundreds of the "virile pueblo of Juchitán" had been killed and hundreds more wounded in combat with the federal army, and now, after spending a month camped out in the rugged interior, they returned to a city stained black by smoke, to find federal soldiers everywhere, and their homes reduced to rubble. Looking beyond the destruction, the Chegomistas found that little had changed in Juchitán, at least for those who could recall the days before the Revolution: the camarilla roja had regained its dominance in local political life, sustained by a federal army swollen in numbers by the conflict and a jefe político imposed from Oaxaca City. While the governor had arrived, ostensibly to find "a jefe político who will fulfill the aspirations of the inhabitants of the district," expectations among the returning rebels were not high. Upon being withdrawn from Juchitán, Cándido Aguilar pessimistically expressed his belief that the governor had been "working in accord with a camarilla of politicians of the old regime" in Juchitán and that "the idea that the sovereignty of the state had been impugned" had simply been a ploy to impose the state's selected jefe político in Juchitán. His instincts proved prescient: upon "checking the public pulse," Governor Juárez Maza left Enrique León as jefe político, to preside over a municipal government saturated by representatives of the partido rojo. To augment federal forces, León established a new volunteer militia called the *colorados* (not to be confused with the rojos), and led by rojo stalwart and acting municipal president, Pablo Pineda. Indeed, just as the Chegomistas had feared, by "returning to past impositions," the state government had left the Revolution unfinished in Juchitán.[69]

While it undermined the Madero regime's attempt to fulfill the revolutionary promise of popular sovereignty, the state government's defense of its sovereignty cannot be simply reduced to the work of reactionaries or advocates of the Old Regime, tugging the Maderistas away from their revolutionary obligations. Apart from the ultraconservative Oaxacan delegation in the national Senate, from the top down the Oaxacan government reflected the revolutionary ascendance of the moderate liberal opponents of the Díaz regime. The governor and the majority of the deputies in the state legislature, all elected after Díaz's resignation, had been associated with moderate liberal opposition organizations during the Porfiriato. They were cut from the same political cloth as Madero and most of his coterie of revolutionary advisers.

So why had the state government risked plunging Oaxaca into a violent confrontation with the federal government over the resolution of the Chegomista Rebellion? On the one hand, the state government's intransigent defense of its sovereignty was critical in establishing the legitimacy and consolidating the authority of the state's new and relatively fragile revolutionary regime. By taking up the cause of state sovereignty, the government of Benito Juárez Maza dissolved party divisions in a deeply fragmented state by winning the support of Oaxaca's powerful conservative oligarchy, anxious to oppose the revolutionary federal government. In this indirect manner, the conservatizing forces of the Old Guard likely exerted some influence over the state government. On the other hand, this hardly accounts for the overwhelming support for the Oaxacan government beyond the state's borders. In attempting to negotiate a peaceful and relatively democratic resolution to the Chegomista Rebellion, the Madero regime faced relentless, impassioned resistance at every turn. But if the president's recommendations were moderate, and limited to local politics, why was public opinion so dead set against the peaceful resolution of the conflict in Juchitán? Answering this question requires an examination of the specific form in which the Chegomista Rebellion entered the public conscience, and the colonial roots of the Mexican political imagination.

5 "More Ignorant Than Guilty"
A "Counterinsurgent" Narrative of the Chegomista Rebellion

On December 4, 1911, the municipal president of San Jerónimo held a reception in honor of the arrival of Governor Benito Juárez Maza, offering him "the sincere votes of adhesion" of the "noble, honorable, and hardworking" people of San Jerónimo and proposing a toast "to peace and hospitality [and] to work and capital, moving firmly toward progress without convulsions, anarchies, and demagoguery." Turning to the audience of about two thousand onlookers, the municipal president declared, "The political revolution has ended; the public right to revolutionize has been extinguished in order to bring the full vigor of constitutional rights." Addressing the crowd, the governor responded that he was "deeply pleased to come to repair the ruins of ignorance and demagoguery, of the myths and the promises for which Mexicans had spilled valiant istmeño blood." The following day an official proclamation was posted on all the corners of the pueblos of Juchitán, declaring "amnesty for the crimes of rebellion and sedition" during the uprising in early November. "Many times," explained the decree, "when pueblos are led into rebellion and disobedience by bastard ends and having as their only motive very personal interests, the law should not make itself felt with all of its rigor because most of the time the unconscious multitudes are fatally pushed to these disasters." Instead, a "forgetfulness for the past is necessary" as a "prescription for forgiveness" and as "a means for resolving the conflict." Within a few days, nearly twenty-five hundred rebels had "turned themselves in, declaring their desire to return to work and to be the first in conserving order."[1]

In the political context of late-1911 Mexico, amnesty represented one side of a "counterinsurgent" response to the persistence of popular violence in the countryside, embodied by the Chegomista Rebellion. If the first wave of popular mobilization had liberated an optimistic, zealous discourse about the promise of democracy and popular sovereignty, continued mobilization into the later months of 1911 produced a more pessimistic, anxious discourse about the dangers of democracy and popular sovereignty, represented by its supposed antithesis, caciquismo. By representing the conflict as the work of an ambitious cacique and his credulous and unwitting followers, the "counterinsurgent" interpretation of the Chegomista Rebellion, to borrow a concept from Ranajit Guha, emphasized the negative aspects of popular violence and denigrated the rebels' capacity for political consciousness, ultimately denying the poor and indigenous Chegomistas agency in their own political activity and representing them as victims of a predatory cacique, "more ignorant than guilty." As the state sought to make sense of the rebellion it did so in familiar terms, describing and interpreting it through a coercive, coded language of pacification that negated all potentially positive aspects of the rebellion and reproduced a narrative that made the security of the state and the restoration of social order its central concerns. Critically, as Guha notes in his analysis of the "primary" historiography of rebellion in nineteenth-century India, in Mexico the "prose of counterinsurgency" was not only disseminated in official language (government dispatches, military reports, and political speeches) but was also reproduced nearly wholesale in nominally neutral and objective texts, such as newspapers. Both sources sought to render the rebellion "legible" from within the same coded framework of liberal republican discourse, which had since Independence been used to mediate the poor and indigenous population's access to political power in lieu of formal, institutional barriers to citizenship.[2]

The counterinsurgent discourse of caciquismo was neither new nor invented, but drew on nineteenth-century debates about the extension of citizenship rights to the masses, articulated in a revolutionary context. This discourse was constructed at the nexus of two broad symbolic dichotomies: the "good" and "bad" pueblo, and "vicious" and "virtuous" elites. Importantly, both of these dichotomies were complicit with the code of counterinsurgency, in that they were concerned primarily with pacification—maintaining security and establishing order. According to Claudio Lomnitz, the difference between good and bad representations of the pueblo hinged on whether or not the popular classes in question were dependent on "good society." While both interpretations broadly understood the popular classes as proto-citizens, lacking the necessary virtue to be true citizens, the good pueblo, connected by bonds of dependency to recognized systems of social distinction, was seen as "abject" and unthreatening. The bad pueblo, on the other hand, was unbound from civil society and thus seen as "dangerous" and a threat to civilization. This basic distinction also applied to elites. While the "virtuous caudillos" of the nineteenth century used their positions of public authority in the service of the common good, to "open the way for the extension of citizenship rights," their inverse, "petty tyrants," used their public authority to advance their self-interest and enhance their power by blocking the extension of citizenship rights to the subordinate classes. These distinctions, which emerged from a time when fractious elites and their armed masses dragged Mexico into a tragic period of prolonged instability, reemerged in 1911 as revolutionary violence threatened to send the nation back down the path of anarchy.[3]

By representing the Chegomista Rebellion as the work of a self-interested demagogue and his "unconscious multitudes," Mexican politicians and the press constructed a narrative of the Chegomista Rebellion that not only justified its repression but did so within the discursive framework of liberal republicanism, thereby delegitimizing the Chegomistas' claims to authority in the name of popular sovereignty. Specifically, by representing Juchitán's poor and indigenous majority as incapable of managing political life—lacking the education to discern their collective self-interest, and the virtue to sublimate their private interest to that of the nation—the counterinsurgent narrative of the Chegomista Rebellion denigrated the value of popular will as a political commodity, empowered to authorize or disauthorize competing claims to liberal-democratic legitimacy. If the poor and indigenous majority were, by their ignorance, incapable of self-governance and "susceptible to suggestion," then the will of the people was not to be obeyed, but managed and mediated by a small, enlightened minority (the gente sensata), capable of defending the national interest from the misguided attacks of the popular classes, and fractious demagogues. Given their degraded state, the principle of popular sovereignty and its promise of equality threatened to unmoor the popular classes from their dependence on "good society," and thereby make them available to the growing influence of "vicious" elites, who preyed on their malleability to expand their own power against that of the nation. No popular movement in Mexico demonstrated more clearly or more publicly the dangers of caciquismo than did the Chegomista Rebellion, which was transformed by the press into a national stage on which the regime worked out its response to persistent popular violence.

The "Bad Pueblo" and "Good Society": The Historical Roots of a Counterinsurgent Discourse

In his work on colonial India, Guha contends that the endemic rebellions that characterized British rule in India represented a series of ruptures in the formative layers of the state, in which a particular "code of insurgency"—generally associated with the idea of "turning the world upside down"—breached the normative code of colonial rule. The act of recording the events of a rebellion and making sense of them required the recorder to make a "principled choice" between this code of insurgency, constituted by a series of inversions of authority, and its opposite, the code of counterinsurgency, a coercive code of pacification. Without fail, primary sources recorded the histories of rebellion in the code of counterinsurgency, making "the security of the state into the central problematic in peasant insurgency," and thereby denying the peasant "recognition as a subject of history in his own right even for a project that was all his own." Specifically, by emphasizing the "terrible" aspects of popular violence and denigrating the political consciousness of the peasant, the elite discourse generated by popular insurgency denied the inherently political nature of popular rebellion while affirming colonial rule and its ideological underpinnings. By defining the peasant outside the domain of the political, the "prose of counterinsurgency" bridged the gap between colonial political practice, which restricted access to the public sphere, and the discourse of liberal nationalism, which promoted equality, laying the groundwork for "a mitigated and second-class citizenship" in India.[4]

During the nineteenth century, Mexican state builders developed a "counterinsurgent" response to the spread of militant movements that mediated the extension of citizenship rights to the popular classes within the "modern" discourse of liberal-democratic revolution. As in India, the Mexican prose of counterinsurgency hinged on a pre-political (and pre-rational) image of the popular classes. Unlike India, however, in Mexico the discourse of counterinsurgency was articulated in the context of national sovereignty rather than direct colonial rule. The challenge for Mexican intellectuals, then, was to justify the persistence of colonial hierarchies beyond Independence in the same language of civic republicanism used to dismantle the remnants of authoritarianism and feudalism that ordered colonial society. By expanding participation in national sovereignty to the popular classes, Mexican state builders made popular sovereignty the new nation's guiding principle—sovereignty embodied in "the people," whose will would be represented by popularly elected officials. In order to accurately gauge the will of the people, the 1812 Constitution of Cádiz legally dissolved the corporate structures of Spanish colonialism and replaced them with individual rights, founded on a broadly inclusive definition of citizenship, rooted in the Spanish notion of *vecindad*, or respectability in the community. By basing citizenship on social prominence rather than uniform, objective criteria, the Constitution of Cádiz established the potential juridical equality of all vecinos, which included indígenas. As a result, nearly all adult males could elect their representative legislative bodies and serve in local government. Unfettered from restrictions to their political participation, Mexico's popular classes flooded the public sphere. However, rather than funnel individual demands through formal, institutional channels, popular politics frequently took the form of collective and direct action: riots in the cities and rebellions in the countryside. As violence engulfed the nation, it was the newly politicized masses, and not the fractious elites who mobilized them, who bore the brunt of the blame.[5]

Alienated by the sudden rise of mass politics, Mexico's *hombres de bien*—loosely defined as relatively wealthy, educated, urban professionals, disconnected from the colonial aristocracy—established an informal social pact bound not by ideology but by common class interest and a shared fear of social dissolution. Together these men of distinction formed a social consensus that interpreted the nation's political instability, rising crime, and fiscal uncertainty as the inevitable outcome of expanding citizenship rights in a society in which the majority of the population lacked the attributes of ideal citizens.[6] Rather than incorporate the collective interests of the popular classes into formal political parties that would represent their sectoral interests in the public sphere, the hombres de bien clung to the ideal of a singular, unified national interest (synonymous with their own class interest) and sought to safeguard the public sphere from popular participation. Beginning in the 1830s, the federal government began instituting income requirements for voting and holding office that effectively reduced electoral participation to a tiny fraction of the population (especially in rural areas) and ensured that elected officials be drawn from a small pool of wealthy property owners.[7]

The constriction of the public sphere made sense within the colonialist logic of Mexico's educated minority, who broadly understood the population of the indigenous periphery as "pre-political"—potential citizens who had not yet achieved the level of civilization needed for self-government, or the level of organization necessary to attain political consciousness. This interpretation of Mexico's indigenous population was embedded in centuries of Spanish political thought that equated civilization with urbanity. In the sixteenth century, lacking legal jurisdiction over the newly encountered indigenous population, Spanish jurists revived Aristotle's theory of natural slavery to justify their political dominion in the Americas. The theory postulated that all races of men existed on a spectrum that ranged from godlike to bestial, with various gradations in between. What separated more perfect men from barbarians was their ability to use reason to control their animal nature—the capacity of their intellect to subdue and restrain their passions. The use of reason required virtue, which could only be learned through participation in urban life: a city. Those who lacked a polis—a physical focal point but also a political and moral community—lived without laws, and alien to any form of virtue. Lacking the moral regulation of a code of law, the virtue by which to subordinate his self-interest to that of the community, and the intellect to subdue his emotions, the natural slave had no means by which to establish communal harmony and concord, save for coercion by brute force. Without harmony and order, natural slaves could not live a life of happiness. Their best hope was to be ruled by rational men and harnessed to the institutions of civil society, by which they could be improved (though not perfected). By the nineteenth century, while Mexico's educated elite did not believe the indigenous masses to be, strictly speaking, natural slaves, they did believe that Spanish colonialism had left them in a state of profound *embrutecimiento*. Denied for centuries access to education, political rights, and private property, and physically isolated from the guiding influence of creole society, Mexico's indigenous population languished in extreme material poverty and cultural degradation, prohibited from becoming independent, rational beings.[8]

This image of the poor and indigenous masses provided the bedrock for the nineteenth-century "code of counterinsurgency," by which Mexico's administrative elite interpreted the political behavior of the popular classes, in general, and justified their continued exclusion from the public sphere. Lomnitz has identified two distinct discourses for the masses generated by the unprecedented spread of popular insurrection following Independence: one for those who remained peaceful and obedient, and one for those who did not. While neither the "good" nor the "bad" pueblo, respectively, were thought capable of managing political life, because it was dependent on "good society," the good pueblo had sovereignty, while the bad pueblo did not. The sovereignty of the good pueblo, however, emanated not from their constitutional rights as individuals but from their "abject" dependence and their need for state protection. They remained proto-citizens in need of elevation, but their obedience granted them the right to be represented by citizens, specifically by local notables capable of discerning their will and aligning it with the general interest.[9]

The bad pueblo, on the other hand—distinguished by a lexicon of negative terms that reinforced their status as an irrational mob, such as *la canalla, la chusma, el populacho*—was unbound from civil society and thus seen as "dangerous" and a threat to civilization. Without the virtue to subordinate their own needs to the common good, and the intellect to pursue their interests through rational discourse, the masses were thought to be pre-political and predisposed to shows of "brute force." Thus denied access to the rational domain of the political, the popular classes could participate in political life in only two ways, apart from passive obedience: by violently advancing their selfish and misguided interests against the general interest (the image of the "erroneous masses"), or as fodder for fractious politicians who preyed on their intellectual malleability to advance their own interest (the image of the "vicious caudillo"). In both cases the political participation of the bad pueblo obstructed the civilizing influence of "good society," thus deferring its own redemption, and undermined the process of social integration, eroding the unanimity of the national interest. As such, the discourse of the bad pueblo negated the political nature of popular rebellion, representing it instead as a "criminal offense." By criminalizing the political activity of the "bad pueblo," elite administrators could easily justify its violent repression as a necessary measure to pave the way for the advance of civilization and the extension of citizenship rights.[10]

One pertinent example of this "counterinsurgent" discourse comes from midcentury Juchitán. Defending his authorization of the army's scorching of the town in 1850, Benito Juárez reasoned that the rebellion in Juchitán "was done neither to carry out a political plan, nor to propose any useful reforms, nor to complain about its current government, nor to change administrative personnel.... It was done to evade obedience to all authority and the healthy burden of the law, and to rob with impunity and engage without obstacles in excesses that morality condemns."[11] By violently rejecting the "healthy burden" of participation in a moral community, ruled by the restraint of law rather than the impunity of force, the rebellion in Juchitán, and popular rebellion in general, "promised no hope of serving well the patria" and functioned only to undermine national unity and circumvent legal channels established to measure popular will. To salvage the nation, the bad pueblo would have to be harnessed to "good society," even forcibly, before being granted the right to be represented in the public sphere by Mexican citizens. By limiting the extension of civil liberties to only the dependent masses, the discourses of the good and bad pueblo constituted a "counterinsurgent" response to the rise of popular politics and a justification for the persistence of colonial hierarchies in lieu of formal colonial institutions.[12]

Following the expulsion of the French in 1867, the consolidation of state power began to take precedence over the expansion of citizenship rights as the key to national redemption. As a new, civilian elite emerged to replace the military caudillos that dominated the midcentury, education and the use of reason replaced military accomplishments as the virtues that authorized certain sectors of society to represent the silent majority in the public sphere. These *hombres de palabra* justified their authority and built their political legitimacy on their capacity to represent public opinion. "Public opinion" represented a transparent signifier of popular sovereignty, but it was also implicitly understood as a reference to the reading public, the gente pensante. Thus, by the beginning of the Porfiriato the "general will" of the people was clearly embodied by a small, enlightened minority. Until the attributes of the ideal citizen were disseminated among the majority, it was the duty of men of education, property, and distinction to discern the popular will and direct it toward the national interest. By controlling the definition of the national interest and the interpretation of the popular will, the gente pensante justified the consolidation of a strong, centralizing state that could ensure political stability and advance the class interests of the educated minority without relinquishing their claims to represent the will of the people.[13]

Once state power was consolidated during the Porfiriato, popular sovereignty and other "metaphysical" ideals were replaced in political discourse by "order and progress." As the fetish of material progress superseded that of citizenship, and faith in the state supplanted social unity as the key to ensuring stability, public opinion lost its value as a political commodity capable of authorizing or disauthorizing elite claims to political legitimacy. In the 1890s a new technocratic elite emerged, steeped in positivist education, and articulated its claims to authority in the language of rationalism and science. Influenced by "scientific" theories of crowd psychology, racial difference, and criminology—all generated in Europe to explain the incapacity of the masses to adapt to "modern" society—Mexico's "científicos" sought to insulate the state from the corrosive and destabilizing effects of public opinion by replacing traditional politics with cold, calculating administration. Rhetorical eloquence and appeals to popular opinion—staples of nineteenth-century political discourse—were increasingly denigrated as instruments of demagoguery, as base attempts to manipulate the gullible masses. With an effective state capable of ensuring material progress and enforcing social order, citizenship became a long-term goal rather than an urgent necessity, popular sovereignty faded from public discourse, and the "prose of counterinsurgency," once critical to mediating access to the public sphere, became increasingly redundant. However, the discourses of the good and bad pueblo did not disappear altogether, but remained just below the surface of public politics, ready to be reactivated whenever the popular classes ruptured the formative layers of the state, or when popular sovereignty emerged to challenge its precepts.[14]

A Counterinsurgent Narrative of the Chegomista Rebellion

With the coming of the Mexican Revolution, the "code of insurgency" once again breached the public sphere, reopening the national debate about the expansion of citizenship rights and the proper role of popular sovereignty in democratic society. Forced by the resurgence of popular violence to make a "principled choice" between the insurgent code of mobilization and the counterinsurgent code of pacification, political chroniclers predominantly (or even subconsciously) chose the latter, recording the events of the Revolution in a linear, legible fashion so as to highlight causality, thus making pacification "the central problematic in peasant insurgency." By reducing the Revolution to a series of "legible" narratives, reporters made sense of the sudden proliferation of popular movements in familiar terms, resuscitating nineteenth-century discourses of the "good" and "bad" pueblo, only now in a revolutionary context. In so doing, they constructed a "record for the regime to refer to so that it could understand the nature and motivation" of rebellion, and "by understanding suppress it." Critically, the revolutionary "prose of counterinsurgency" saturated not only official accounts of the rebellion but also non-official sources, such as newspapers, which often maintained the pretense of being purely descriptive, and thus neutral or objective. Despite their straightforward nature and claims to objectivity, because their ways of making sense of the Revolution derived from the same body of colonialist knowledge and operated in the same reactionary code of counterinsurgency, newspaper accounts of the Revolution were indistinguishable from policy, and both official and non-official discourses of rebellion worked together as an affirmation of state power.[15]

In the forty days that followed the initial uprising on November 2, the Chegomista Rebellion entered the national conscience as the lead story in the national press. Under Madero the press enjoyed unprecedented freedom: new dailies and magazines appeared overnight, anti-Porfirian newspapers resurfaced with renewed energy, and the Old Regime's propaganda organs remained largely unchanged, resulting in a deeply polemical and partisan press. Despite its factionalism and critical freedom, however, the press's representations of the Chegomista Rebellion effectively performed the function of official texts, even when being explicitly critical of the government's handling of the rebellion: they varied tremendously from metonymical, indicative accounts (descriptions of events by correspondents) to more metaphorical, interpretive commentaries (editorials and reports of political speeches), and from newspapers that were directly official or nominally "revolutionary" (*El Demócrata Mexicano* and *El Diario*) to more conservative holdovers from the Porfiriato (*El Imparcial* and *El País*). However, all reproduced a narrative of the Chegomista Rebellion that functioned as a defense of order and justified the repression of the rebellion. By emphasizing the terrible aspects of popular violence and mobilizing the language and symbols of caciquismo to (mis)represent insurgent political actions, the press worked within the same code of counterinsurgency as the state, and even in criticizing the regime it functioned to reaffirm an exclusive interpretation of citizenship that marginalized the popular classes from the domain of the political. What follows is an aggregated reproduction of the counterinsurgent narrative of the Chegomista Rebellion, gleaned from a wide array of national and regional newspapers that reported daily on events in Juchitán, and a few contemporaneous political speeches and testimonies.[16]

"One of the Most Fearsome and Arbitrary Caciques": Che Gómez

By 1911, as the thrust of the Revolution shifted from the urban realm of formal politics and into the hands of what Frank Tannenbaum called "small groups of Indians under anonymous leaders," the term "cacique" emerged in public discourse as a broad, descriptive label for these otherwise "anonymous leaders." Originally an Arawak word for "chief," under the Spanish "cacique" was a relatively neutral term for the indigenous rulers who mediated the space between the colonial administration and their indigenous pueblos. Following Independence the term came to signify generic "political bosses," losing its ethnic connotations while maintaining its relative neutrality. At the same time, a new class of rural warlords, known as "caudillos," emerged from the wars of Independence to replace caciques as the most prominent interlocutors between the state and the rural poor. As their power and grandeur eclipsed that of local caciques, caudillos also shouldered much of the blame for Mexico's political instability. The worst of them were represented as "petty tyrants" who used their personalist authority and their control of vast resources to maintain extensive networks of clients, whom they mobilized to advance their self-interest against the common good. In so doing, caudillos undermined attempts to organize the popular classes into ideologically based political parties and impeded the extension of citizenship rights down the social hierarchy. "Vicious caudillos" were seen as obstacles to national unity who would have to be subdued militarily and subordinated to the state in order to have political stability. Such was the case under Porfirio Díaz (the "Last Caudillo"), who brought an end to the Golden Age of the caudillos, pushing them to the margins of political life and discourse. However, when popular violence returned to challenge the pillars of state authority with the Revolution, so too did the negative discourse of "vicious elites," only now directed at undifferentiated "caciques" and their rustic, often indigenous followers.[17]

By late 1911, caciques had become the symbolic scourge of the Revolution, threatening to destabilize the delicate political balance by fomenting popular unrest, and using the spread of violence as an opportunity to expand their own private fortunes at the public's expense. The term "caciquismo" itself had become political shorthand for demagoguery. It was from within this context that Che Gómez emerged from obscurity on the pages of the nation's newspapers. According to newspaper reports, Gómez was a typical cacique: an ambitious and restless member of the científico elite who sought to use his privileged status and sharp intellect to usurp public functions and use them for personal gain. His primary objective was to win the appointment to the jefatura política, which required him to establish vertical relations of patronage with the federal and state governments, both controlled by nominal revolutionaries. To do so, Gómez eschewed his status within the científico establishment and cloaked himself in the ideology of the Revolution, posing as a Maderista. Although his cynical maneuverings fooled some within the federal government, the state government of Oaxaca, many of whom had personal relationships with Gómez, was less susceptible to his deceptions.

Before the national press corps arrived in Juchitán to cover the rebellion, Che Gómez was unknown outside the Isthmus. The early accounts of newspaper correspondents from before they had access to Juchitán indicate that, given the popular nature of the rebellion, Che Gómez was assumed to be indigenous, a "Zapotec leader" of Zapotec followers. *El País* even reported that Gómez "speaks a depraved castellano, and is inclined to Zapotec, which is his natural language." This image dissolved once the press was allowed into Juchitán. Based on interviews with locals, the regional correspondent for *El Demócrata Mexicano*, Aldo Baroni, clarified that "contrary to what is supposed, [Gómez] is not an illiterate misled by ideas of dissolution, but rather a qualified lawyer, a cultivated man of great prestige among the inhabitants of the Isthmus." After meeting Gómez face-to-face, Baroni fleshed out his image: "He is a man who appears physically and intellectually like doctor Vázquez Gómez. His culture is vast and he speaks with ease about any topic. Refuting that he is a half-literate and bloodthirsty Indian, as all the readers of *El Demócrata* presume the Indiada would be, I will clarify that he is a learned, illustrious Juchiteco, and has exercised politics and used his influence with firmness." Leopoldo Zea, writing for the more conservative *El Imparcial*, was sparser in his commentary. He noted that Gómez seemed eager to be interviewed, and described him simply as being of "medium height, robust complexion, olive color, and ... clear cunning and sharpness." Together, these descriptions established that Gómez was intellectually, culturally, and ethnically distinct from his followers.[18]

Gómez's cultural and intellectual distinction reflected his elevated status as a member of the científico elite. This characterization of

Gómez owed, no doubt, to his personal relationship with prominent científico Rosendo Pineda, which the press thoroughly explored. In the immediate aftermath of the rebellion, multiple newspapers reported that Pineda, in fact, had funded the rebellion. Though these rumors were short-lived, Gómez became regularly identified as a "científico," especially in the regional press. Oaxaca's most widely distributed daily, *El Avance*, described Gómez as "the spoiled child of the camarilla científica" who had parlayed the "favoritism of the fallen regime" into a series of prestigious political positions under Díaz, accounting for his exalted status in Juchitán. However, despite being "one of the favorites of cientificismo," Gómez was notably "inquieto" and had been "a disturbing element in the city of Juchitán" for quite some time. His "perverse" or "bellicose temperament" made him "the most unruly, turbulent, and scheming man on the Isthmus." Uniformly, Gómez's restlessness was attributed to his ambition.[19]

In the context of revolutionary Mexico, ambition was by no means a neutral or passive descriptor. Ambition was the descriptive hallmark of the "vicious" elite and a synonym for the self-interest that distinguished him from his "virtuous" mirror image. The ambition of elites identified as caciques or caudillos was widely blamed for the factionalism that had corroded national unity in the days before Díaz, and threatened to do so again as revolutionary violence continued to destabilize the countryside. Ambition fractured the unity of the general interest and led weaker members of the elite to appropriate the public for private use. Che Gómez's image as an ambitious and corrosive elite—a cacique—was established descriptively in the texts of the nation's newspapers. He was regularly referred to simply as ambitious, or an "ambitious cacique," and his ambitions were qualified by a host of descriptive adjectives referencing his "unruly," "exorbitant," or "selfish ambitions."[20] In fact, ambition was written as Gómez's defining quality. More interpretative texts clarified the precise object of his ambition: his "compulsive aspiration to occupy the post of jefe político of the District of Juchitán."[21] He wanted "to monopolize all authority in Juchitán, in order to use it for his personal benefit and that of his partisans, excluding from public business and tyrannizing all of those not devoted to his caciquismo."[22] Gómez achieved the first step toward his ultimate goal in May 1911, when he was elected municipal president. "Once in possession of his office," testified General Telésforo Merodio, the jefe de armas on the Isthmus, "his first measure was to remove all personnel of the administration subject to his authority, and fill the vacancies with his relatives and associates, in this way reducing the means of repression of the political authorities and augmenting for his part his prestige."[23] Gómez's nepotism, anathema to ideologically committed liberals, was a common theme: after he "ignominiously sacked the existing police, [he] organized another to his liking, commanded by his cousin"; he got his stepson elected to the state legislature; and he named his brother municipal president. According to *El País*, "in this situation he exploited the entire district and developed there the most coarse caciquismo that has been established up to today, that has converted the cabecera [Juchitán] into a little Republic, where neither the state nor the federal government can intervene."[24] This command of the region, perverting public office for private interest, defined Gómez as a "demagogue" and a "despot."[25]

However, despite his command of the region, Gómez could not fully consolidate his authority until he usurped its highest office, the jefatura política. To assume this political post, an appointed position, Gómez intrigued at winning the patronage of the federal and state governments by refashioning himself as a committed Maderista. "After having been an adorer of Rosendo Pineda," reported *El Avance*, Gómez "converted himself into an interested sympathizer of the present regime." Gómez's transformation into a Maderista coincided with the July arrival of the insurgent army to Juchitán: "From this moment on, Che Gómez modified his plan: shamelessly stripping his Porfirista clothing and hiding his 'científica' affiliation, he disguised himself and disguised his people as Maderistas, and presented them to [the insurgent army] as allies." On their visits to the rebel encampments, correspondents noted that the rebels greeted them almost compulsorily with spirited "vivas" to Madero, despite the fact that when questioned by Leopoldo Zea of *El Imparcial*, "the rebels did not know that Señor Madero is the President of the Republic." If Zea remained unconvinced, Gómez persuaded many within the revolutionary regime. The president himself later admitted that the rebels' shouts of "Viva Madero!" had led him to mistakenly "believe that they were supporters of my government."[26] Those within the state government, however, many of whom had long-standing and rancorous relationships with Gómez, would not be so easily fooled. When it came time to promote a new jefe político in Juchitán, the governor passed him over. Frozen out of formal political authority, Gómez looked to prove his political value by demonstrating his support among the popular classes. It was here, in his nefarious work among the popular classes, that Gómez earned his reputation as "one of the most fearsome and arbitrary caciques."[27]

"A Magician, Who Fascinates the Rudimentary Beings around Him": Gómez and His Followers

At no point was the counterinsurgent character of the narrative of the Chegomista Rebellion clearer than in the descriptions of the relationship between Che Gómez and his popular following. The Chegomista rebels were nearly always described in coded terms for the "bad pueblo," intended to convey their class and ethnic character, while underscoring their ignorance and incapacity for political consciousness. Their ignorance and broad representation as "rudimentary beings" highlighted their vulnerability to the manipulations of the predatory cacique, who "tricked" them into following him by making a series of false and unsustainable promises. Moreover, given the naïveté of the poor, uneducated, Indian masses and their predisposition to autocracy and vertical power relations, their devotion to Gómez was inherently irrational and fanatical. Ultimately, then, the Chegomista Rebellion, despite its legitimate demand for popular sovereignty (which was completely absent from press accounts of the rebellion), was represented as a pre-political movement that harnessed the brutish energies of the pueblo to the advancement of the private, selfish interests of a cacique, rather than the general interest, or even the collective interest of the pueblo itself.

The use of coded and ideologically loaded indices and adjectives as simple descriptors of Che Gómez's followers laid bare the counterinsurgent code in which both newspapers and politicians worked. Gómez's followers were described almost invariably through an elaborate colonial discourse aimed at marking them not only socioeconomically and ethnically but also as representative of the "bad pueblo," untethered from civil society, ignorant, and incapable of managing political life. Many of the simple indices used to identify the Chegomistas were colonial terms for the anonymous, uncivilized popular classes, all variations of the "rabble," the "crowd," or the "mob": *la chusma, el populacho, las turbas, el muchedumbre, los multitudes, la plebe, las masas populares, la masa humana, los rudos, las chusmas iresponsables,* and *las clases más rudas.*[28] The indigenous character of the rebels was accepted as a fact and was almost always noted by the relatively mild (if not neutral) term *indígenas,* or the less-mild *indios.* However, other ethnically coded terminology was applied to the rebels to make clear their "dangerous" nature. These terms included *salvajes, tribus salvajes, indios alzados, indígenas levantados, indígenas armadas,* or *desgraciados indígenas.*[29] Most telling of the counterinsurgent code employed by the press was the expansive lexicon used to underscore the ignorance and coarseness of the rebels. The Chegomistas were regularly referred to as *las clases analfabetas, la gente más ignorante, la gente simple, las ignaras chusmas, el pueblo ignorante,* and *la gente estulta,* all terms aimed at conveying their ignorance, and thereby their susceptibility to the suggestions of a powerful cacique.[30] This denigration of the rebels' political consciousness had more direct descriptive forms, such as *las multitudes inconcientes, indígenas inconcientes, inconcientes mesnadas, los ciegos,* and *gentes susceptibles de sugestión.*[31] This negative lexicon used to describe the Chegomistas coexisted with a positive terminology used to describe their middle-class opponents and the poor who chose not to join the rebellion, which, in juxtaposition with descriptions of the rebels, emphasized either their advanced level of civilization and education—*la gente sensata, los habitantes sensatos, la sociedad sensata, la gente pensante, las clases sanas*[32]—or, their more honorable, abject nature, as *los ciudadanos pacíficos, el pueblo laborioso, el verdadero pueblo*, and *el pueblo honrado*.[33]

To advance his prestige among the naive popular classes, Che Gómez made a series of "vain" and "impossible promises," claiming to represent the demands and interests of Juchitán's poor, indigenous, and "rudimentary" population and to have the power to make their demands satisfied. To the popular classes, Gómez "promised liberties, gratification . . . in short, whatever was possible to promise." Specifically, "he announced to his Indians his certain ascension to the jefatura, from where he would never be removed and from where he would shower them with goods, consisting of lands and salt flats that the rich had apparently stripped from the poor pueblo; in absolute freedom to do with impunity as they wanted, with complete exemption from taxes and public services." This basic interpretation of Gómez's manipulations echoed through newspaper accounts of the rebellion, gaining traction even in the radical press. In *Regeneración*, Enrique Flores Magón explained, "In order to get the Indian brothers of that region to follow him in his enterprise of establishing the Republic of Tehuantepec, of which he would be the president, Che Gómez promised them that upon his triumph he would give them the land, water, salt flats and forests of that region for them to enjoy without the burden of more masters." This narrative skeleton was repeated with a few variations in detail.[34]

Gómez's success in winning the support of the popular classes depended on a combination of his talents for demagoguery and the natural credulity of the ignorant masses. Or, in other words, Gómez's ability to gain popular support depended on his ability to lie and the popular classes' innate gullibility and predisposition to believe his lies. On the first count, based on interviews it seems that Gómez's singular talent for manipulation and dissimulation was well known among politicians in Oaxaca. "With perfect naturalness he transforms himself from a raging Porfirista into a Maderista, Vazquista, and *reyista*," complained one of his opponents. "He is apt to exercise wickedness and later appear as the victim to evade responsibility."[35] As Miguel Bolaños Cacho, the governor's personal aide, noted, "The danger of Gómez did not lie, does not lie in his popularity, nor in him being loved nor esteemed by the district in reference, but rather, by the natural sagacity of his character, and by the profound understanding that he has had and has of the customs, quarrels, and motives of the inhabitants of that region, he has always had an aptitude for using these means to [play] one group against the other." In fact, Porfirio Díaz, "a profound judge of men," recognized Gómez's talents for causing trouble and intentionally kept him far from the region.[36] While Gómez's manipulations fell flat among the gente sensata of Juchitán, they clearly found their mark "among the classes most rude and susceptible to suggestion." By "exercising great influence and suggestion over the indígenas, all of whom are illiterate," Gómez established an "ominous prestige" among "the ignorant chusmas Juchitecas." According to *El Imparcial*, Gómez "had always been a disturbing element in the city of Juchitán, where he enjoys some prestige among the most ignorant people, [who] by their illiteracy, are always disposed to let themselves be fooled, if one makes them an alluring promise, no matter how absurd."[37]

The coarse nature of Gómez's followers carried serious implications for the nature of political rule in Juchitán. Specifically, the evolutionary interpretation of the masses presumed that the poor and indigenous population lacked the necessary level of civilization for democratic rule and thus tended naturally toward autocracy. This natural tendency made them especially vulnerable to caciquismo. The "unconscious indígenas" that comprised Che Gómez's following invested in him the absolute authority of a "czar" and "obeyed him as a chief," pledging to him a "fanatical" devotion. This all-encompassing devotion was reflected in common use of possessive determiners in describing the relationship between Che Gómez and "his chusmas," "his indios," or, most telling "his Indiada." In *El Demócrata Mexicano*, Aldo Baroni illustrated the vertical nature of this relationship with an anecdotal comparison to Victor Hugo's *Les misérables*: "The Juchiteco is a pueblo that allows itself to be swayed more than any other... so much so that when they seized a Saint Chamond-Mondragón cannon, on the suggestion of licenciado Gómez, a rival of the Parisian Gavroche wet himself as bullets whistled by furiously." The reference to Gavroche, the young boy who flung himself into the fire of the French army to retrieve cartridges for the student protesters, was meant to underscore the Chegomistas' total devotion to Gómez.[38]

The indigenous character of the Chegomistas added an air of messianism to the movement, shot through with heavy-handed racialized references. The "unconscious Indians" of Juchitán deified Che Gómez, "who is everything there, who is constantly acclaimed, to whom they throw flowers when he passes, they kiss his hands, and the women receive him in masses like a god." For the people of Juchitán, noted Baroni, "Gómez was an apostle, one of those types of Zapotec idols that sends good crops to the countryside of the ancient and glorious Oaxacan land." His popularity "derived from the thousand commitments of autosuggestion of a people who had come to see in Che Gómez its only savior." This sort of deification was not unique to Juchitán, but typical among the indigenous masses of the countryside: the Chegomistas "represent the common case among savage tribes of a priest, or a magician, who fascinates the rudimentary beings that surround him, them believing in him as in God and not allowing anyone else to govern or administer them."[39]

Lomnitz has noted that "the situation of the 'bad pueblo' was compared to that of a young woman who was not under the tutelage of a man" and thus susceptible to the "seductions" of the predatory elite. This comparison was brought into full, illustrative relief by Baroni:

> The pueblos have the need for a Savior every few years, like young women for a boyfriend; these things are natural.... Boyfriend and Savior come decked out in promises, filling their head and their heart with illusions, giving them five minutes of hope and for that they adore them, they squeeze them in passionate embraces...

(it is true that the embraces of a pueblo are often mortal . . .) Che Gómez was the thousandth savior of the Zapotec people; he promised liberties, leisure . . . in short, everything that was possible to promise; the people followed him and he allowed himself to be swept away by popularity until the day came in which Oaxaca sent he who should succeed him.[40]

Che Gómez, according to Baroni, was not unique, but the product of rural life on Mexico's indigenous periphery. Gómez himself was neither "a bandit" nor "a great man and a patriot," but a man with "the average mind of a fighter and politician with the garnish of a demagogue, one of those minds of which there are many in our provincial pueblos; they have a certain native indolence, in general, in a golden mean, but chance sometimes launches them to popularity, carrying them to Glory or to jail, indifferently, depending on the moment. Because the most normal mind allows itself sometimes to be swept away by the gale of popularity and popularity is a guide that when one trusts it is not so easy to give up." Ultimately, then, the indigenous periphery, degraded and desperate for salvation, invested even the most average of men with the prestige of popularity and the power of a messiah. The weaker of these men, unable to resist the newfound power conveyed by popularity, rode it either to "Glory" or "to jail." Che Gómez had tasted a modicum of glory, but jail seemed to be imminent, the result of the "mortal" embrace of the pueblo.[41]

By establishing the relationship between Che Gómez and his followers as a typical relationship between a cacique and his unconscious, ignorant Indians, the official narrative excluded the Chegomista movement from the domain of the political, defining it as the work of a personalist cacique and his unconscious masses. As a result, the Chegomista Rebellion, in the words of Governor Juárez Maza, was a "sterile fight" that "did not seek out a principle, that did not have a justified cause to rebel." As such, the rebellion was a criminal act, more akin to banditry than politics. Even before he arrived in Juchitán, the correspondent for *El País* degraded the political legitimacy of the movement, writing: "Che Gómez is truly criminal and deserves a severe punishment ... because he has aroused the unconscious indígenas, the stultified and ignorant people who do not pursue any goal, who do not long for their improvement nor that of their fellow man, but rather who follow the voice of an ambitious vulgarian, of a cacique from the Porfirian times, who ... without caring [about] the numerous victims that he is causing, does not lay down his criminal attitude, but continues instigating these masses of indígenas, in order to defend a usurpation, an illegality, an outrage." Several weeks later, an editorial in *El Avance* echoed these sentiments: "The Juchiteco revolt is unjustifiable, as it does not pursue any noble idea, nor redeeming principles, nor altruistic or righteous goals." *El Avance* rejected the peace negotiations of the federal government, in particular, as they "implied a recognition of the belligerence of [the rebels] that they do not deserve, because they are not, properly speaking, revolutionaries, but seditious criminals who have cowardly consummated horrifying murders, who have uselessly caused the sacrifice of a multitude of lives useful to the patria, who have made Juchitán, on the path to progress, fall back, ruining it and discrediting it before the nation and the civilized world. The agreement sought, in this case, is tactless, immoral, and, above all, dangerous."[42]

At the same time, as the conflict between the federal and state government came to a head over how best to resolve the situation in Juchitán, the state legislature of Oaxaca outlined an official interpretation of the rebellion that justified its own actions. "We wish for [the federal government] to declare which side is correct," began the official statement of the state legislature to the national Chamber of Deputies:

> On one side [is] the uncontrollable, selfish, and perverse ambitions of a cacique with inexplicable refinements and intentions, of a cacique whose intentions do not include protecting the lives of authorities, the honor of families, the property of residents, the honorable name of oaxaqueños, or the decency that the patria claims

like an afflicted mother, for the love and protection of all of her children. On the other side is the government that adapts its actions to the precepts of the law, that in the orbit of its faculties and far from absolutism has watched over the effective performance of its institutions. On one side the treachery, the boundless ambitions, the exploitation of the naïveté of the ignorant masses; on the other side governmental integrity ... rectitude in its proceedings, the constant observation of the law.[43]

These were the conclusions drawn from the counterinsurgent narrative: if Gómez was an ambitious cacique who used false promises to mobilize an unwitting and unconscious mass of Indians who were too ignorant to penetrate his manipulations, then the resulting rebellion was not political, but personal. It pursued the interests of Che Gómez, diametrically opposed to the general interest, and divorced even from the collective interest of his followers themselves. Thus, the Chegomista Rebellion took place outside the domain of the political, in the realm of criminality.

"A Borrachera de Niño": Degeneration and Indian Violence

While popular violence continued to be interpreted through a classical, colonial framework—as the only political language available to pre-political peoples—by the time of the Revolution images of "Indian violence," more specifically, began to reflect the growing influence of the medicalized, European discourse of degeneration. The concept of degeneration emerged in Europe in the nineteenth century as a way of making sense of the rising crime rates and political instability that accompanied the transition to "modern" living. Largely the domain of criminologists and psychiatrists, theories of degeneration proposed that the adaptation of simple, rural people to complex, urban society created a "division between the human body and social conditions."[44] This division stimulated or disinhibited "latent atavisms" that had been repressed through education and discipline but continued to lurk in the subconscious, or in primitive neurological centers, of the poor and other "lamentably alien" populations. These atavisms—primitive instincts thought to have long disappeared—manifested themselves in a wide variety of "criminally deviant" behaviors, generally implying among men the "recrudescence of bloodlust."[45]

The discourse of degeneration carried obvious appeal for Porfirian intellectuals, who used it to justify the implementation of rigid social controls and the growth of the state's disciplinary apparatus as the pace of the nation's modernization projects accelerated. In Mexico the fear of degeneration specifically targeted the "primitive" indigenous population. While Mexican intellectuals symbolically acknowledged the greatness of past indigenous civilizations, thereby recognizing the abstract potential for civilization among contemporary indígenas, they feared the latent hatreds and degraded customs that the indigenous population had developed over centuries of economic exploitation, cultural isolation, and violent political instability. Through education and discipline—the pillars of civilization—the indigenous population had learned to repress these regressive hatreds and habits, but they persisted in the subconscious, waiting to be brought to the surface by some external stimulus, like a nervous tic. This gave rise in Mexico to a schizophrenic image of the contemporary Indian, on the one hand noble and brave, and on the other savage and violent. The key to coaxing out the Indian's nobility and suppressing his savagery, then, lay in controlling his exposure to aggravating stimuli. With this in mind, Porfirian lawmakers sought to ban bloody public spectacles, such as bullfighting, and prohibit the consumption of intoxicants, like marijuana, that were thought to trigger retrograde behavior. However, if the tutelage of a progressive state administered by an enlightened elite could protect the indigenous population from its primitive instincts, the stimulus of revolutionary violence under the patronage of imprudent, ambitious caciques threatened to destabilize the whole project by "turning back the evolutionary clock" and calling forward "human passions in their most criminal and degraded aspect." Nowhere was the influence of the discourse of degeneration more evident than in descriptions of the Chegomistas' violence.[46]

Juchitán represented both the potential and the peril of bringing modern life to Indian Mexico: its people were at once proud and naturally brave, yet capable of the most savage cruelty. The "sons of Juchitán" were the inheritors of Zapotec blood and a long history of violent conflict, and under the influence of legally constituted authorities their "Spartan bravery" was a potential resource to be tapped in defense of the nation. Against the French, for example, Juchitán lent "a brave contingent of the bold valor of its sons" to the war effort, where they "demonstrated themselves to be dignified descendants of their heroic ancestors." However, under the influence of fractious politicians, warned one congressman from Oaxaca, the primitive "temperament and character of the Juchitecos" could be unleashed, as it was in 1882, "which resulted in the deaths of many innocent people." The danger of triggering this latent bloodlust was not lost on the editors of *El Ahuizote*, who in reference to Juchitán warned against the consequences of "shaking from their lethargy the various dozens of battling, arrogant, valiant, powerful pueblos of warriors from birth." The "stoicism of their race," which made them insensitive to pain and able to "confront danger with indifference," could manifest itself as either extreme bravery or brutality, depending on the quality of external stimuli; they represented two sides of the same coin.[47]

The discourse of degeneration provided a neat framework within which to interpret the violence of the Chegomista Rebellion. From the beginning, Che Gómez had exercised a "pernicious influence" over the poor and indigenous of Juchitán, grotesquely distorting their "Spartan bravery" into "wanton acts of savagery." According to this narrative, the effects of Gómez's influence came to the surface in July, when the federal army and the gente bien—the only remaining remnants of civilization in Juchitán—evacuated the city, granting "license, licentiousness, and impunity" to the "rebellious Indians." Over the course of the summer of 1911, Gómez and his "most blind and simple partisans" intimidated and persecuted their enemies, stoning houses, carrying out "predatory homicides," and "committing real offenses even against women." The respectable families of

Juchitán remained in exile all summer, fearing that they "could not return to their homes without being beaten to death." The violence of the summer was mild, however, compared to that unleashed by the battle with the federal army.[48]

If simple liberty from the restraints of civilization disinhibited the latent violent tendencies of the Chegomistas, open combat with the federal army gave them full vent, completing their transformation into a "bloodthirsty mob." Without directly referencing degeneration in his report in *El Demócrata Mexicano*, Baroni gave a pitch perfect description of the condition: "The people of Juchitán, upon seeing that [the government] wanted to remove their idol, rebelled, and rebelled as the pueblos rebel: killing, burning, throwing themselves like wild beasts upon the tireless Mausers of the federales." During the conflict "the Indians sacked without consideration," moving about the city "burning buildings, raping, killing, and mocking the cadavers of their innocent victims." According to Baroni, they even reproduced "peculiar scenes of cannibalism" that recalled long-extinct pre-Columbian ritual practices.[49]

The appearance in newspaper accounts of postmortem cannibalism, in particular, and mutilation, more generally, reflected the influence of criminology on elite understandings of the pathology of popular violence. Italian criminologist Cesare Lombroso, whose work was widely read in Mexico, noted among the atavisms of what he called "born criminals" "the desire not only to extinguish life in the victim, but to mutilate the corpse, tear into the flesh, and drink its blood."[50] The physical manifestation of these savage desires, attributed to the Chegomistas, was a recurrent theme in the newspapers' coverage of the rebellion. In fact, no story connected to the rebellion drew more ink from the press or was fleshed out in more detail than that of Leonides Argüello, the surgeon for the Fifteenth Battalion. Known throughout the region for his humanitarian efforts, Argüello spent the first days of the rebellion tending to the wounded on both sides, until he was lured into the home of a young rebel who claimed his wife had been injured in the crossfire. There the young man shot Argüello in the chest and spat on, kicked, and cursed his body. The rebels then mutilated his corpse before dragging it through the streets to the cheers of raucous onlookers. This bloodlust was not an isolated incident. Newspapers reported that the local judge and the paymaster of the Twenty-Fifth Battalion suffered similar fates at the hands of the "bloodthirsty mob," being dragged through the streets after having their ears and noses chopped off with machetes. Days later, the White Cross identified the judge's body, hacked to pieces and burned, by the river. Whether real or imagined (correspondents depended on rumors and purported witness testimony to piece together these stories), these incidents starkly demonstrated for the reading public the terrifying outcome of Indian recidivism.[51]

The trope of degeneration found further expression in comparisons of rebel violence to that of animals and diminished or incompletely formed humanity. When questioned by *El Demócrata Mexicano* about the brutality of Argüello's murder, one rebel responded simply, "When the bitch is hot ...." When asked why the paymaster of the Twenty-Fifth Battalion was killed and dismembered, Che Gómez himself responded plainly, "That's how the people work." Baroni likened the rebels to children, and their rebellion to "a borrachera de niño" (a child's drunken spree)—irrational and unavoidable in Mexico's indigenous pueblos, in the absence of proper authorities. This form of Indian recidivism had two possible outcomes: "from the borrachera de niño can come vice as indifferently as virtue: abstinence or alcoholism, depending on which moral remedy is more or less violent and effective." If the indigenous population was indifferent (and unconscious), steering them toward virtue and halting their regression to vice would depend on the moral stimulation of external authorities.[52]

"Popular Will Will Be Personified Only in the Chusmas": Democracy and Demagoguery

The resolution of the Chegomista Rebellion carried critical symbolic implications for the future of democracy in Mexico. By advancing the principles of the Revolution (popular sovereignty and local autonomy) through informal political practice (such as mass demonstrations, shows of force, and ultimately, violent rebellion), the Chegomista movement circumvented formal channels for redressing grievances and measuring popular opinion (such as elections), and rendered moot conventional democratic institutions. However, conservative politicians and the anti-Maderista press made clear in their speeches and countless editorials that the blame for this lay not with the Chegomistas per se but with the revolutionary government now in power. The Chegomistas, by their ignorance incapable of comprehending advanced political principles and concepts such as rights and citizenship, misinterpreted (through the eager translation of caciques like Che Gómez) the revolutionary government's promise of sovereignty embodied in the people to imply total liberation from the obligations and restraints of "good society," represented by civic institutions and wage labor. Unmoored from "good society," the Chegomistas became vulnerable to a predatory cacique who represented himself to the poor and indigenous masses as uniquely fitted to fulfill these untenable promises. The Chegomista Rebellion was a monster of the regime's own making and a warning about the dangers inherent in the expansion of citizenship rights. By promising popular sovereignty to a citizenry unprepared for democracy, the revolutionary regime had ironically rendered impossible its own promises.

The mobilization of the popular classes around a cacique represented a fundamental threat to the consolidation of democracy: by privileging "traditional" political forms for advancing their claims and seeking redress for grievances, the Chegomistas circumvented formal democratic institutions and processes. Specifically, by organizing the masses to advance their claims legally through demonstrations, emotional appeals, and petitions, and extralegally by harassment, censorship, shows of armed force, and rebellion, the Chegomista movement suppressed free political expression in the public sphere and rendered useless formal means of redressing grievances and gauging popular opinion. Descriptions of "archaic" forms of mass politics—"the convocation of the chusmas, telegrams of protest, arrogant threats, demonstrations of force"—filled the public record and press coverage of the Chegomista movement. Gómez used the "noisy apparatus" of the masses to manipulate supposed public opinion in his favor. When he learned that the state government was sending someone to replace him, "he convoked his 'indiada,' insinuating to them that the governor was going to impose as jefe político an enemy of the Juchiteco people, who would undoubtedly oppress them, [and] deny them all benefits, and after spouting similar deceptions, he asked the people if they accepted such a grand imposition with all of the sad consequences that he had evoked: the chusma, faced with the disagreeable perspective of his frustrated ambitions, answered that they would reject any political agent of the government who was not Che Gómez." He also employed classic populist tactics to launch the rebellion itself. With the federal army holed up in the local barracks, and "the masses being armed and once again brought together in front of the [municipal] palace and adjacent streets, Gómez ascended to the balcony and directed a violent discourse at the people, exhorting them to spill up to their last drop of blood before losing their autonomy. Overcome with rage by Gómez's seditious words, the multitude pounced on the barracks." These forms of populist manipulation, perhaps best captured by the image of a cacique inciting a mob of armed Indians from his balcony, ensured that "so long as gomismo, that is caciquismo, remains afoot, legal order will be impossible in Juchitán."[53]

Speaking to a large assembly in Mexico City, Jorge Vera Estañol addressed the conflict in Juchitán and its potential impact on the future of democracy in Mexico. He expressed his fears that the Madero regime's attempts to reconcile with the Chegomistas had established a dangerous precedent in local politics by privileging informal forms of popular politics over formal political institutions and procedures. Vera Estañol took particular exception to the federal government's efforts to impose a jefe político in Juchitán in contradiction to the state government's official appointment, on the grounds that the state's candidate "was unpopular." With this type of federal intervention, he argued, from this moment [forward] the nation will no longer manifest the will of its people in constitutional forms ... but rather through convulsive forms and with the spasmodic jolting of rebellions, revolts, and uprisings wherever. Who can say what is the popular will of the District of Juchitán? ... Has somebody recounted the votes of will in favor of León or in favor of Gómez ... in order to know who has the majority? Or is [the government] trying to say that ... popular will is going to be personified only in the chusmas that have the audacity to rise up in arms against the constituted authorities, most of the time to satisfy the personal and spurious ambitions of intriguing demagogues? Does [the government] want to say that peaceful men, men of order, men who respect the constituted authorities, will not be an integral part of the pueblo, they will not be able to figure into the popular will and will be unpardonably passed over for the seditious and rebels?[54]

Vera Estañol's argument cut the feet out from under the Chegomista Rebellion, challenging the assumption, asserted by the Chegomistas themselves and admitted even by their opponents, that Che Gómez represented the will of the people. So long as popular forms of political organization and expression continued to submerge formal, reliable means of gauging public opinion, popular will would be impossible to determine; or worse, it would be subject to the manipulations of demagogues, who could justify their intrigues in the name of popular will, whether real or invented. Of course, the effect of this would be to drive peaceful citizens away from the voting booth and toward rebellion—the only viable means of political expression in a nation where "demagoguery has been enthroned in the executive power."[55]

Conservative politicians and the anti-Maderista press interpreted the resurrection of demagoguery as a failure of the Madero regime, or more broadly as the inevitable outcome of revolution in a nation with an ignorant, unconscious citizenry. The Maderistas, according to their opponents, took control of Oaxaca "with the sympathy of the popular classes ... convinced that the new governor was going to remove them from their humble condition, to redeem them from their poverty and servitude. The other classes watched the movement with suspicion ... but as luck would have it, the program was not just unrealizable, but dangerous, simply upon its announcement. And what had to happen happened."[56] The promise of redemption, "simply upon its announcement," awakened the people of Juchitán from their lethargy, leading them to renounce their dependent, abject position in society ("their humble condition") and its corresponding "poverty and servitude." *El Mañana* carried the argument a step further, proposing that Madero's democratic discourse had awoken "the credulous consciousness of the popular masses, making them believe that public administration can survive without taxes, and that, as a consequence, contributions are odious and nobody should pay them; that the large properties have been made to placate the disordered appetite that the poor suffer for land and water; that the Golden Age was going to begin, and that all of Mexico would be converted into a branch of the land of milk and honey [Jauja], without jefes políticos, without gendarmes, without tax collectors, with effective suffrage, with democracy in abundance, with liberties by the ton, with infinite goods and inexhaustible fortunes that would crush us under the weight of an immense well-being." The Revolution had promised redemption, which the ignorant masses of Juchitán interpreted as liberation from the obligations and restrictions of "good society"—freedom from taxation and public administration, from the restrictions of private property and wage labor, and from obedience to political authority and the burden of law. By driving a wedge between the "good pueblo" and civil society, the Revolution promised a tyranny of the masses, characterized by "democracy in abundance, with liberties by the ton," and embodied in the legendary land of Jauja, where the people lived without having to labor.[57]

What was "fine" for the masses, however, was "terrible" for the government. By divorcing the popular classes from civil society and releasing them from their obligations and responsibilities, the promise of democracy made the people "available" to the seduction of caciquismo, in Juchitán and elsewhere. Vera Estañol concluded his speech by warning that so long as the new regime continued its policy of reconciliation toward popular revolutionaries, "the nation is lost . . . the coup of the plebe will substitute the coup of the army, and this neopraetorianism, each time recruiting itself from the lowest, most abject, and most irresponsible classes of society, will end by annihilating all truly patriotic elements, all sound personality, and all spirit of order . . . the most minor fiasco of a *déclassé*, will push him to the head of a group of discontents, the revolt will be sparked, sedition will explode everywhere in the Republic, forming a portrait of anarchy, ruin, and desolation."[58] As they had in the previous century, liberal promises of democracy and popular sovereignty had already begun to lead Mexico on the path to self-destruction.

"They Work Unconsciously, Directed by Their Instigators": The Chegomistas as Victims

On December 5, as order returned to Juchitán, brought by the flood of rebels returning to their homes, a declaration of "amnesty for the crimes of rebellion and sedition" was posted on all of the street corners of Juchitán. As described earlier, amnesty for the Chegomista rank and file was predicated on two assumptions: first, that the Chegomistas did not participate willingly in the rebellion, but had to be "led" or "pushed" into disobedience by a selfish cacique; and second, that the selfish work of the cacique had "dragged" them from a more natural state of abjectivity (and order), which could be restored (and already was being restored) by replacing arbitrary rule and personalism with the rule of law and civil society. The offer of amnesty and the restoration of order appealed to a parallel, abject interpretation of the poor and indigenous people of Juchitán that coexisted with the dangerous interpretation, and underscored their patriotism, progressive work ethic, and masculine honor. No less "counterinsurgent" than the "bad" image of the pueblo, the counter-image of the "good pueblo" represented the return of the status quo in Juchitán as a return to the natural order of things.

The assumption that the Chegomistas were unwitting and unconscious victims of caciquismo was uniformly accepted by the press and political authorities, and as we have seen, ubiquitous in the language used to describe the rebels. That Che Gómez compelled them to rebel for his own "bastard ends" was evidenced in the various iterations of the verb *engañar*, meaning "trick," "deceive," or "mislead." Examples of this language abounded in the press. *El Avance* referred to the Chegomistas as "these beings who suffered the *engaño* of a vulgar careerist." In *El Imparcial* Leopoldo Zea wrote, "my mission here is to tell the truth, and the truth is that the partidarios of Gómez have been *engañado*." Thus deceived, according to Benito Juárez Maza, the Chegomistas naturally "did not understand the actions of the government, [which were not] to impose any determined person, but rather to redeem them from a caciquismo that, potent and audacious, came to agitate them." However, if the people of Juchitán had been "dragged" from their peaceful dependence on civil society by the deceptions of a single agitator, there was still some hope that order could be restored.[59]

The state government and other officials in Juchitán sought to persuade the rebels to reenter good society as dependents by mobilizing a paternal discourse of patriotism, progress, and masculine honor that appealed to an abject interpretation of the Chegomistas. Governor Juárez Maza, in preparing for his peacekeeping mission to Juchitán, captured the paternalist spirit of this discourse, stating that his goal in Juchitán was to get "the strays to return to work and their homes." He explicitly targeted the "disgraced indígenas, many of whom [were] miserably deceived by the disastrous Che Gómez," and aimed "to open their eyes so that the light can reach those poor inhabitants of the region."[60] It was the state government's duty to enlighten the poor indígenas and return them to an abject state of dependence. When Pancho León appealed to the rebels to lay down their arms, he brought into full relief the abject interpretation of the Chegomistas:

Juchitecos! You are being villainously cheated! They have made you believe in a patriotic deed, when in reality you are committing a crime against the patria for which your fathers sacrificed themselves. You have fallen to your exploiters, and for that reason you have armed yourself against the legally constituted powers. I invite you to put aside your bellicose attitude in exchange for reasonable and patriotic conduct.

Exchange your tools of war for those of farming, and make yourself recipients of a most ample and generous amnesty. Understand that fratricidal wars bring only the ruin and desolation of the villages, just as peace and compliance bring progress to the villages in all branches of human activity. Unite, then, to search for peace based in the most ample justice, progress, and well-being of our villages![61]

León's appeal established a dichotomy between the outcomes of the good and bad tendencies of the people of Juchitán. The influence of Che Gómez had led them to commit crimes against the nation and legal authorities, resulting in fratricide, ruin, and desolation. However, it left open the possibility that under other influences the Chegomistas were capable of "reasonable and patriotic conduct" and participation in and compliance with the regime of progress and well-being. If Juchitán's poor and indigenous majority had gone from "good" to "bad" under the influence of a cacique, they could be brought back under the influence of civil society and wage labor. The direct relationship between work and peace echoed throughout the appeals to the Chegomistas, challenging their masculine honor by implying that by choosing rebellion over work they were leaving "more homes in destitution and more children and wives without bread."[62] Amnesty gave the Chegomistas the opportunity to redeem themselves by resuming their dual roles as wage laborers and heads of household, and thereby transforming themselves from the "bad" pueblo to the "good."

Official support for the policy of amnesty was justified by representing the Chegomistas as victims, "more ignorant than guilty."[63] "In the name of the people of Juchitán," Ricardo León appealed to President Madero to approve amnesty for the "poor people" of Juchitán, for they "by their ignorance, are not guilty, they work unconsciously, directed by their instigators. They are deserving of protection."[64] General Merodio also favored offering amnesty for the rebels, reasoning that they "were deceived into rising up in arms" and that "the majority of them are friends of the government and are inclined to sustain order." The steady stream of rebels returning to Juchitán reinforced the belief that the popular classes of Juchitán were abject by nature, and "realizing the bad faith with which Lic. Gómez operates," they were eager to return to their dependent status. As rebels flooded into Juchitán to surrender themselves to the federal army, General Merodio reported that "almost all of those who had revolted have returned to their homes," reiterating his belief that "many of those who follow Gómez, do so out of genuine fear," and once they realized the "senselessness" of the struggle, the Chegomistas were now "inclined to submit themselves and file charges against Lic. Gómez."[65] The justification of amnesty in a paternalist discourse of victimhood that fetishized order and the dependency of the popular classes provided a fitting final chapter to the counterinsurgent narrative of the Chegomista Rebellion. By offering amnesty for "political crimes," the state government explicitly degraded the rebels' capacity for political consciousness and denied them agency in their own political actions. In so doing, the counterinsurgent narrative of the Chegomista Rebellion justified the restoration of the Porfirian status quo and the expansion of the state's disciplinary apparatus in the name of peace and order.

Conclusion

On December 12 President Madero wrote a letter of apology to Ricardo León, excusing his "primitive attitude in relation to Lic. Gómez" and supporting a general amnesty for the rebel rank and file. "According to reports," he explained, Gómez's "partidarios mobilized to the shout of 'Viva Madero!' and death to the imposition of the jefe . . . which led me to believe that they were supporters of my government." With the situation resolved, the president now understood that the rebels "operated only by pressure, of which they were victims."[66] Madero's about-face regarding the Chegomistas reflected the growing contradictions between continued popular mobilization and the president's "outmoded concept of democracy." Madero and his coterie of doctrinaire liberal reformers had hoped that the installation of democratic institutions in the aftermath of Díaz's resignation would facilitate the emergence of formal, ideologically coherent political parties to compete for popular constituencies, and in the process, inculcate the popular classes in the universalism of the legal order. This form of indoctrination would not only provide the popular classes with the republican virtue necessary to sublimate their collective self-interest to the common good, but would also dissolve their corporate identities and unlock their potential as autonomous individuals. However, when the popular classes proved unwilling to participate in their own gradual redemption, and gravitated instead toward personalist leaders like Che Gómez, unafraid to appeal to their collective interests, Madero no longer considered "the makeup of his movement... to be representative of either his cause or the interests of Mexico."[67]

The participation of the uneducated masses and their populist leaders in the political sphere violated bourgeois "assumptions about who should and should not govern a model liberal regime."[68] Galled by the uppishness of popular rebels, and terrified by the prospect of social dissolution, Mexico's reading public—the *república pensante*—struck an informal social pact, reminiscent of the nineteenth century. Likewise trapped between the promise of popular sovereignty and dominant assumptions about the degraded state of their social and ethnic subordinates, the gente bien of all political and ideological stripes circled their wagons to protect their shared class interest against the deleterious effects of *baja democracia*. As it played out on the national stage, the Chegomista Rebellion provided Mexico's educated minority the opportunity to express its anxiety about the changing role of the poor and indigenous population in Mexican society and to articulate a definitive response to the problem of persistent popular violence. As such, the "counterinsurgent" narrative of the Chegomista Rebellion represented a broad social consensus regarding the nation's unresolved

"Indian problem" and provided the new revolutionary state with a discursive framework by which to "put the tiger back in the cage" without undermining its commitment to liberal-democratic reform.

By negating the political nature of the Chegomista Rebellion, denying the agency of the popular classes in their own political activity, and placing the blame for popular "rebellion and disobedience" on one agitator, the discourse of caciquismo allowed the regime to ignore the structural bases of popular discontent and cling to the belief that the misguided masses could be redeemed by reharnessing them to civil society. By eliminating caciquismo and returning the "strays" to the flock, the revolutionary regime sought to unlock the abject "good nature" of the Chegomistas and reintegrate them into society as wage laborers and responsible breadwinners, but not yet as citizens. It was here in Juchitán, during the first month of Madero's rule, that the dream of democratic consolidation gave way to the harsh realities of the *república posible* and the liberal-democratic experiment was superseded by a new brand of redemptive authoritarianism, distinguished from the old brand by its dedication to revitalizing civil society through democratic institutions and practices, but by which the redemption of the poor, indigenous masses would still be carried out at the end of a rifle. Here in Juchitán, in response to the Chegomista Rebellion, the revolutionary regime defined the limits of democratic reform in a society it deemed, in its majority, unfit for democracy.

Conclusion
Political Assassination and the Limits of Revolutionary Democracy

On December 5, 1911, at about 8 p.m., Che Gómez's train pulled into the station at Rincón Antonio, en route to Mexico City, where he was due to meet with President Madero. Gómez had long dreaded this moment, fearing that he would never make it out of Rincón Antonio, where for weeks his enemies had been summarily searching all passing trains, hoping to prevent him from making it to the capital. Now, despite the presidential writ of safe-conduct in his hand and the escort of armed rurales by his side, his deepest fears were realized. A massive crowd awaited his train on the platform, where "an infinity of rifles glistened" in the late-afternoon sun. A contingent of "the infuriated multitude"—some municipal police, but most not—boarded the train, forcibly removed Gómez and his ten travel companions, and deposited them in the local jail. The rurales, sent by the president to protect Gómez, offered little resistance. This much was known and agreed upon. The following morning a group of campesinos discovered the bodies of Che Gómez and eight of his companions riddled with bullets and strewn along the "dusty and deserted" road to nearby Petapa. How their bodies ended up there—on a secluded plain called Paso Guayabo—was less known and certainly not agreed upon. In the coming days, the chain of events connecting Gómez's arrest to the discovery of his remains became the subject of heated debate and "the most absurd conjectures" in the nation's capital, where the assassination of Che Gómez produced "an enormous sensation."[1]

"On the wings of popular fantasy," news of the assassination took flight, spreading through the region "with extraordinary velocity" and making its way to the capital, where it "took on incredible proportions." "In theaters and cafés, on the thoroughfare and the streetcars," wrote one observer in *El Diario*, "the topic of all conversations ... is nothing else: the death of Che Gómez, and on him are embroidered the most passionate commentaries, the most acrid opinions, the most energetic censures."[2] In lieu of credible sources of information, newspaper reporters stoked the fires of public passion, weaving elaborate, detailed accounts of Gómez's capture and assassination from the most fine-spun threads of rumor and innuendo. The bulk of these initial reports attributed Gómez's death to the work of a vindictive lynch mob, drawn variably from his own disgruntled followers or the "honorable workers" of the region, "to whom he had caused much damage." "Over one thousand in number," according to *El Imparcial*, the angry mob poured in from surrounding municipalities, wresting Gómez and his companions from the rurales, dragging them behind the railroad station, and unloading over one hundred rounds on them while shouting "Viva Oaxaca libre!" As evidence of their fury, the mob left four thousand pesos in Gómez's pocket and fifty-two bullet holes in his body, "from which poured long streams of blood that stained the ground." The rabble then dragged the bodies to Paso Guayabo and dispersed before they could be identified. By attributing blame to a nameless, faceless mass of the very same people he claimed to represent, this version of the story represented Gómez's death as the logical outcome of populist politics—the natural price to pay for conniving at demagoguery. Given the "feelings of hostility that Rincón Antonio had against" him, wrote Leopoldo Zea of *El Imparcial*, Gómez's death there "had already been foretold" the minute he got on the train.[3]

Over the next few days, as new sources of information opened up and details trickled in, it became clear, even to Zea, that the assassination happened in "a form very different from what has up to today has been accepted as true."[4] New accounts in the Maderista press focused on the role of the state government in Gómez's death. *El Demócrata Mexicano* confirmed that Gómez died as the result of "a true lynching," his body "ripped to pieces" in "a rain of bullets," then hacked up and trampled for good measure. "So horrifying" was the scene that the correspondent could "not remember another like it in the United States." However, he noted, this was not simply "a collective killing committed in a moment of popular fury. Behind this fury was the long work of preparation." "In hushed voices and among the gente consciente," he continued, it was common knowledge that Gómez's death had been "a true summary execution"—an application of the infamous *Ley fuga*—"ordered by people of 'high status' in the government of Oaxaca" and carried out by a small group of volunteer police.[5] On December 8 even *El Imparcial* conceded that Gómez had, in fact, been killed by a group of volunteer police and that it was the same group that Governor Juárez Maza had sent to remove Gómez from the protective custody of the rurales.[6] Just as peace had been restored, lamented the editors of *El Ahuizote*, news of Gómez's "imprisonment and lynching in Rincón Antonio, by a band of so-called volunteers who persecuted him on the orders of the governor of Oaxaca," had "come to complicate [matters] to an extremely dangerous degree."[7] Governor Juárez Maza admitted ordering Gómez's arrest, and defiantly justified his decision as a defense of state sovereignty, but he steadfastly denied any responsibility for Gómez's death. Nonetheless, the implication of the governor's complicity (or worse) raised serious questions about the circumstances surrounding the assassination.

"Death to Demagoguery!": The Anatomy of a Political Assassination

The provisions of the agreement reached between the state and federal governments on November 28 stipulated that although the federal army stationed in Juchitán would be put at the disposal of the state government, Che Gómez would be granted a writ of safe-conduct to travel to Mexico City and meet personally with President Madero. Despite Madero's personal guarantee that Gómez "would not go unpunished for the common crimes he has committed," the state government was skeptical, interpreting the meeting as an "obvious invasion of the sovereignty of Oaxaca on the part of the executive."[8]

Many believed the new president was too soft on popular revolutionaries, and even Carlos María Gil, Oaxaca's lead negotiator in the accord, publicly expressed his belief that Gómez would ultimately be pardoned for his crimes. The prospect of Gómez's acquittal caused great consternation among Gómez's enemies on the Isthmus, who urged the governor to take special measures to ensure that Gómez would not reach the capital. Nonetheless, on December 3, after weeks of anticipation, Gómez's passports arrived, signed by the president himself. The following day, Gómez decamped from Unión Hidalgo and departed for Mexico City with ten of his closest supporters and a small contingent of rurales.[9]

As fate would have it, Gómez and his escort passed through the train station in San Jerónimo on the same day that Governor Juárez Maza arrived on the Isthmus on his peacekeeping mission. Several days prior, Gómez had cabled the governor in anticipation of his arrival on the Isthmus, promising to greet him "with the tenderness and respect that you deserve as governor and as a friend." Juárez Maza refused Gómez's offer, warning him through a mutual friend "that during my stay on the Isthmus, do not even approach me." Considering the matter dealt with, Juárez Maza later explained that "upon descending" to the platform in San Jerónimo, he "was rudely surprised by a warning that Gómez was at the same station . . . accompanied by an escort of perfectly armed men." When Gómez approached him, ignoring his warning, in defense of his "personal honor" and the "decorum" of his position, Juárez Maza not only rebuffed Gómez's advances but ordered General Merodio, who was at the train station to welcome the governor, to arrest him and his companions on the spot. Forced once again into a familiar predicament, Merodio refused the governor's order, explaining "clearly and frankly" that he could not arrest Gómez or any of his men, as they all had passports from the president. "Seeing [the governor's] lack of elements, surrounded by force, [and] . . . supported morally by the [federal army]," Juárez Maza later testified, Gómez "calmly and casually boarded his train . . . with the objective of escaping from the Isthmus and leaving justice cheated."[10]

As Gómez headed toward the capital, Juárez Maza's secretary, Heliodoro Díaz Quintas, headed to the telegraph station. In code, Díaz Quintas wired Enrique León in Juchitán, ordering him to take "urgent measures" to ensure the detention of Gómez and his companions before they left the district. The jefe político immediately wired municipal authorities in Petapa, Palomares, and Rincón Antonio—the three municipalities in the district with access to the Tehuantepec National Railway—ordering them to use all "the elements at [their] disposal [including] the assistance of residents" to detain Gómez and his men. Writing from San Jerónimo, *El Imparcial*'s correspondent, Leopoldo Zea, expressed his confidence that "Gómez will be apprehended en route" to Mexico City. A few hours later, while Juárez Maza was being toasted at a banquet in his honor, he received the good news: the municipal authorities of Rincón Antonio had "apprehended and detained" Che Gómez and his companions.[11]

To those familiar with istmeño politics, Gómez's arrest in Rincón Antonio came as no surprise. Animosity ran deep between Gómez and the authorities of Rincón Antonio, and especially with local cacique Josué Esteva. Favored by the partido rojo, Esteva parlayed his standing within the group into political office, serving as the *alcalde* (mayor) of Rincón Antonio for much of the Porfiriato. Now, as "the intellectual alcalde of his people," Esteva continued to dominate politics in Rincón Antonio, a role that brought him into direct conflict with Che Gómez. The enmity between the two came to a head with the vice-presidential elections on October 15. As one of the official electors representing Rincón Antonio, Esteva complained that Gómez had prevented him from casting his vote, arrested him, and even tried to have him executed.[12] Esteva escaped, and in the aftermath of the Chegomista Rebellion he led municipal authorities of Rincón Antonio in the formation of a volunteer militia, armed and equipped by the state government. Despite its explicit objective of protecting the people of Rincón Antonio from the depredations of the Chegomistas, the Club Justicia la Unión de la Fuerza, as the irregular force called itself, was characterized by one source (unaffiliated with the Chegomistas) as a

Conclusion 235

band of enforcers, "henchmen" paid for their labor by the partido rojo, and specifically by the Maqueo Castellanos family, who owned most of the lands of Rincón Antonio and the surrounding municipalities. Led by Esteva and Tomás Carballo, the Club Justicia served as "the right arm of this legion of wretched *ricos* [and the] terror of honorable men," nothing more than "a band of thieves who enrich themselves marauding around the ranges of the Isthmus, which they know brush for brush."[13] During the last two weeks of November, hoping to prevent Gómez or any of his emissaries from reaching the capital, the Club Justicia began forcibly stopping and searching all trains on the Tehuantepec National Railway, despite the complaints of the railroad company. Fully aware of his enemies' activities, Che Gómez was afraid to travel through Rincón Antonio, refusing Madero's invitations to the capital until he had a guarantee of safe passage and an escort of rurales. Even then, when Gómez departed for Mexico City he did so only reluctantly. Perhaps tellingly, when León sent orders to detain Gómez, he included only one civilian, Josué Esteva.[14]

News of Gómez's pending arrest had spread throughout the region, and as his train pulled into the station in Rincón Antonio, a crowd gathered ominously on the platform in anticipation of his arrival. When the train came to a stop, three gendarmes boarded the train, accompanied by "many" volunteers, including the municipal president, Ventura Cano, who positively identified Gómez. After a brief scuffle that left two of Gómez's escort injured, the volunteers forcibly disarmed Gómez and his companions, placed them under arrest, and escorted them to the waiting room of the train station, despite the protests of the rurales. Cano met privately with Almagino Tovar, the captain of the rurales, and likely presented him with a copy of the governor's arrest warrant. Apparently satisfied, Tovar consented to have Gómez and his men transferred to the municipal jail, and placed in separate cells. The captain's tepid resistance to municipal authorities was never sufficiently explained (he changed stories many times), making his complicity the subject of much speculation. Regardless, once Gómez was successfully detained in the local jail, Cano wired

Díaz Quintas, requesting that an auxiliary force be sent immediately to assist the municipal police in guarding the prisoners against any outside threats.[15]

In San Jerónimo, Díaz Quintas snapped into action, ordering the jefes políticos of Juchitán and Tehuantepec to send any forces they had at their disposal to Rincón Antonio to help the municipal police relocate the prisoners to "a more adequate place"—ostensibly somewhere with a competent judge and sufficient police. Although the jefe político of Juchitán declined, fearing unrest there, in Tehuantepec the jefe político quickly gathered a force of thirty-nine men, "perfectly equipped and armed," and put them on the first train to San Jerónimo. At 9:30 that night, the train from Tehuantepec arrived in San Jerónimo on its way to Rincón Antonio. When Díaz Quintas arrived at the train station to review the militia, he was surprised to find a contingent of forty federal soldiers boarding the train. The jefe de armas, General Merodio, had clearly been informed of Gómez's apprehension, and now sent a detachment of men to Rincón Antonio with the aim of taking the prisoners into federal custody, with the express objective of "protecting the life of licenciado Gómez." As the two forces headed to Rincón Antonio on the same train, Governor Juárez Maza, through his secretary, took the necessary measures to ensure that Gómez would not fall into the hands of the federal army and once again "cheat justice."[16]

Faced with unexpected competition from the federal army—Merodio had assembled his men without briefing the governor or his secretary—Díaz Quintas immediately wired municipal president Cano, commanding him not to turn the prisoners over to any outside authorities without direct orders from the governor. He reminded Cano of "the role of the federal forces in this matter" and advised him that the federal army was coming "to protect the life licenciado Goméz, but without orders to collect the prisoner." In other words, if the federal army wanted to help protect the prisoners from harm, that was fine, but he was not to turn the prisoners over to them under any circumstances. However, sometime between the train's departure from San Jerónimo and its arrival in Rincón Antonio, the governor and his secretary changed plans. Fearing that the federal forces would overwhelm the assemblage of volunteers, Díaz Quintas ordered Cano to relocate the prisoners: "I urge you to remove Gómez from [Rincón Antonio] and put him outside the reach of any element that favors him." When the train carrying the federal army and the volunteer militia of Tehuantepec arrived in Rincón Antonio a few hours later, they found "neither authorities, nor the prisoner." "His whereabouts are unknown," reported the chief of the Tehuantepec militia.[17]

At some point before the arrival of the train from San Jerónimo, the Club Justicia la Unión de la Fuerza arrived at the municipal jail on horseback to transfer the prisoners. The group of eight to ten men, led by Josué Esteva and Tomás Carballo, tied the prisoners together in pairs and began to march them into the dead of night. The riders claimed they were headed to the courthouse in Petapa, five miles away, but the prisoners likely knew that there was no real destination. Having caught wind of the Club Justicia's not-so-secret motives, a small group of campesinos followed closely behind with morbid curiosity. As they passed through a secluded plain known as Paso Guayabo, a few of the men on horseback split from the pack, riding off into the darkness. After a few quiet minutes, a group of mounted "bandits" descended on the posse and opened fire while shouting "Death to demagoguery!" By all accounts, the "bandits" let off an exorbitant number of rounds, gunning down Gómez and the other prisoners while the Club Justicia cleared out. The "rain of bullets" was enough to scatter the crowd of onlookers. When they returned running to Rincón Antonio, the municipal president, Cano, refused to take their statements, insisting instead that they go home and get some rest. When a few members of the Club Justicia arrived a short while later, they informed Cano that they had been "surprised by more than one hundred men, [who] took the prisoners." The municipal president immediately relayed this story to his superiors, writing that the volunteers had returned to Rincón Antonio fleeing, having been attacked by "a group of unknown men." Early the next morning, the municipal authorities of Ranchería Barrancón informed Cano that they had found the bodies of Che Gómez and eight of his companions in the road. Two had escaped, but their whereabouts were unknown. Even as the volunteers collected the bodies to be taken back to town, rumors swirled that the prisoners had been shot more than one hundred times, and that Gómez alone had received fifty-two gunshots. This false detail, remarkably, continues as part of Che Gómez's lore to the present day.[18]

That afternoon the authorities of Juchitán set into motion the wheels of justice, but to little effect. Local volunteers transported the bodies to Rincón Antonio, where they would remain pending an autopsy. Juárez Maza gave the municipal president explicit instructions to ensure that the bodies remained unmoved until a judge and a coroner could be appointed to the case. Specifically, he was not to allow any of Gómez's friends, family, or partisans to take custody of the body, or allow the body to be returned to Juchitán for a burial. Meanwhile, León appointed a coroner to the case and sent the circuit judge of Juchitán to Rincón Antonio to open an official investigation. The investigation, however, never got off the ground. The autopsy revealed that, contrary to popular reports, Gómez had been shot three times, each potentially mortal: once in the abdomen, once in the heart, and once in the face. None of his companions had been hit by more than four bullets. While it quickly became "common knowledge" in Juchitán that Josué Esteva had orchestrated the killing and Tomás Carballo had pulled the trigger on Gómez, nobody was willing to testify against them. Cano detained the witnesses for questioning, but none could positively identify the assailants, claiming it was too dark to make out details. According to Cano, they could say "nothing, absolutely nothing" about the men who had attacked Gómez's escort, except that they were from Juchitán. On December 8 the circuit judge issued subpoenas for the testimonies of all members of the Club Justicia, but neither Esteva nor Carballo was anywhere to be found. Lacking eyewitness testimony, little could be done. Gómez had a lot of enemies, reasoned local authorities, and suspects and motives were limitless. After a brief investigation,

Gómez's death was dismissed as a case of "popular justice." It would be more than three years before anyone would be brought to trial in connection to the assassination of Che Gómez.[19]

"A Delinquent Who Deserved to Die": Public Reaction to the Assassination

As news of Che Gómez's assassination made its way into the national consciousness, debate about the governor's actions in the matter polarized popular opinion and resurrected the question of state sovereignty. While it became generally understood in the wake of Gómez's death that Governor Juárez Maza had played some role in the assassination, it was much less clear what, exactly, his role had been. National commentaries stopped far short of defending Che Gómez, but they roundly condemned the circumstances surrounding his "villainous assassination." Very few pointed the finger directly at Juárez Maza, but many in the press openly criticized the governor for his "caprice and lack of tact" in handling the affair. Even *El Ahuizote*, which had been effusive in its support of Juárez Maza's defense of state sovereignty and relentlessly critical of the Chegomistas, refused to justify Gómez's "semi-lynching." "Justice should judge the guilty under the precedents established by the law, in conformity with the practices of humanity and civilization," opined *El Ahuizote*, "and these riots against defenseless men that are already under the safeguard of justice ... are savage acts, condemnable, stupid, and cowardly, undignified of a people who wants to be democratic, or believes itself to be so." Ultimately, the ends did not justify the means: "No, in no way do we applaud the tragic death of Lic. José F. Gómez, regardless of the crimes to which his rebellion had given place." The conservative *Siglo XX* echoed this criticism: "Che Gómez was a delinquent and surely deserved to die for the great evils that he inflicted on his countrymen, and the blood of innocent beings that he spilled. His intrigues, his lies ... cut down more than five hundred lives. Yes, for sure, he deserved death, but applied by the hand of the law, after a truly legal trial, within the practice of justice." As it was, Gómez's assassination represented an "infamously odious attack that cannot be excused," and "a crime dignified of 'apaches.'" *Siglo XX* reminded its readers that regardless of how they felt about Che Gómez, the "assassination of his eight compañeros, perpetrated brutally, in summary execution, in the most unjust and cowardly way, without motive, without a reason for being, like the infamous work of jackals; [was] a result so wicked, so perverse, so inhumane and cruel, that there will never exist the sufficiently energetic words to condemn it." The editorial concluded by calling for those responsible to "be punished equally, be they who they may."[20]

In his official report, Juárez Maza admitted taking measures to block the federal government's attempts to remove Gómez from the state's jurisdiction, but justified his actions as a defense of state sovereignty. Specifically, he ordered General Merodio to arrest Gómez, but Merodio refused, citing presidential orders. This refusal, reasoned Juárez Maza, violated the terms of the agreement reached the previous week, in which Madero agreed to put the federal army at the governor's disposal in compliance with Article 116 of the Constitution. Upon being rebuffed by Merodio, the governor immediately wired news of the events to the state legislature. In an extraordinary session, the state congress discussed Merodio's actions, and agreed to lodge an official complaint against the "mockery that Madero makes of our government [by] giving a passport to Gómez." By drawing on the issue of state sovereignty, Juárez Maza deflected blame for the assassination to the federal government, reasoning that the denial of federal assistance left the state government in the lurch, forcing the governor to arm and mobilize groups of volunteers, on very short notice, to detain Gómez and his well-armed escort. By putting Gómez's fate in the hands of armed volunteers, the governor (only reluctantly, according to him) left Gómez and his companions vulnerable to the reprisals of his myriad enemies, particularly those of Rincón Antonio. By leaving resolution of the conflict in the hands of the underequipped state government, the governor explained, the Madero regime was indirectly responsible for Gómez's death. Juárez Maza's justification of his actions in the matter was predicated on the overriding belief that if Gómez were allowed to leave the state's jurisdiction, he would never be held responsible for his crimes.[21]

Juárez Maza's defense fell on deaf ears in Oaxaca, where the celebration had already begun. In Oaxaca City, politicians and the public rallied behind their beleaguered governor, offering their unflinching support and defending his actions in bringing Gómez to justice. For two consecutive nights, masses of the "honorable people, of work and order" filled the streets of the capital, marked by impassioned speeches in support of their governor, and shouts of protest against the federal government, aimed at Madero. On both nights, reported *El Imparcial*, the protests lasted well into the night with "the same ardor as which they began." In a well-attended session of the state congress, on December 5 the deputies of the state legislature resolved unanimously to "congratulate the governor of the state for the energetic attitude that he has assumed in this matter" and to "maintain, at all costs, in accordance with the governor, the sovereignty of the state and to not allow the federation to interfere in local affairs." The members of Oaxaca's deputation in Mexico City echoed these sentiments. While admitting to not having access to the details of the assassination, "all of the deputies," in a series of interviews with *El Diario*, "opined that the attitude of Governor Juárez is within the mandates of the law ... [and] that it is entirely anti-constitutional that the Supreme Chief of the Republic had ordered the chief of federal forces in Juchitán, General Merodio, to give safe passage and all types of protections to 'Che' Gómez." The overwhelming sentiment of the Oaxacan delegates was that, "to give guarantees to a revolutionary who disturbs the peace of the state in the federation is clearly indicated as an invasion of the sovereignty of the state." Those interviewed by *El Diario* further emphasized that regardless of what details the investigation turned up, their support of the governor "will not change in the least."[22]

The Madero regime rebutted the charges of the Oaxacan government with a palpable sense of exasperation, but ultimately it capitulated, not wanting to prolong the conflict when peace seemed imminent. On the one hand, the federal government pointed out that while their accord with the state government did make federal forces available to the governor, it also made explicit provisions for Gómez's safe passage to the capital to meet with Madero. Juárez Maza himself had ratified this agreement, though clearly believing that the provisions of Article 116 of the Constitution would trump those of the accord. In other words, Governor Juárez Maza seemed to believe that the federal government's recognition of Article 116 would give him complete autonomy over the federal army stationed in Oaxaca, even to contradict federal mandate. According to Madero, this was simply not the case. At the same time, Madero bristled personally at the implication that upon his arrival in Mexico City, Gómez would be absolved of his crimes. Che Gómez had launched his rebellion against the federal army in Juchitán, and thus his crimes were, primarily, federal crimes "of military character." Thus, Madero reasoned, the federal government was well within its rights to remove Che Gómez from the state's jurisdiction and force him to stand trial for federal crimes first, and if found innocent, "he would have been put at the disposal of the authorities of Oaxaca." However, with Gómez dead and hostilities subsiding in the region, the president seemed anxious to put the conflict behind him. Writing to Juárez Maza, Madero expressed his "best wishes of cordiality toward Oaxaca" and informed the governor that he had "already given the orders" to put the federal army fully at the state's disposal. With this, the president hoped, "the conflict between federal and local powers is considered over."[23]

From the beginning Juárez Maza maintained his innocence in the assassination, claiming that after learning of Gómez's apprehension he had done all within his power to ensure the safety of the prisoner. While there is no evidence directly contradicting the governor's claims, it is possible to deduce at least a degree of complicity in the execution. Given that hostility in Rincón Antonio was public knowledge, as was the presence of an aggressive armed force of Gómez's enemies, and that the governor himself admitted his fear that Gómez would fall under attack in the municipal jail, ordering Gómez's transfer to Petapa in the middle of the night seems curious. Juárez Maza almost certainly knew that the transfer would jeopardize the lives of Gómez and his companions, and thus he could not legitimately claim to have done all within his power to protect the prisoners. However, there was no paper trail directly connecting the governor to Che Gómez's death, and his exact role is, to this day, unclear. It was clear, though, that Juárez Maza believed that the assassination was justified. He offered no apologies, and lamented only that Gómez's death had denied the state the chance to try him "and make him take responsibility for what he incurred, launching the pueblo into a struggle of personal ambitions, and sacrificing, at the altar of these [ambitions] many good citizens, whose widows and orphans are today found in the state of greatest helplessness."[24]

"Healthy Social Prophylaxis": Order, Progress, and the Mano Dura

Benito Juárez Maza used his December 6 visit to Juchitán to vindicate his hard-line stance toward Che Gómez. Despite postponing his arrival by one full day and canceling all official celebrations, about five thousand people turned out to greet Juárez Maza at the train station in Juchitán, dressed in full festive regalia and carrying flowers for the governor. His visit was brief, but according to *El Imparcial*, Juárez Maza's presence "calmed a little bit the indignation" in Juchitán.[25] The governor's official report underscored the pacifying effect of his visit. By Juárez Maza's own account, he used his trip to Juchitán "to get closer" to the people, who, "finding in the governor the loyalty and good faith that are his characteristics, saw their error.... [T]he conduct observed by the Governor bore its fruits; since then families began to return" to their homes. Within a few days of Juárez Maza's visit, 2,474 rebels had "turned themselves in, declaring their desire to return to work and to be the first in conserving order." The state's report described the governor's visit to Juchitán as "commendable on all counts," because it "revealed that the labor of the governor bore its fruits, and also made clear the good sense of the pueblo Juchiteco....

After the death of its cabecilla . . . that virile people that fought with so much valor has learned that its struggle was sterile." Only with Gómez's death could the "good sense" of the people be liberated from the degrading effect of caciquismo and begin to regenerate the ruins left behind by their rebellious adventure. When Juárez Maza arrived in Juchitán, according to his report, the city was "almost abandoned," but "today it comes back to life, and not in a slow and painful way, but in a spontaneous and honest way; not with distrust for the future, but rather the contrary, with great hopes for tomorrow; the pueblo Juchiteco will know, in the future, to respect the law and esteem the labor of the government as the work of justice and redemption."[26] By reestablishing the bond of trust between governor and governed, a bond severed by Gómez's pernicious influence, the state government had reharnessed their misguided energies to "good society" and unlocked their true character as a peaceful and working people, respectful of law and order, and capable of being redeemed by an enlightened state and its institutions.

After a brief interlude, the old order had been restored. While the image of a popular political leader being shot fifty-two times in cold blood conjured horrifying memories of the recent past—a past the Revolution was supposed to leave behind—even Madero's apologists could not deny that Gómez's death would restore peace to a region that only days before had threatened to destabilize the regime. When asked if the assassination would reestablish peace in Juchitán, Madero's minister of the interior, Abraham González responded, "that is undoubted, as Gómez was the only element of rebellion there was in Oaxaca." This sentiment echoed through the highest levels of government and in the Maderista press. *El Diario*, which had been most harsh in its criticism of the Oaxacan government, even conceded that "with the death of Che Gómez, and with the conduct of señor Juárez, the conflict has ended." Making clear the obvious advantages of democratic liberty and absolute rule of law, the editorial defended Gómez's assassination as an unfortunate necessity in a society incapable of managing political life: "We Mexicans are not fit for democracy! And if we are not fit to manage ourselves ... we must accept that only one hand governs us and that one arm directs us."²⁷

In 1908, in his infamous interview with James Creelman, Porfirio Díaz addressed the necessity of violence in preparing Mexico for peace and progress, justifying his use of the mano dura by explaining, "It was better that a little blood be shed that much blood should be saved. The blood that was shed was bad blood, the blood that was saved was good blood."²⁸ Now, only six months after the forces of democratic restoration had toppled Díaz, the leading newspaper of the new regime struck a conspicuously similar chord. Commenting on the assassination of Che Gómez, *El Diario* called on its readership to unite behind the new president—once the "Apostle of Democracy"—as he picked up the constable's staff, left behind by Díaz, and endeavored to save Mexico from itself:

> So many uprisings are registered daily in different parts of the country; so many acts of banditry and anarchy are ceaselessly noted that society shudders with fear, and asks, with cries of anguish, that this painful situation come to an end as soon as possible, and that an iron hand close its fist and in a formidable reversal leave the insolent disturbers of order in the ground.
>
> "Che" Gómez riddled with fifty-two bullets ... [is an example] of healthy social prophylaxis.
>
> And if to [Gómez] are added ... all of those who in agitating the masses induce them to disturb order and sow the weeds of civil war, then we would say that the Republic should feel secure having at the front of its destinies a man who, despite his placid bearing and melancholy smile, has in his chest a heart that was not even frightened before the dangerous Díaz....
>
> There is Clemenceau, in France; Canalejas, in Spain; ... and so many other statesmen who, when the occasion arrived, imperatively pronounced the tragic word: fire!
>
> Then ... rifles discharge, delinquents fall, and societies are pacified. This is what we want, us Mexicans of order and national

progress. It is hard to say it; the fire of a Mauser is needed to make disappear the "Che" Gómezes, the Zapatas ... who are affronts to cultivated nations.

The death of Che Gómez, we believe we are not wrong to say, will give lost peace back to the state of Oaxaca. And if this is true, what is the summary execution of a man who puts himself outside of the law worth, in exchange for the return of peace to frightened homes, for the powerful current that once again drives commercial life, and for the drops of sweat that anew water the fields?

Whether it was Governor Juárez who ordered the death of Gómez; or the populacho who took him from prison to sacrifice him ... society is satisfied and applause resounds and will resound for a long time, in honor of the righteous hand that cut down one dangerous life for the public well-being.[29]

For a public uneasy with the changing role of the poor and indigenous population in Mexican society, and eager to see its new president apply the mano dura, the assassination of Che Gómez represented not a circumvention of the democratic process but rather a case of "healthy social prophylaxis"—a selective shedding of "bad blood" to save "Mexicans of order and national progress" from "affronts to cultivated nations"; to save a society that "shudders with fear" from "acts of banditry and anarchy"; and to save "the powerful current that once again drives commercial life" from those who "disturb order and sow the seeds of civil war." In response to the challenge of Che Gómez, the high principles of liberal republicanism gave way to the familiar pessimism of "order and progress," forcing popular revolutionaries back into the bonds of degraded citizenship. This was the lesson to be learned from the Chegomista Rebellion: that democracy had its limits, especially in a nation where the vast majority were not fit for democracy.

NOTES

Abbreviations

AGN   Archivo General de la Nación, Mexico City
AGOM   Archivo de Gildardo y Octavio Magaña, Archivo Histórico de la UNAM, Mexico City
AGPEO   Archivo General del Poder Ejecutivo del Estado de Oaxaca
AJFG   Archivo José F. Gómez, Biblioteca Francisco de Burgoa, Oaxaca City
APJEC   Archivo del Primer Jefe del Ejército Constitucionalista, Fondo XXI, CONDUMEX
CONDUMEX   Centro de Estudios de Historia de México, Mexico City
CP   Censos y Padrones, Distrito: Juchitan, 1890
DHRM   *Documentos históricos de la Revolución Mexicana: Revolución y Régimen Maderista.* Ed. Isidro Fabela. Vol. 6. Mexico City: Editorial Jus, 1964–65.
FBJM   Fondo Benito Juárez Maza, Biblioteca Francisco de Burgoa, Oaxaca City
FPRO   Fondo Periodo Revolucionario de Oaxaca, AGPEO

Introduction

1. *El Imparcial*, Nov. 8, 1911.
2. Testimony in Matus Gutiérrez, "La Revolución en Juchitán," 90. All translations from Spanish to English are the author's unless otherwise indicated.
3. José F. Gómez to Heliodoro Diaz Quintas, Oaxaca, June 21, 1911, AJFG.
4. *El Imparcial*, Nov. 26, 1911.
5. Lomnitz, *Deep Mexico, Silent Mexico*, 65–71.
6. Delgado Aguilar, *Jefaturas políticas*; Falcón, "Force and the Search for Consent"; Falcón, "Jefes políticos y rebeliones campesinas."

7. Reprinted in Ramírez, *Historia de la Revolución*, 45–57.
8. Ruiz, *The Great Rebellion*, 23; Waterbury, "Non-revolutionary Peasants."
9. For example, Chassen-López, *From Liberal to Revolutionary Oaxaca*. Earlier revisionist works include Chassen, *Los precursors de la Revolución*; Martínez Medina, "Genesis y desarrollo del maderismo"; Reina and Abardía, "Cien anos de rebelión"; Chassen and Martínez, "El desarrollo económico de Oaxaca"; Sánchez Silva, "Estructura de las propiedades agrarias."
10. For example, de la Cruz, "Che Gómez y la rebelión"; and de la Cruz, "La rebelión de los juchitecos." See also Campbell, *Zapotec Renaissance*; and various essays in Campbell et al., *Zapotec Struggles*.
11. For example, Knight, *The Mexican Revolution*; and Purnell, "The Chegomista Rebellion in Juchitán."
12. Rubin, *Decentering the Regime*; Bailón and Zermeño, *Juchitán*; Campbell, *Zapotec Renaissance*.
13. López Monjarin, "Juchitán," 67; Campbell, "Class Struggle," 216.
14. López Monjardín, "Juchitán," 67, 75.
15. De la Cruz, "La rebelión de los juchitecos," 69.
16. Since the 1980s Juchitán has been the subject of approximately fifty monographs (in several languages), dozens of scholarly articles, and a handful of dissertations, documentaries, and museum exhibits.
17. Tutino, "Ethnic Resistance," 41.
18. Campbell, *Zapotec Renaissance*, 3.
19. Tutino, "Ethnic Resistance," 42, 58.
20. Knight, *The Mexican Revolution*, 368–82.
21. Knight, *The Mexican Revolution*, 368; Friedrich, "The Legitimacy of a Cacique," 247; Knight, "Caciquismo in Twentieth-Century Mexico."
22. Knight, *The Mexican Revolution*, 375.
23. Purnell, "The Chegomista Rebellion in Juchitán," 53.
24. Purnell, "The Chegomista Rebellion in Juchitán," 68.
25. Purnell, "The Chegomista Rebellion in Juchitán," 52.
26. Nuñez Ríos, "Apuntes geográficos"; Binford and Campbell, Introduction, 4, 6, 8.
27. Campbell notes that approximately 80 percent of Juchitán's current population are Zapotec; see *Zapotec Renaissance*, xi. This figure is relatively stable, dating back to the eighteenth century—Tutino notes that in 1743 there were about 13,000 people on the Isthmus classified as indigenous and about 1,300 classified as Spanish and mulatto; in 1793

the district of Tehuantepec listed 16,189 indígenas in the region, 2,226 Spaniards, and 3,316 mulattoes; see Tutino, "Ethnic Resistance," 50–51.
28. Whitecotton, *The Zapotecs*, 219.
29. Zeitlin, "Colonialism," 78; Chance, "La dinámica étnia," 69; Marcus and Flannery, "An Introduction to the Late Postclassic," 217; Whitecotton, *The Zapotecs*, 140–43.
30. Williams, *The Isthmus of Tehuantepec*, 251.
31. Jiménez López, *Historia de Juchitán*, 33–35.
32. Studies from other regions in Mexico include French, *A Peaceful and Working People*; Lomnitz, *Deep Mexico, Silent Mexico*, 263–86; and Overmyer-Velázquez, *Visions of the Emerald City*. For a synthetic examination, see Buffington and French, "The Culture of Modernity."
33. Weber, "Class, Status, Party."
34. This type of cultural mediator represents what Antonio Gramsci called "organic intellectuals." See Gramsci, "The Formation of Intellectuals."
35. Mallon, *Peasant and Nation*, 317. Mallon refers to this distinction as a competition between "enforcers" and "counterhegemonic heroes" (286, 316–17). See also Lomnitz, *Deep Mexico, Silent Mexico*, 263–86.
36. Lomnitz, *Exits from the Labyrinth*, 275–76.
37. For an explanation of the "domain of sovereignty," see Chatterjee, *The Nation and Its Fragments*, 6. See also Rubin, *Decentering the Regime*, 46, 63.
38. According to Jürgen Habermas, this form of "civic republicanism" tied to a unified public interest precedes and stands in contrast to "liberal" democracy, which allowed for the public representation of competing, private interests. See Habermas, "Three Normative Models of Democracy."
39. This interpretation draws on the work of François-Xavier Guerra, *México: Del Antiguo Régimen a la Revolución*, and "Mexico from Independence to Revolution." See also LaFrance, *The Mexican Revolution in Puebla*. In particular, Matthew Karush's study of Rosario, Argentina, offers several striking parallels to this study, though in an urban setting and without the ethnic component. See Karush, *Workers or Citizens*.

1. A Tale of Two Cities

1. Juán Sánchez to Francisco Madero, Nov. 27, 1911, AGN, Archivo Madero, caja 61, expediente 680 [61.680].
2. Lomnitz, *Exits from the Labyrinth*, 276.

3. Nancy Farriss pioneered the "second conquest" narrative in *Maya Society under Colonial Rule*. See also Carmagnani, *El regreso de los dioses*; Tutino, *From Insurrection to Revolution*.
4. For example, Sánchez Silva, *Indios, comerciantes y burocracia*; and Chassen-López, *From Liberal to Revolutionary Oaxaca*. Counter-interpretations of the "second conquest" in Yucatán include Rugeley, *Yucatán's Maya Peasantry*; and Caplan, *Indigenous Citizens*.
5. Zeitlin, "Ranchers and Indians," 39; Taylor, *Landlord and Peasant*; Hamnett, *Politics and Trade*; Tutino, "Ethnic Resistance."
6. Chassen-López, "Una derrota juarista?" 42-43; Reina and Abardía, "Cien años de rebelión," 457, 460-62; Tutino, "Ethnic Resistance," 53.
7. Tutino, "Ethnic Resistance," 53; de la Cruz, *La rebelión de Che Gorio Melendre*, 10; Chassen-López, "Una derrota juarista?" 44.
8. Orozco, *Tradiciones y leyendas*, 27; Chassen-López, "Una derrota juarista?" 42-43; de la Cruz, *La rebelión de Che Gorio Melendre*, 10; Tutino, "Ethnic Resistance," 55-57; López Gurrión, *Efeméridas Istmeñas*, 53, 59.
9. Chassen-López, "Una derrota juarista?" 45-46; Fortson, *Los gobernantes de Oaxaca*.
10. Chassen-López, "Una derrota juarista?" 47-48; de la Cruz, *La rebellion de Che Gorio Melendre*, 29-31.
11. Jiménez López, *Historia de Juchitán*, 21-24; de la Cruz, *La rebelión de Che Gorio Melendre*, 13-16, 46-50; Chassen-López, "Una derrota juarista?" 51-56; Chassen-López, *From Liberal to Revolutionary Oaxaca*, 323.
12. Chassen-López, "Una derrota juarista?" 59-60; de la Cruz, *La rebelión de Che Gorio Melendre*, 18-21; Chassen-López, *From Liberal to Revolutionary Oaxaca*, 325-26; López Gurrión, *Eferméridas Istmeñas*, 68, 70.
13. Chassen-López, "Una derrota juarista?" 65-67. For a discussion of the persistence of "pactismo" and the transfer of sovereignty in post-Independence Mexico, see Annino, "The Two-Faced Janus," 67-74; and Guerra, "Mexico from Independence to Revolution," 130-37.
14. Covarrubias, *Mexico South*, 160.
15. Mallon, *Peasant and Nation*; Thomson, "Popular Aspects of Liberalism in Mexico"; Thomson, "Bulwarks of Patriotic Liberalism"; Thomson and LaFrance, *Patriotism, Politics, and Popular Liberalism*; Guardino, *Peasants, Politics*; Hernández Chávez, *La tradición republicana*.
16. Mallon, *Peasant and Nation*, 23-62; Thomson, "Bulwarks of Patriotic Liberalism."

17. Chassen-López, "Una derrota juarista?" 61; Jiménez López, *Historia de Juchitán*, 36–44; Chance, "La dinámica étnia," 169; Dennis, *Intervillage Conflict in Oaxaca*, 21–22.
18. Jiménez López, *Historia de Juchitán*, 55–73.
19. Juárez, *Documentos*, 15:480–82; Jiménez López, *Historia de Juchitán*, 81–109.
20. Taracena, "Evocaciones de la vida de ayer."
21. Juárez, *Documentos*, 15:411–12, 480–81; Chassen-López, "Una derrota juarista?" 63.
22. Hale, *The Transformation of Liberalism*; Mallon, *Peasant and Nation*, 321–22.
23. Chassen-López, *From Liberal to Revolutionary Oaxaca*, 45–48; Campbell, *Zapotec Renaissance*, 43–46.
24. Quoted in Chassen-López, "Una derrota juarista?" 62.
25. Orozco, *Tradiciones y leyendas*, 35.
26. Quoted in Jiménez López, *Historia de Juchitán*, 108.
27. Jiménez López, *Historia de Juchitán*, 100–105.
28. Katz, "The Liberal Republic and the Porfiriato," 74–76.
29. Coatsworth, *Growth against Development*.
30. Ruiz, *The Great Rebellion*, 23.
31. Chassen-López, *From Liberal to Revolutionary Oaxaca*; Chassen and Martínez, "El desarrollo económico de Oaxaca"; Sánchez Silva, "Estructura de las propriedades agrarias."
32. Chassen-López, *From Liberal to Revolutionary Oaxaca*, 45–48; Campbell, *Zapotec Renaissance*, 43–46.
33. Chassen-López, *From Liberal to Revolutionary Oaxaca*, 60–71; Chassen and Martínez, "El desarrollo económico de Oaxaca," 291–93.
34. Chassen-López, *From Liberal to Revolutionary Oaxaca*, 104–9; Chassen-López also provides an ample summary of the diversity of commercial agriculture in Oaxaca in chapter 3, pages 133–86; Sánchez Silva, "Estructura de las propriedades agrarias," 115–16, 122.
35. Esparza, "Las tierras de los hijos," 404–5; Chassen and Martínez, "El desarrollo económico de Oaxaca," 300; Chassen-López, *From Liberal to Revolutionary Oaxaca*, 175–77; Campbell, *Zapotec Renaissance*, 58.
36. Garner, *La Revolución en la provincia*, 28; Chassen and Martínez, "El desarrollo económico de Oaxaca," 300; Esparza, "Las tierras de los hijos," 429–34.

37. Hale, *The Transformation of Liberalism*; Cosio Villegas, *Historia moderna de México*; Katz, "The Liberal Republic and the Porfiriato."
38. Katz, "The Liberal Republic and the Porfiriato," 81–83; Buffington and French, "The Culture of Modernity," 404–6, 410; Vanderwood, *Disorder and Progress*.
39. Delgado Aguilar, *Jefaturas políticas*, 13–25; Guerra, *México: Del Antiguo Régimen a la Revolución*, 122–25; Falcón, "Force and the Search for Consent"; Falcón, "Jefes políticos y rebeliones campesinas"; Hernández Chávez, "La querella de Coahuila"; Blanco, *Revolución y contienda política en Guanajuato*; Chassen-López, *From Liberal to Revolutionary Oaxaca*, 428–30.
40. Delgado Aguilar offers an excellent overview of the expanding functions and growing powers of the jefe político in Aguascalientes. See Delgado Aguilar, *Jefaturas políticas*, 191–278.
41. Wells and Joseph, *Summer of Discontent*.
42. Reina, "Local Elections and Regime Crises," 99–113.
43. Coatsworth, "Railroads, Landholding, and Agrarian Protest," 55.
44. Terrones López, "Istmeños y subversión en el Pofiriato," 144–49; Jiménez López, *Historia de Juchitán*, 119–20.
45. Jiménez López, *Historia de Juchitán*, 120–21, 221–22.
46. Jiménez López, *Historia de Juchitán*, 159–62.
47. Jiménez López, *Historia de Juchitán*, 216–22; Knight, *The Mexican Revolution*, 374.
48. Overmyer-Velázquez, *Visions of the Emerald City*, 4, 6; Buffington and French, "The Culture of Modernity," 425.
49. Buffington and French, "The Culture of Modernity," 422–25; Overmyer-Velázquez, *Visions of the Emerald City*, 2, 7–11. See also French, *A Peaceful and Working People*; Delgado Aguilar, *Jefaturas políticas*, 211–51.
50. Buffington and French, "The Culture of Modernity," 407, 411. The regulation of new urban populations included new notions of crime and criminality that were fundamental to the interpretation of citizenship. See Buffington, *Criminal and Citizen*; and Piccato, *City of Suspects*.
51. Chassen-López, *From Liberal to Revolutionary Oaxaca*, 240–43; Jiménez López, *Historia de Juchitán*, 223–24.
52. Jiménez López, *Historia de Juchitán*, 130–39.
53. Sánchez to Madero, AGN, Archivo Madero, 61.680; Ríos Pineda, "Descripción de Xavishende"; Covarrubias also noted this spatial organization in *Mexico South*, 159.
54. Sánchez to Madero, AGN, Archivo Madero, 61.680.

55. According to the census, Juchitán had 1,434 labradores and 100 jornaleros (93.5 percent and 6.5 percent, respectively); AGPEO, CP 1.1.
56. Lomnitz, *Exits from the Labyrinth*, 274-77.
57. Mallon, *Peasant and Nation*, 317.
58. Sánchez to Madero, AGN, Archivo Madero, 61.680.
59. Matus Gutiérrez, "La Revolución en Juchitán," 76.
60. Díaz's program was established on January 17, 1867, and Pineda was part of the first class. See Jiménez López, *Historia de Juchitán*, 77.
61. Esposito, "Death and Disorder in Mexico City," 90.
62. Jiménez López, *Historia de Juchitán*, 234.
63. Jiménez López, *Historia de Juchitán*, 237.
64. Maqueo Castellanos, *Algunos problemas nacionales*, 80; Reina and Abardía, "Cien años de rebelión," 461-63; Tutino, "Ethnic Resistance," 56.
65. The information here is gleaned from a number of sources, including G. P. del Pino to Venustiano Carranza, Feb. 26, 1915, APJEC, carpeta 29, legajo 3117 [29/3117]; testimonies in Matus Gutiérrez, "La Revolución en Juchitán"; and Jiménez López, *Historia de Juchitán*, 161-64.
66. APJEC 29/3117, Feb. 28, 1915; APJEC 13/1379, Feb. 28, 1915; APJEC 27/2831, Feb. 11, 1915; *Causa contra Tomás Carballo (a) Matanche*, 14.
67. Matus Gutiérrez, "La Revolución en Juchitán," 77, 92.
68. Vicente Matus to Francisco León de la Barra, July 7, 1911, AGOM, caja 36, expediente 196 [36.196].

2. The Rise of the Chegomista Movement

1. *El Avance*, June 9, 1911.
2. Knight, *The Mexican Revolution*, 239.
3. Knight calls "the emergence of these new men . . . one of the remarkable features of the Madero revolution." See Knight, *The Mexican Revolution*, 197.
4. Albino Orozco y socios to Heliodoro Díaz Quintas, June 30, 1911, FPRO, legajo 7, expediente 13, documento 31 [7.13.31].
5. Carlos Rodríguez to Díaz Quintas (encrypted), July 3, 1911, FPRO 7.13.80-84.
6. For a summary of the internal politics of the Porfiriato, see Katz, "The Liberal Republic and the Porfiriato," 81-88. For an intellectual history, particularly regarding the científico faction, see Hale, *The Transformation of Liberalism*. For the radicalization of Mexican liberalism and the rise of the PLM, see Cockroft, *Intellectual Precursors*, 91-156. See also Bartra, *Regeneración, 1900-1918*; Albro, *Always a Rebel*; Raat, *Revoltosos*.

7. Ross, *Francisco I. Madero*, 64-79; Cumberland, *Mexican Revolution*, 55-69.
8. Ross, *Francisco I. Madero*, 3-45; Cumberland, *Mexican Revolution*, 30-54; Madero, *La sucesión presidencial*.
9. Ross, *Francisco I. Madero*, 80-112.
10. Frank Tannenbaum wrote that "the Mexican Revolution was anonymous. It was essentially the work of the common people. No organized party presided over its birth. No great intellectuals prescribed its programme." He adds: "*small groups of Indians under anonymous leaders were the Revolution.*" See Tannenbaum, *Peace by Revolution*, 115, 119. For synthetic analysis of the Madero Revolt in the countryside, see Brading, "Introduction"; LaFrance, "Many Causes, Movements, Failures"; Knight, *The Mexican Revolution*, 171-227. For the foco in Chihuahua, see Katz, *The Life and Times of Pancho Villa*, 57-125; Meyer, *Mexican Rebel*.
11. Ross, *Francisco I. Madero*, 150-70; Knight, *The Mexican Revolution*, 201-4;
12. Ross, *Francisco I. Madero*, 170-73, 176-77; Henderson, *In the Absence of Don Porfirio*, 45-47.
13. Chassen-López, *From Liberal to Revolutionary Oaxaca*, 406-9.
14. Chassen-López, *From Liberal to Revolutionary Oaxaca*, 460-80.
15. Chassen-López, *From Liberal to Revolutionary Oaxaca*, 466. For the similar case of Yucatán, see Wells and Joseph, *Summer of Upheaval*, especially chapter 2.
16. Quotes in Chassen-López, "Benito Juárez Maza of Oaxaca," 22; Martínez Medina, "La campaña electoral para gobernador."
17. Martínez Medina, "Génesis y desarrollo del maderismo."
18. Martínez Medina, "Génesis y desarrollo del maderismo"; Chassen-López, *From Liberal to Revolutionary Oaxaca*, 465-66, 537.
19. AGPEO, CP 1.1; Iturriaga, *La estructura social y cultural de México*; *División territorial de los Estados Unidos Mexicanos*.
20. *Regeneración*, Dec. 17, 1904; E. Gurrión, "Memorias," 3-6; *Archivo de Adolfo C. Gurrión*, 7-9.
21. Fernando de Gyves to Porfirio Díaz, April 4, 1906, *Archivo de Adolfo C. Gurrión*, 23-24.
22. *La Semecracia*, March 25, 1906; Adolfo C. Gurrión to Porfirio Díaz, June 20, 1906, and Francisco Carrasco to Porfirio Díaz, June 18, 1906, *Archivo de Adolfo C. Gurrión*, 34-36; *El Colmillo Público*, April 22, 1906; *El Paladín*, June 15, 1906; E. Gurrión, "Memorias," 8-11.
23. J. P. del Pino to Venustiano Carranza, Feb. 28. 1915, APJEC, 29/3117; Jiménez López, *Historia de Juchitán*, 163; Chassen-López, *From Liberal*

to Revolutionary Oaxaca, 472, 485; Reina, "Sin propiedad comunal"; Carlos Marín to José P. del Pino, June 22, 1911, AJFG; José F. Gómez to Heliodoro Díaz Quintas (multiple correspondence), AJFG.

24. Chassen-López derives the term (somewhat tongue-in-cheek) from Francisco Bulnes's quip that Oaxacans were for Díaz "what the Jesuits have been for the Pope." See Chassen-López, *From Liberal to Revolutionary Oaxaca*, 362.

25. De la Cruz, "La rebelión de los juchitecos," 57–61; de la Cruz, "Che Gómez y la rebelión," 234; Knight, *The Mexican Revolution*, 375.

26. Juan Puerto to Porfirio Díaz, Dec. 11, 1893, and Edmundo Bermúdez to Díaz, May 21, 1895, Colección Porfirio Díaz, legajo 18, caja 38, documento 18832, and legajo 20, documento 727.

27. Quoted in Valadés, *El Porfirismo*, 282; de la Cruz, "Che Gómez y la rebelión," 252–53.

28. De la Cruz, "Che Gómez y la rebelión," 248–55.

29. Rosendo Pineda to Severo Castillejos, Jan. 28, 1905, and Julio González to José F. Gómez, May 1, 1908, AJFG.

30. De la Cruz, "La rebelión de los juchitecos," 69.

31. Ruiz Cervantes, "De la bola a los primeros impartos," 368–69.

32. For a few examples, see *El Demócrata Mexicano*, Nov. 17, 1911; *Diario del Hogar*, Nov. 19, 1911; *Regeneración*, Dec. 16, 1911.

33. Hobsbawm, *Primitive Rebels*.

34. Ranajit Guha identifies three prerequisites for political consciousness in "elitist" interpretations of peasant rebellion: conscious leadership, some well-defined aim, and "a programme specifying the components of the latter as particular objectives and the means of achieving them." Failing to meet these criteria, "the activity of the masses ... may then be characterized as unconscious, hence pre-political." See *Elementary Aspects of Peasant Insurgency*, 5.

35. Guha argues that this act of inversion, "a task in which the existing power nexus had to be turned on its head as a necessary condition for the redress of any particular grievance," was "essentially a political task." See *Elementary Aspects of Peasant Insurgency*, 8.

36. Testimonies in Matus Gutiérrez, "La Revolución en Juchitán," 77, 92.

37. Matus Gutiérrez, "La Revolución en Juchitán," 77.

38. Ricardo León to Francisco Madero, Nov. 8, 1911, DHRM, no. 396.

39. Matus Gutiérrez, "La Revolución en Juchitán," 77.

40. Ricardo León to Francisco Madero, Nov. 8, 1911, DHRM, no. 396; "Cartas contra Che Gómez,"; Henestrosa de Webster, *Juchitán*, 75; de la Cruz, "Che Gómez y la rebelión," 251–52; Purnell, "The Chegomista Rebellion in Juchitán," 61; Jesus Fernández to Benito Juárez Maza, Nov. 23, 1911, FPRO 7.13.255; Jiménez López, *Historia de Juchitán*, 176, 179.
41. Lomnitz, *Deep Mexico, Silent Mexico*, 71.
42. De la Cruz, "La rebelión de los juchitecos," 61.
43. Quoted in Gutiérrez Montes, "La Revolución Mexicana en Juchitán, Oaxaca," 69.
44. Vicente Matus to Francisco León de la Barra, July 1, 1911, AGOM 36.196.
45. Matus Gutiérrez, "La Revolución en Juchitán," 77–78.
46. Ricardo León to Madero, Nov. 8, 1911, DHRM, no. 396; Vicente Matus to León de la Barra, July 1, 1911, AGOM 36.196; de la Cruz, "Che Gómez y la rebelión," 259.
47. For examples see Knight, *The Mexican Revolution*, 233–38.
48. V. Matus to Díaz Quintas, June 30, 1911, and V. Matus to León de la Barra, July 1, 1911, AGOM 36.196.
49. *El Demócrata*, July 1, 1911.
50. *El Demócrata*, July 1, 1911.
51. De la Cruz, "La rebelión de los juchitecos," 62.
52. Carlos Rodríguez to Díaz Quintas, Oaxaca, June 25, 28, 1911, FPRO 7.13.93–95; de la Cruz, "Che Gómez y la rebelión," 258.
53. Gómez to Díaz Quintas, June 27, 29, 1911, FPRO 7.13.24–25, 27;
54. V. Matus to León de la Barra, July 1, 1911, AGOM 36.196.
55. R. León to Madero, Nov. 8, 1911, DHRM, no. 396.
56. De la Cruz, "La rebelión de los juchitecos," 63.
57. Matus Gutiérrez, "La Revolución en Juchitán," 91.
58. Albino Orozco y socios to Díaz Quintas, June 30, 1911, FPRO 7.13.30–35.
59. Gómez to Díaz Quintas, Oaxaca, June 22, 1911, AJFG. León vehementely denied Gómez's claim in *El Avance*, November 14, 1911.
60. Díaz Quintas to Albino Orozco y socios, June 30, 1911, FPRO 7.13.37.
61. Ricardo León to Díaz Quintas, July 1, 1911, and Rodríguez to Díaz Quintas, July 2, 1911, FPRO 7.13.38, 42–43;
62. Gómez to Díaz Quintas, July 2, 1911, FPRO 7.13.45–55; de la Cruz, "Che Gómez y la rebelión," 260; Purnell, "The Chegomista Rebellion in Juchitán," 62.
63. Ricardo León to Madero, Nov. 8, 1911, DHRM, no. 396.

64. Quote from *El Diario del Hogar*, Nov. 19, 1911; Evaristo Matus to Díaz Quintas, July 2, 1911, Gabino Matus Gallegos to Díaz Quintas, July 2, 1911, Rodríguez to Díaz Quintas, July 2, 1911, Ricardo León, Vicente Matus, y socios to Díaz Quintas, July 2, 1911, and Mauro Ortega to Díaz Quintas, July 2, 1911, FPRO 7.13.57, 59, 61, 67–69, 71.
65. Ayuntamiento de Juchitán to Díaz Quintas, July 3, 1911, FPRO 7.13.73–78; Ricardo León to Madero, Nov. 8, 1911, *DHRM*, no. 396.
66. Rodríguez to Díaz Quintas (encrypted), July 3, 1911, FPRO 7.13.80–84.
67. *El Demócrata Mexicano*, July 1, 1911.
68. Vicente Matus to Díaz Quintas, July 3, 1911, FPRO 7.13.86–87; Ricardo León to Madero, Nov. 8, 1911, *DHRM*, no. 396.
69. Federico Sandoval to Díaz Quintas, July 3, 1911, FPRO 7.13.88.
70. Díaz Quintas to Emilio Vázquez Gómez, July 4, 5, 1911, FPRO 7.13.89, 100.
71. Rodríguez to Díaz Quintas, July 5, 1911, and Díaz Quintas to Rodríguez, July 8, 1911, FPRO 7.13.101, 120.
72. Gabriel Gavira to Díaz Quintas, July 5, 1911, and Emilio Vázquez to Díaz Quintas, July 7, 1911, FPRO 7.13.105, 114.
73. Matus to León de la Barra, July 7, 1911, AGOM 36.196.
74. Rodríguez to Díaz Quintas, July 6, 7, 1911, and Sandoval to Díaz Quintas, July 7, 10, 1911, FPRO 7.13.107, 109, 116, 119, 130.
75. General Merodio to Díaz Quintas, July 9, 1911, and Díaz Quintas to Merodio, July 10, 1911, FPRO 7.13.125, 126; de la Cruz, "Che Gómez y la rebelión," 263.
76. *El Diario del Hogar*, Nov. 20, 1911.
77. Gómez to Díaz Quintas, July 10, 1911, FPRO 7.13.127–28; Matus Gutiérrez, "La Revolución en Juchitán," 87, 88.
78. Vicente Matus and Ricardo León to Emilio Vázquez Gómez, July 11, 1911, FPRO 7.13.151–52.
79. Scott, "Gender"; Alonso, *Thread of Blood*, 73–75.
80. Gómez to Diaz Quintas, Oaxaca, June 21, 1911, AJFG.
81. Lomnitz, *Deep Mexico, Silent Mexico*, 175–76.
82. José F. Gómez to Heliodoro Díaz Quintas, Oaxaca, June 22, 1911, AJFG; Albino Orozco y socios to Díaz Quintas, June 30, 1911, FPRO 7.13.34.
83. Gómez to Díaz Quintas, Oaxaca, June 22, 23, 26, 1911, AJFG.
84. Albino Orozco y socios to Díaz Quintas, June 30, 1911, FPRO 7.13.30–35; Gómez to Diaz Quintas, Oaxaca, June 22, 1911, AJFG.

85. Gómez to Diaz Quintas, Oaxaca, June 21, 1911, AJFG.
86. Albino Orozco y socios to Díaz Quintas, June 30, 1911, FPRO 7.13.31.
87. Pitt-Rivers, "Honour and Social Status," 37; Alonso, *Thread of Blood*, 82–84.
88. Albino Orozco y socios to Díaz Quintas, June 30, 1911, FPRO 7.13.31.
89. Pánfilo Ríos y socios to de la Barra, Oct. 31, 1911, AGOM 19.206.
90. Gómez to Francisco León de la Barra, Oct. 24, 1911, AGOM 26.142.
91. Matus Gutiérrez, "La Revolución en Juchitán," 85.
92. *El País*, Nov. 6, 1911.
93. Von Tempsky, *Mitla*, 284; Juárez, *Documentos*, 1:671-74.
94. Augustín Valdivieso y socios to Díaz Quintas, Oaxaca, June 20, 1911, AJFG.
95. Gómez to Díaz Quintas, Oaxaca, June 23, 26, 1911, AJFG.
96. Lomnitz, *Deep Mexico, Silent Mexico*, 175-76.
97. Gómez to Díaz Quintas, Oaxaca, June 22, 23, 26, 1911, AJFG.
98. Gómez to Díaz Quintas, Oaxaca, June 22, 23, 26, 1911, AJFG.
99. "To be or no to be" appears several times in Gómez's letters to Díaz Quintas, always in imperfect English; Gómez to Díaz Quintas, June 22, 26, 1911, AJFG.
100. Matus to León de la Barra, July 7, 1911, AGOM 36.196.
101. Matus to León de la Barra, July 7, 1911, AGOM 36.196.

3. The Chegomista Rebellion

1. Felix Gómez to Francisco Léon de la Barra, Oct. 21, 1911, and José Gómez to de la Barra, Oct. 24, 29, 31, 1911, AGOM 26.142; Pánfilo Ríos y socios to Benito Juárez Maza, Oct. 31, 1911, AGOM 19.206; Ramírez Castañeda, *Cuarenta días*, 119.
2. *Periódico Oficial*, Feb. 17, 1912.
3. *Diario del Hogar*, Nov. 20, 1911.
4. Failing to find a documented connection between Che Gómez and the Vázquez Gómez brothers, historians Víctor de la Cruz and Héctor Zarauz López have denied any alliance between the two. See de la Cruz, "Che Gómez y la rebelión"; and Zarauz López, "El Porfiriato y la Revolución Mexicana," 169-204.
5. Ross, *Francisco I. Madero*, 203; Knight, *The Mexican Revolution*, 249.
6. Ross, *Francisco I. Madero*, 48, 73, 78, 90-91, 98-100; Knight, *The Mexican Revolution*, 51, 60; Cumberland, *Mexican Revolution*, 62-63; E. Vázquez Gómez, *La reelección indefinida*.
7. F. Vázquez Gómez, *Memorias políticas*, 50-51.

8. Quoted in Ross, *Francisco I. Madero*, 108, 110.
9. Ross, *Francisco I. Madero*, 119–20, 135, 155–61; Cumberland, *Mexican Revolution*, 120, 146, 148, 153; Henderson, *In the Absence of Don Porfirio*, 39–44.
10. Henderson, *In the Absence of Don Porfirio*, 54–63; Knight, *The Mexican Revolution*, 231–33.
11. Ross, *Francisco I. Madero*, 182–86; Henderson, *In the Absence of Don Porfirio*, 58–63, 68, 70; Knight, *The Mexican Revolution*, 249.
12. LaFrance, *The Mexican Revolution in Puebla*, 115–21; Henderson, *In the Absence of Don Porfirio*, 63–68.
13. Ross, *Francisco I. Madero*, 203–8; Cumberland, *Mexican Revolution*, 159–60, 162–63; Henderson, *In the Absence of Don Porfirio*, 71–72; Knight, *The Mexican Revolution*, 249–50.
14. Federico Sandoval to Heliodoro Díaz Quintas, July 3, 1911, Díaz Quintas to Emilio Vázquez Gómez, July 4, 5, 1911, Carlos Rodríguez to Díaz Quintas, July 5, 1911, Gabriel Gavira to Díaz Quintas, July 5, 1911, E. Vázquez Gómez to Díaz Quintas, July 7, 1911, and Díaz Quintas to Rodríguez, July 8, 1911, FPRO 7.13.88, 89, 100, 101, 105, 114, 120; Knight, *The Mexican Revolution*, 63, 188–89, 272–73; Gavira, *General de brigada Gabriel Gavira*.
15. Díaz Quintas to Rodríguez, Juchitán, July 4, 5, 1911, FPRO 7.13.92–93.
16. General Merodio to Díaz Quintas, July 9, 1911, and Díaz Quintas to Merodio, July 10, 1911, FPRO 7.13.125–26.
17. Gavira to Díaz Quintas, July 8, 1911, FPRO 7.13.121–22.
18. *Diario del Hogar*, Nov. 20, 1911; *El Avance*, Nov. 25, 1911.
19. Díaz Quintas to E. Vázquez Gómez, July 8, 1911, FPRO 7.13.124.
20. Federico Sandoval to Díaz Quintas, July 15, 1911, and Ambielly to Díaz Quintas, Aug. 24, 1911, FPRO 7.13.162–63, 198–99.
21. *El Avance*, Nov. 25, 1911.
22. *El Imparcial*, Dec. 10, 1911.
23. Fragment from *El Demócrata*, written by Julio Fernet, found in AGOM 36.196.
24. *Diario del Hogar*, Nov. 20, 1911.
25. Vicente Matus to de la Barra, Aug. 2, 1911, AGOM 36.196.
26. E. Vázquez Gómez to Díaz Quintas, July 15, 1911, Díaz Quintas to E. Vázquez Gómez, July 17, 1911, Iturribarria to Jefe Político, July 18, 1911, and Julio Gónzalez to Díaz Quintas, July19, 21, 1911, FPRO 7.13.158–60, 169–70, 183–86, 194; Amable Matus to Germán Matus, September 8, 1911, AGOM 36.196.

27. Julio Fernet, clipping from *El Demócrata* in AGOM 36.196.
28. Vicente Matus to de la Barra, Aug. 2, 1911, AGOM 36.196.
29. Aurelio López to Díaz Quintas, July 28, 1911, and Concepción López to Díaz Quintas, July 28, 1911, FPRO 7.13.203–4, 206.
30. Alfredo Terán to Díaz Quintas, Aug. 2, 1911, FPRO 7.13.229–31; *Diario del Hogar*, Nov. 20, 1911.
31. Esteban Maqueo Castellanos to President Francisco León de la Barra, July 26, Aug. 4, 9, 1911, AGOM 35.192; Rodríguez to Díaz Quintas, July 12, 1911, and de la Llave to Jefe Político, July 13, 1911, FPRO 7.13.154–55.
32. *El Imparcial*, Oct. 11, 1911.
33. González to Díaz Quintas, July 20, 29, 1911, FPRO 7.13.200, 213–14.
34. E. Vázquez Gómez to Díaz Quintas, July 18, 1911, FPRO 7.13.187–88.
35. Various communications, FPRO 7.13.153, 157, 165, 179, 181, 190–91, 197, 201–2, 204, 207, 209–10, 217–18, 225.
36. Martínez Medina, "Génesis y desarrollo del maderismo"; Ramírez, *Historia de la Revolución*, 33–34; Chassen-López, "Benito Juárez Maza of Oaxaca," 25–27; Henderson, *Félix Díaz*, 31–39.
37. Carlos Marín to José P. del Pino, June 22, 1911, AJFG.
38. Juárez Maza to de la Barra, n.d., AGOM 24.90.
39. Martínez Medina, "Génesis y desarrollo del maderismo"; Chassen-López, "Benito Juárez Maza of Oaxaca," 25–27; Alejandro Morales, "Benito Juárez Maza," *Oaxaca Gráfico*, Apr. 25, 1955.
40. Chassen-López, *From Liberal to Revolutionary Oaxaca*, 573.
41. Medina Martínez, "Génesis y desarrollo del maderismo"; de la Cruz, "Che Gómez y la rebelión," 263–64; Ramírez, *Historia de la Revolución*, 34.
42. Womack, *Zapata and the Mexican Revolution*, 106.
43. Henderson, *In the Absence of Don Porfirio*, 73, 83–104; Ross, *Francisco I. Madero*, 197–99; Womack, *Zapata and the Mexican Revolution*, 106–7.
44. Ross, *Francisco I. Madero*, 206–11; Cumberland, *Mexican Revolution*, 162–64; Henderson, *In the Absence of Don Porfirio*, 129–30; Knight, *The Mexican Revolution*, 249–50, 398.
45. Ross, *Francisco I. Madero*, 215–16; Cumberland, *Mexican Revolution*, 168–69; Knight, *The Mexican Revolution*, 256–57.
46. *El Avance*, Oct. 17, 1911; *Diario del Hogar*, Nov. 20, 1911.
47. *El Imparcial*, Nov. 9, Dec. 10, 1911; *Diario del Hogar*, Nov. 20, 1911.
48. Porsch, Tapachula, Feb. 23, 1912, U.S. State Department, Records Relating to the Internal Affairs of Mexico, 1910–1929, 812.00/3050.
49. Ramírez Castañeda, *Cuarenta días*, 118.

50. Matus Gutiérrez, "La Revolución en Juchitán," 93.
51. *El Imparcial*, Nov. 14, 1911.
52. *El Diario*, Nov. 27, 1911; *El Imparcial*, Oct. 27, 1911.
53. Matus Gutiérrez, "La Revolución en Juchitán," 91; *El Avance*, Nov. 14, 1911.
54. Juárez Maza to Merodio, Oct. 25, 1911, FBJM, caja 3, documentos 46, 48 [3.46, 48]; Juárez Maza to de la Barra, Oct. 29, 1911, AGOM 19.5; de la Cruz, "Che Gómez y la rebelión," 264; Ramírez, *Historia de la Revolución*, 38-39; Purnell, "The Chegomista Rebellion in Juchitán," 64.
55. Juárez Maza to de la Barra, Oct. 29, Nov. 1, 1911, AGOM 19.5, 13.
56. Plan de Tacubaya in Román Iglesias González, recopiliación, *Planes políticos, proclamas, manifiestos y otros documentos de la Independencia al México moderno, 1812-1940* (Mexico City: UNAM, 1998), 626.
57. Juárez Maza to de la Barra, Oct. 31, 1911, and Juárez Maza to Ministro de Hacienda, Oct. 31, 1911, FBJM 3.226, 231; Juárez Maza to de la Barra, de la Barra to Juárez Maza, Oct. 31, 1911, AGOM 19.174.
58. Chassen-Lopez, *From Liberal to Revolutionary Oaxaca*, 242.
59. Prida, *From Despotism to Anarchy*, 78.
60. Juárez Maza to de la Barra, Oct. 29, 1911, AGOM 19.5.
61. The October 31 headline of *Correo del Sur* read, "Juchitán and Tehuantepec Declare Their Independence from the State," but the story failed to elaborate. This theme would be repeated in the press over the next month.
62. *Correo del Sur*, Oct. 30, 1911.
63. Díaz Quintas to León, Juchitán, Nov. 1, 1911, Gómez to E. León, Juchitán, Nov. 2, 1911, and León to Gómez, Juchitán, Nov. 2, 1911, AJFG; *El Demócrata Mexicano*, Nov. 10, 12, 1911; *Diario del Hogar*, Nov. 21, 1911.
64. Félix Gómez to de la Barra, Oct. 21, 31, 1911, AGOM 26.142; Pánfilo Ríos y socios to de la Barra, Oct. 31, 1911, AGOM 19.206; Gómez to Enrique León, Nov. 1, 1911, AJFG.
65. Gómez to de la Barra, Oct. 24, 29, 31, Nov. 1, 1911, AGOM 26.142.
66. *Periódico Oficial*, Feb. 17, 1912.
67. Juárez Maza to de la Barra, Oct. 31, 1911, and Juárez Maza to Ministro de Hacienda, Oct. 31, 1911, FBJM 3.226, 231.
68. Gómez to de la Barra, de la Barra to Gómez, Nov. 2, 1911, AGOM 26.142; E. León to Gómez, November 2, 1911, AJFG.
69. *Diario del Hogar*, Nov. 21, 1911; Ramírez Castañeda, *Cuarenta días*, 119.
70. *Diario del Hogar*, Nov. 21, 1911; *El Imparcial*, Nov. 4, 1911; *El País*, Nov. 4, 1911; *El Demócrata Mexicano*, Nov. 10, 1911; Matus Gutiérrez, "La Revolución en Juchitán," 79-80, 85.

71. *El Imparcial*, Nov. 3, 8, 1911; *El País*, Nov. 3, 5, 6, 1911; *Diario del Hogar*, Nov. 21, 1911; *El Diario*, Nov. 4, 1911; *El Avance*, Nov. 5, 1911; Ramírez Castañeda, *Cuarenta días*, 118–19; Matus Gutiérrez, "La Revolución en Juchitán," 89.
72. *El Demócrata Mexicano*, Nov. 6, 1911; *El País*, Nov. 4, 5, 7, 1911; *Diario del Hogar*, Nov. 21, 1911; *El Diario*, Nov. 13, 1911; *Siglo XX*, Nov. 12, 1911; *Regeneración*, Dec. 16, 1911; Ramírez Castañeda, *Cuarenta días*, 109–12, 118; Matus Gutiérrez, "La Revolución en Juchitán," 95; de la Cruz, "Che Gómez y la rebelión," 267.
73. Matus Gutiérrez, "La Revolución en Juchitán," 81, 90.
74. *El Imparcial*, Nov. 8, 9, 1911; *El Demócrata Mexicano*, Nov. 7, 9, 1911; *Diario del Hogar*, Nov. 21, 1911; Ramírez Castañeda, *Cuarenta días*, 119–20, 128–32; Matus Gutiérrez, "La Revolución en Juchitán," 81, 86, 90, 94–95; de la Cruz, "Che Gómez y la rebelión," 266; Knight, *The Mexican Revolution*, 375–76.
75. Ramírez Castañeda, *Cuarenta días*, 128–32, 136; Haskell, Salina Cruz, Nov. 6, 1911, U.S. State Department, Records Relating to the Internal Affairs of Mexico, 1910–1929, 812.00/2497.
76. *El Demócrata Mexicano*, Nov. 9, 1911.
77. Ross, *Francisco I. Madero*, 218–19.
78. Knight, *The Mexican Revolution*, 264–66; Henderson, *In the Absence of Don Porfirio*, 120.

4. State Sovereignty and the Peace Process

1. *El País*, Nov. 20, 1911; *El Imparcial*, Nov. 17, 19, 20, 21, 1911; Enrique León to Benito Juárez Maza, Nov. 20, 1911, AJFG.
2. Benito Juárez Maza to Enrique León, Nov. 23, 1911, AJFG; *Periódico Oficial del Gobierno del Estado Libre y Soberano de Oaxaca*, Mar. 20, 1912; *El Imparcial*, Nov. 23, 24, 25, 1911; *Boletín de Avance*, Nov. 24, 1911.
3. *El Mañana*, Nov. 28, 1911.
4. The reading of Madero's executive report was reprinted in *El Diario*, Nov. 25, 1911, *El Imparcial*, Nov. 25, 1911, and Ramírez, *Historia de la Revolución*, 45–57.
5. Ramírez, *Historia de la Revolución*, 71–81.
6. *El Demócrata Mexicano*, Nov. 9, 1911. *El País*, Nov. 8, 1911; *Correo del Sur*, Nov. 8, 1911; *El Imparcial*, Nov. 7, 14, 1911.
7. *El Imparcial*, Nov. 8, 14, 15, 1911; *El Demócrata Mexicano*, Nov. 9, 10, 12, 1911; *El País*, Nov. 9, 12, 1911; Haskell, Salina Cruz, Nov. 6, 8, 11, 1911,

U.S. State Department, Records Relating to the Internal Affairs of Mexico, 1910–1929, 812.00/2497, 2498, 2528.
8. *El Imparcial*, Nov. 8, 14, 1911; *El País*, Nov. 9, 10, 13, 14, 1911; *El Demócrata Mexicano*, Nov. 9, 10, 12, 14, 15, 1911.
9. *El País*, Nov. 7, 9, 10, 11, 16, 1911; *El Diario*, Nov. 9, 1911; *El Imparcial*, Nov. 10, 1911; *El Demócrata Mexicano*, Nov. 7, 10, 11, 14, 1911; *Nueva Era*, Nov. 12, 1911; *El Avance*, Nov. 10, 1911; *Correo del Sur*, Nov. 10, 1911.
10. *El Imparcial*, Nov. 14, 18, 1911; *El Demócrata Mexicano*, Nov. 12, 16, 17, 1911.
11. *El Imparcial*, Nov. 13, 14, 1911; *El País*, Nov. 12, 1911; *El Demócrata Mexicano*, Nov. 14, 16, 1911.
12. *El Avance*, Nov. 25, 1911; *Nueva Era*, Nov. 9, 12, 1911; *El Imparcial*, Nov. 8, 9, 13, 15, 16, 1911; *El País*, Nov. 10, 12, 15, 16, 1911; *El Demócrata Mexicano*, Nov. 9, 10, 11, 12, 15, 1911; Juchitecos to Presidente de la República, Nov. 8, 1911, *Archivo de Adolfo C. Gurrión*, 58–59.
13. The animosity between Gómez and Merodio dated back to 1893, when Gómez successfully petitioned to have Merodio transferred to Sonora following a street brawl in Juchitán in which federal soldiers opened fire on a crowd of Juchitecos. See Jiménez López, *Historia de Juchitán*, 192. This animosity was undoubtedly stoked by the death of Merodio's son in combat with the Chegomistas. See *El Demócrata Mexicano*, Nov. 10, 1911.
14. *El País*, Nov. 15, 16, 1911; *El Avance*, Nov. 25, 1911; *El Demócrata Mexicano*, Nov. 15, 1911; *El Imparcial*, Nov. 9, 13, 15, 16, 1911.
15. *El Imparcial*, Nov. 17, 1911; *El País*, Nov. 17, 1911.
16. *El País*, Nov. 20, 1911; *El Imparcial*, Nov. 21, 1911; Enrique León to Benito Juárez Maza, Nov. 20, 1911, AJFG.
17. Juárez Maza to Enrique León, Nov. 17, 18, 1911, AJFG.
18. Juárez Maza to Gregorio Ponce de León, Nov. 22, 1911, FBJM 4.279.
19. León to Juárez Maza, Nov. 23, 1911, AJFG.
20. Juárez Maza to León, Nov. 23, 1911, AJFG.
21. *El Diario*, Nov. 25, 1911; *El Imparcial*, Nov. 23, 24, 1911.
22. *Periódico Oficial*, March 20, 1912.
23. *Boletín de Avance*, Nov. 24, 1911.
24. The executive report is reprinted in Ramírez, *Historia de la Revolución*, 46–57.
25. Ramírez, *Historia de la Revolución*, 49–51.
26. Ramírez, *Historia de la Revolución*, 49–51, 55.
27. Ramírez, *Historia de la Revolución*, 51, 55.
28. *El Diario*, Nov. 25, 1911; this part of the report does not appear in Ramírez, *Historia de la Revolución*.

29. *El Diario*, Nov. 25; Ramírez, *Historia de la Revolución*, 51–52.
30. Ramírez, *Historia de la Revolución*, 49.
31. Ramírez, *Historia de la Revolución*, 53–57.
32. *El Imparcial*, Nov. 25, 1911.
33. *Boletín de Avance*, Nov. 24, 1911; El Diario, Nov. 25, 1911; *El Imparcial*, Nov. 25, 1911; *El País*, Nov. 25, 1911.
34. *Nueva Era*, Nov. 26, 1911; *El Imparcial*, Nov. 25, 26, 1911; *El Diario*, Nov. 27, 1911; *El País*, Nov. 25, 26, 1911.
35. Ruiz Cervantes, "El Batallón Sierra Juárez," 16–18.
36. *El Diario*, Nov. 25, 27, 1911; *El País*, Nov. 25, 1911; *El Imparcial*, Nov. 27.
37. *El Ahuizote*, Nov. 29, 1911; *El Imparcial*, Nov. 27, 28, 1911; *El Manana*, Nov. 28, 1911; *El Diario*, Nov. 28, 1911.
38. *El Imparcial*, Nov. 9, 14, 16, 24, 1911; *El Avance*, Nov. 25, 1911; *Regeneración*, Nov. 18, 1911; *Correo del Sur*, Nov. 18, 1911.
39. The speeches from the conference were reprinted in multiple daily newspapers. I am using the transcription in *El Imparcial*, Nov. 26, 1911.
40. *El Imparcial*, Nov. 26, 27, 28, 1911; *El País*, Nov. 26, 27, 1911.
41. *El Avance*, Nov. 25, 1911; *El País*, Nov. 9, 1911; *El Ahuizote*, Nov. 11, 18, 29, 1911; *Regeneración*, Nov. 18, 1911; *El Diario*, Nov. 29, 1911.
42. *El Avance*, Nov. 25, 1911; *El Ahuizote*, Nov. 29, 1911; *El Imparcial*, Nov. 26, 1911.
43. Ramírez, *Historia de la Revolución*, 54.
44. *El Ahuizote*, Dec. 2, 1911; *El Manana*, Nov. 28, 1911; *El Diario*, Nov. 25, 1911; *El País*, Nov. 28, 1911.
45. *El Imparcial*, Nov. 26, 1911; *Regeneración*, Nov. 18, 1911.
46. Congreso del Estado Libre y Soberano de Oaxaca, Nov. 25, 1911, FPRO 7.13, unnumbered.
47. *El Avance*, Nov. 25, 1911.
48. Ramírez, *Historia de la Revolución*, 83–84; *El Diario*, Nov. 26, 1911.
49. *Periódico Oficial*, March 27, 1912.
50. *El País*, Nov. 28, 1911; Ramírez, *Historia de la Revolución*, 72.
51. Ramírez, *Historia de la Revolución*, 72, 74–76, 78, 81.
52. *El País*, Nov. 26, 1911. A turiferario is a priest's incense bearer; as a colloquialism it is meant to convey one's subservience to another.
53. *El Avance*, Nov. 26, 1911; *Nueva Era*, Nov. 29, 1911; *El Imparcial*, Nov. 26, 1911.
54. *El Imparcial*, Nov. 29, 1911; *El País*, Nov. 29, 1911; *El Demócrata Mexicano*, Nov. 29, 1911; *Nueva Era*, Nov. 29, 1911.
55. Ramírez, *Historia de la Revolución*, 72–73; Bolaños Cacho, *La causa de Oaxaca*.

56. León to Juárez Maza, Nov. 29, 1911, AJFG.
57. *El Imparcial*, Dec. 1, 5, 1911.
58. *El Imparcial*, Dec. 1, 1911; *El País*, Dec. 3, 1911.
59. *El País*, Dec. 3, 1911.
60. Ramírez, *Historia de la Revolución*, 76.
61. *El Imparcial*, Nov. 30, 1911.
62. *El Diario*, Dec. 1, 1911; *El Imparcial*, Dec. 1, 1911.
63. *El Imparcial*, Dec. 2, 1911.
64. *El Imparcial*, Dec. 1, 1911.
65. Juárez Maza to Ignacio Luchichí, Nov. 27, 1911, FBJM 4.242–43.
66. *El Imparcial*, Nov. 26, Dec. 1, 1911; *El Diario*, Nov. 27, Dec. 3, 1911; *El País*, Nov. 29, Dec. 3, 4, 1911; *Nueva Era*, Nov. 29, 1911; *El Avance*, Dec. 1, 20, 1911; León to Secretario del Despacho, Dec. 2, 1911, León to Presidente Municipal de Ixtepec, Dec. 1, 1911, and Heliodoro Díaz Quintas to León, Dec. 3, 1911, AJFG.
67. *Diario del Hogar*, Nov. 21, 1911; *El Imparcial*, Dec. 6, 1911.
68. *El Imparcial*, Dec. 5, 1911.
69. *El País*, Dec. 3, 1911; *El Diario*, Dec. 1, 1911; *El Imparcial*, Nov. 29, 1911.

5. A "Counterinsurgent" Narrative

1. *El Imparcial*, Dec. 5, 1911; *El Avance*, Dec. 21, 1911.
2. Guha, "The Prose of Counterinsurgency," 46–48.
3. Lomnitz, *Deep Mexico, Silent Mexico*, 65–71.
4. Guha, *Elementary Aspects of Counterinsurgency*, 2–3, Guha, "The Prose of Counterinsurgency," 53–57, 70.
5. Annino, "The Two-Faced Janus," Annino, "Cádiz y la revolución territorial"; Hernández Chávez, "From res publicae to Republic"; Guerra, *México: Del Antiguo Régimen a la Revolución*, 182–245; Reína, "Local Elections and Regime Crisis," 93–99.
6. Pablo Piccato calls this the "paradox of equality." See Piccato, *The Tyranny of Opinion*, 16.
7. According to Richard Warren, federal electoral reforms drafted in 1830 and 1836 "disenfranchised the vast majority of the rural peasantry" while excluding about 80 percent of the urban population from the polls. See Warren, *Vagrants and Citizens*, 101–3; 143–44. For a definition of the hombres de bien see Costeloe, *The Central Republic in Mexico*, 15–23; Fowler, "Dreams of Stability"; Annino, "Ciudadanía 'versus' gobernabilidad republicana en México."

8. Pagden, *The Fall of Natural Man*, 15–56; Hale, *Mexican Liberalism*, 215–47.
9. Lomnitz, *Deep Mexico, Silent Mexico*, 65–71.
10. Lomnitz, *Deep Mexico, Silent Mexico*, 65–71.
11. "The Juchitecos as Seen by Benito Juárez," in Campbell et al., *Zapotec Struggles*, 124.
12. Quoted in Chassen-López, "Una derrota juarista?" 59. The Parián Riot provided another prominent example of this "counterinsurgent" discourse. See Arrom, "Popular Politics in Mexico City."
13. Piccato, *The Tyranny of Opinion*, 23–156; Guerra, *México: Del Antiguo Régimen a la Revolución*, 386–94.
14. Piccato, *The Tyranny of Opinion*, 157–253; Hale, *The Transformation of Liberalism*; Lomnitz, *Deep Mexico, Silent Mexico*, 79.
15. Guha, "The Prose of Counterinsurgency," 58–59, 62, 70–71; Guha, *Elementary Aspects of Counterinsurgency*, 3.
16. Knight, *The Mexican Revolution*, 389–91; Ross, *Francisco I. Madero*, 232; Rutherford, *Mexican Society during the Revolution*, 142–45.
17. Tannenbaum, *Peace by Revolution*, 118–19. For the definitions of "cacique" see Knight, "Caciquismo in Twentieth-Century Mexico"; Friedrich, *The Princes of Naranja*; Friedrich, "A Mexican Cacicazgo"; Smith, *Pistoleros and Popular Movements*; Chance, "The Caciques of Tecali."
18. *El País*, Nov. 6, 1911; *El Demócrata Mexicano*, Nov. 7, 17, 1911; *El País*, Nov. 6, 1911; *El Imparcial*, Nov. 14, 1911.
19. *El Avance*, Nov. 12, 1911; *El País*, Nov. 6, 1911; *El Imparcial*, July 4, Nov. 9, 1911; *Siglo XX*, Nov. 12, 1911.
20. *Diario del Hogar*, Nov. 19, 21, 1911; *El Avance*, Nov. 12, 25, Dec. 6, 1911; *El Ahuizote*, Nov. 25, 1911; *El Demócrata Mexicano*, Nov. 10, 17, 1911; *El Imparcial*, Nov. 4, 8, 26, 1911.
21. *El Imparcial*, July 4, 1911.
22. *El Avance*, Nov. 25, 1911.
23. Merodio's testimony in Ramírez Castañeda, *Cuarenta días*, 118.
24. *Diario del Hogar*, Nov. 19, 1911; *El País*, Nov. 5, 1911; *El Ahuizote*, Nov. 25, 1911; *El Imparcial*, Nov. 26, 1911; Ramírez Castañeda, *Cuarenta días*, 118.
25. *El Imparcial*, July 4, Nov. 26, 1911; *El Avance*, Nov. 25, 1911; *Diario del Hogar*, Nov. 19, 1911; *El País*, Nov. 5, 1911; *El Ahuizote*, Nov. 25, 1911; Ramírez Castañeda, *Cuarenta días*, 118.
26. Madero to Telésforo Merodio, San Gerónimo, Dec. 12, 1911, DHRM, no. 474.

27. *El Imparcial*, July 4, 1911.
28. Translations for these terms are variations of "mob" or "rabble," including the multitudes, the popular masses, the human mass, rude people, the irresponsible mob, and the most rude classes.
29. Savages, savage tribes, insurgent Indians, armed Indians, and disgraced Indians.
30. The illiterate classes, the most ignorant people, the simple people, the ignorant rabble, the ignorant "people," and the stultified people.
31. The unconscious multitudes, unconscious Indians, unconscious followers, the blind, and people susceptible to suggestion.
32. The reasonable or sensible people, inhabitants, society, the thinking people, the sane or wise classes.
33. Peaceful citizens, the hardworking people, the true people, and the honorable people.
34. *El Demócrata Mexicano*, Nov. 17, 1911; *Diario del Hogar*, Nov. 19, 1911; *Regeneración*, Dec. 16, 1911.
35. *El Avance*, Nov. 12, 1911; *Diario del Hogar*, Nov. 19, 1911; *El Imparcial*, Nov. 14, 1911; *El Demócrata Mexicano*, Nov. 17, 1911; *El País*, Nov. 6, 1911.
36. Bolaños Cacho, *La causa de Oaxaca*.
37. Ramírez Castañeda, *Cuarenta días*, 118; *El Imparcial*, Nov. 4, 14, 1911; *El Avance*, Nov. 12, 1911.
38. *El Ahuizote*, Nov. 11, 18, 1911; *El Demócrata Mexicano*, Nov. 17, 1911.
39. *El Ahuizote*, Nov. 11, Dec. 2, 1911; *El Demócrata Mexicano*, Nov. 17, 1911.
40. *El Demócrata Mexicano*, Nov. 17, 1911.
41. *El Demócrata Mexicano*, Nov. 17, 1911; Lomnitz, *Deep Mexico, Silent Mexico*, 71.
42. *El Avance*, Nov. 25, Dec. 20, 1911; *El País*, Nov. 7, 1911.
43. Congreso del Estado Libre y Soberano de Oaxaca, Nov. 25, 1911, FPRO 7.13, unnumbered.
44. Pick, *Faces of Degeneration*, 24.
45. Campos, *Homegrown*, 128. For a discussion of the European origins of the concept see Pick, *Faces of Degeneration*, 109–39; Lombroso, *Criminal Man*.
46. The internal orientalization of Mexico's indigenous populations is noted in Tenorio-Trillo, *Mexico at the World's Fairs*, 70; Buffington, *Criminal and Citizen*, 145–49; and Campos, *Homegrown*, 128–33. The most comprehensive examination of Mexican "atavisms" can be found in Guerrero, *La genesis del crimen en México*.

47. *El Ahuizote*, Nov. 11, 18, 29, 1911; Juchitecos to Presidente de la Republica, Mexico, Nov. 8, 1911, *Archivo de Adolfo C. Gurrión*, 58; *Regeneración*, Nov. 18, 1911; *El Imparcial*, Nov. 21, 29, 1911; *El Demócrata Mexicano*, Nov. 17, 1911.
48. *Diario del Hogar*, Nov. 19, 20, 1911; *El País*, Nov. 6, 1911; Ramírez Castañeda, *Cuarenta días*, 118.
49. *El Demócrata Mexicano*, Nov. 10, 11, 17, 1911; *El Avance*, Nov. 9, 1911; *El Ahuizote*, Nov. 12, 1911.
50. Quoted in Pick, *Faces of Degeneration*, 122. Lombroso's impact on Mexican criminology is discussed in Buffington, *Criminal and Citizen*; and Piccato, *City of Suspects*.
51. *El Demócrata Mexicano*, Nov. 10, 12, 1911; *Diario del Hogar*, Nov. 12, 1911; *El País*, Nov. 11, 1911.
52. *El Imparcial*, Nov. 18, 1911; *El Demócrata Mexicano*, Nov. 17, 1911.
53. *El Diario del Hogar*, Nov. 19-21, 1911; *El Avance*, Nov. 25, 1911.
54. *El Imparcial*, Nov. 26, 27, 1911.
55. *El Imparcial*, Nov. 27, 1911.
56. *El Imparcial*, Nov. 18, 1911.
57. *El Manana*, Dec. 1, 1911.
58. *El Imparcial*, Nov. 27, 1911.
59. *El Avance*, Nov. 17, Dec. 20, 1911; *El Imparcial*, Nov. 14, 1911.
60. Benito Juárez Maza to Ignacio Luchichí, Nov. 27, 1911, FBJM 4.242-43.
61. Ricardo León to Francisco Madero, 8 Nov. 1911, DHRM, no. 396.
62. *El País*, Nov. 20, 1911; *El Avance*, Nov. 7, 1911.
63. *El Ahuizote*, Nov. 25, 1911.
64. León to Madero, Nov. 8, 1911, DHRM, no. 396.
65. *El Imparcial*, Nov. 24, Dec. 3, 1911; Ramírez Castañeda, *Cuarenta días*, 120.
66. Madero to Merodio, Dec. 12, 1911, DHRM, no. 474.
67. LaFrance, *The Mexican Revolution in Puebla*, 243.
68. Knight, *The Mexican Revolution*, 266.

Conclusion

1. *El Imparcial*, Dec. 6, 1911; *El Diario*, Dec. 6, 1911; *Causa contra Tomás Carballo*, 12-13.
2. *El Diario*, Dec. 6, 1911.
3. *El Imparcial*, Dec. 6, 7, 1911; *El Avance*, Dec. 6, 1911; *El País*, Dec. 7, 1911.
4. *El Imparcial*, Dec. 8, 1911.
5. *El Demócrata Mexicano*, Dec. 7, 1911; *El Diario*, Dec. 6, 7, 1911.

6. *El Imparcial*, Dec. 8, 1911.
7. *El Ahuizote*, Dec. 10, 1911.
8. *El Diario*, Dec. 5, 1911; Bolaños Cacho, *La causa de Oaxaca*.
9. *El Demócrata Mexicano*, Nov. 29, 1911; *El País*, Nov. 29, 1911; *El Imparcial*, Dec. 5, 1911.
10. *El Avance*, Dec. 20, 21, 1911.
11. Díaz Quintas to León, Dec. 4, 1911, León to Josué Esteva, Catarino Abad, Ventura Cano, Dec. 4, 1911, and Esteva to León, Dec. 4, 1911, AJFG; *El Imparcial*, Dec. 5, 1911.
12. *El Imparcial*, Dec. 10, 1911; *Diario de Hogar*, Nov. 20, 1911.
13. G. P. del Pino to Venustiano Carranza, Feb. 28, 1915, CONDUMEX, APJEC, 29/3117.
14. *El País*, Nov. 13, Dec. 10, 1911; *El Imparcial*, Nov. 17, 18, 1911; *El Demócrata Mexicano*, Nov. 23, 1911; León to Esteva, Dec. 4, 1911, AJFG.
15. *El Imparcial*, Dec. 5, 6, 9, 10, 1911; *El Demócrata Mexicano*, Dec. 6, 1911; Bolanos Cacho, *La causa de Oaxaca*; Cano to León, Dec. 4, 1911, AJFG.
16. Díaz Quintas to León, Dec. 4, 1911, AJFG; *El Avance*, Nov. 20, 21, 1911.
17. León to Díaz Quintas, Díaz Quintas to León, Dec. 4, 1911, AJFG; *El Avance*, Nov. 20, 21, 1911.
18. *Causa contra Tomás Carballo*, 12-13, 15-16; Cano to León, Dec. 5, 1911, AJFG; Everardo Ruiz y socios to Juárez Maza, Feb. 3, 1912, FBJM 7.380; *El Imparcial*, Dec. 5, 1911; *El Demócrata Mexicano*, Dec. 6, 1911; Ramírez, *Historia de la Revolución*, 108; Knight, *The Mexican Revolution*, 377.
19. *El Imparcial*, Dec. 7, 9, 10, 11, 12, 1911; *El Avance*, Dec. 21, 1911.
20. *El Ahuizote*, Dec. 10, 1911; *Siglo XX*, Dec. 10, 1911.
21. *El Avance*, Dec. 5, 20, 21, 1911.
22. *El Diario*, Dec. 7, 1911; *El Imparcial*, Dec. 6, 1911.
23. *El Demócrata Mexicano*, Dec. 6, 1911; *El Diario*, Dec. 6, 1911; *El Imparcial*, Dec. 8, 1911.
24. *El Avance*, Dec. 21, 1911.
25. *El Imparcial*, Dec. 7, 1911.
26. *El Avance*, Dec. 21, 1911.
27. *El Diario*, Dec. 6, 8, 1911.
28. Creelman, "President Díaz," 244.
29. *El Diario*, Dec. 7, 1911.

BIBLIOGRAPHY

Archives

Archivo General de la Nación, Mexico City
    Ramo de la Administración Pública, Presidentes
        Archivo Madero
Archivo General del Poder Ejecutivo del Estado de Oaxaca, Oaxaca City
    Censos y Padrones, Distrito: Juchitán, 1890
    Fondo Periodo Revolucionario de Oaxaca
Archivo Histórico de la UNAM, Mexico City
    Archivo de Gildardo y Octavio Magaña
        Fondo Francisco León de la Barra
Biblioteca Francisco de Burgoa, Oaxaca City
    Archivo de José F. Gómez
    Fondo Benito Juárez Maza
    Fondo Hemerográfico "Manuel Brioso y Candiani"
Biblioteca Miguel Lerdo de Tejada, Mexico City
    Hemeroteca
Centro de Estudios de Historia de México, Mexico City
    Archivo del Primer Jefe del Ejército Constitucionalista
        Fondo XXI
Colección Porfirio Díaz, Mexico City
Hemeroteca Pública de Oaxaca, Oaxaca City
U.S. State Department, Washington DC
    Records Relating to the Internal Affairs of Mexico, 1910–1929

Published Works

Albro, Ward S. *Always a Rebel: Ricardo Florés Magón and the Mexican Revolution*. Fort Worth: Texas Christian University Press, 1992.

Alonso, Ana María. *Thread of Blood: Colonialism, Revolution, and Gender on Mexico's Northern Frontier.* Tucson: University of Arizona Press, 1997.

Annino, Antonio. "Cádiz y la revolución territorial de los pueblos mexicanos, 1812–1821." In *Historia de las elecciones en Iberoamérica, siglo XIX: De la formación del espacio político nacional,* ed. Antonio Annino, 177–226. Buenos Aires: Fondo de Cultura Económica, 1995.

———. "Ciudadanía 'versus' gobernabilidad republicana en México: Los orígenes de un dilema." In *Ciudadanía política y formación de las naciones: Perspectivas históricas de América Latina,* ed. Hilda Sabato, 62–93. Mexico City: El Colegio de Mexico, 1999.

———. "The Two-Faced Janus: The Pueblos and the Origins of Mexican Liberalism." In *Cycles of Conflict, Centuries of Change: Crisis, Reform, and Revolution in Mexico,* ed. Elisa Servín, Leticia Reina, and John Tutino, 60–90. Durham: Duke University Press, 2007.

Archivo de Adolfo C. Gurrión. Oaxaca City: Ediciones Toledo, 1983.

Arrom, Silvia. "Popular Politics in Mexico City: The Parián Riot, 1828." *Hispanic American Historical Review* 68, no. 2 (May 1988): 245–68.

Bailón, Moisés J., and Sergio Zermeño, eds. *Juchitán: Limites de una experiencia democrática.* Mexico City: Universidad Nacional Autónoma de México, 1987.

Bartra, Armando, ed. *Regeneración, 1900–1918: La corriente más radical de la Revolución Mexicana a través de su periódico de combate.* Mexico City: Era, 1977.

Beezley, William H. "Kaleidoscopic Views of Liberalism Triumphant, 1862–1895." In *The Divine Charter: Constitutionalism and Liberalism in Nineteenth-Century Mexico,* ed. Jaime E. Rodríguez O., 167–79. Lanham MD: Rowman and Littlefield, 2005.

Binford, Leigh, and Howard Campbell. Introduction. In *Zapotec Struggles: Histories, Politics, and Representations from Juchitán, Oaxaca,* ed. Howard Campbell, Leigh Binford, Miguel Bartolomé, and Alicia Barabas, 1–21. Washington DC: Smithsonian Institution Press, 1993.

Biografía de Adolfo C. Gurrión. Juchitán, Oaxaca: H. Ayuntamiento Popular de Juchitán, 1985.

Blanco, Monica. *Revolución y contienda política en Guanajuato, 1908–1913.* Mexico City: El Colegio de México, 1995.

Bolaños Cacho, Miguel. *La causa de Oaxaca.* Oaxaca City: Imprenta del Estado, 1911.

Brading, David A. "Introduction: National Politics and the Populist Tradition." In *Caudillo and Peasant in the Mexican Revolution,* ed. Brading, 1–16. Cambridge: Cambridge University Press, 1980.

———. "Liberal Patriotism and the Mexican Reforma." *Journal of Latin American Studies* 20, no. 1 (May 1988): 27–48.
Buffington, Robert. *Criminal and Citizen in Modern Mexico*. Lincoln: University of Nebraska Press, 2000.
Buffington, Robert, and William E. French. "The Culture of Modernity." In *The Oxford History of Mexico*, ed. Michael C. Meyer and William H. Beezley, 397–432. New York: Oxford University Press, 2000.
Campbell, Howard. "Class Struggle, Ethnopolitics, and Cultural Revivalism in Juchitán." In *Zapotec Struggles: Histories, Politics, and Representations from Juchitán, Oaxaca*, ed. Howard Campbell, Leigh Binford, Miguel Bartolomé, and Alicia Barabas, 213–31. Washington DC: Smithsonian Institution Press, 1993.
———. *Zapotec Renaissance: Ethnic Politics and Cultural Revivalism in Southern Mexico*. Albuquerque: University of New Mexico Press, 1994.
Campbell, Howard, Leigh Binford, Miguel Bartolomé, and Alicia Barabas, eds. *Zapotec Struggles: Histories, Politics, and Representations from Juchitán, Oaxaca*. Washington DC: Smithsonian Institution Press, 1993.
Campos, Isaac. *Homegrown: Marijuana and the Origins of Mexico's War on Drugs*. Chapel Hill: University of North Carolina Press, 2012.
Caplan, Karen. *Indigenous Citizens: Local Liberalism in Early National Oaxaca and Yucatán*. Stanford: Stanford University Press, 2009.
Carmagnani, Marcello. *El regreso de los dioses: El proceso de reconstitución de la identidad étnica en Oaxaca, siglos XVII y XVIII*. Mexico City: Fondo de Cultura Económica, 1988.
Causa contra Tomás Carballo (a) Matanche. Juchitán, Oaxaca: H. Ayuntamiento Popular de Juchitán, 1983.
Chance, John. "The Caciques of Tecali: Class and Ethnic Identity in Late Colonial Mexico." *Hispanic American Historical Review* 76, no. 3 (1996): 475–502.
———. "La dinámica étnia en Oaxaca colonial." In *Etnicidad y pluralismo cultural: La dinámica étnica en Oaxaca*, ed. Miguel Bartolomé and Alicia Barabas, 145–211. Mexico City: Consejo Nacional para la Cultura y las Artes, 1986.
Chassen, Francie. *Los precursores de la Revolución en Oaxaca*. Oaxaca City: Instituto de Administración Pública de Oaxaca, 1985.
Chassen, Francie, and Héctor Martínez. "El desarrollo económico de Oaxaca a finales del Porfiriato." *Revista Mexicana de Sociología* 48, no. 1 (1986): 285–305.

Chassen-López, Francie. "Benito Juárez Maza of Oaxaca: A Revolutionary Governor?" In *State Governors in the Mexican Revolution, 1910-1952*, ed. Jurgen Buchenau and William H. Beezley, 19-42. Lanham MD: Rowman and Littlefield, 2009.

———. "Una derrota juarista? Benito Juárez vs. los juchitecos." In *Los pueblos indígenas en los tiempos de Juárez*, ed. Antonio Escobar Ohmstede, 37-68. Mexico City: Universidad Autónoma Metropolitana y Universidad Autónoma "Benito Juárez" de Oaxaca, 2007.

———. *From Liberal to Revolutionary Oaxaca: The View from the South, Mexico, 1867-1911*. University Park: Penn State University Press, 2004.

Chatterjee, Partha. *Nationalist Thought and the Colonial World: A Derivative Discourse?* Tokyo: Zed Books for United Nations University, 1986.

———. *The Nation and Its Fragments: Colonial and Postcolonial Histories*. Princeton: Princeton University Press, 1993.

Chopitea, José María. *Guieshuba: Jazmín del Istmo*. Mexico City: Manuel M. Flores, 1960.

Coatsworth, John. *Growth against Development: The Economic Impact of Railroads in Porfirian Mexico*. DeKalb: Northern Illinois University Press, 1981.

———. "Railroads, Landholding, and Agrarian Protest in the Early Porfiriato." *Hispanic American Historic Review* 54, no. 1 (February 1974): 48-71.

Cockroft, James D. *Intellectual Precursors of the Mexican Revolution, 1900-1913*. Austin: University of Texas Press, 1981.

Cosio Villegas, Daniel. *Historia moderna de México: El Porfiriato: Vida Política Interna*. Mexico City: Editorial Hermes, 1972.

Costeloe, Michael. *The Central Republic in Mexico, 1835-1846: Hombres de Bien in the Age of Santa Anna*. Cambridge: Cambridge University Press, 1993.

Covarrubias, Miguel. *Mexico South: The Isthmus of Tehuantepec*. New York: Knopf, 1946.

Creelman, James. "President Díaz: Hero of the Americas." *Pearson's Magazine* 19, no. 3 (March 1908): 231-77.

Cumberland, Charles. *Mexican Revolution: Genesis under Madero*. Austin: University of Texas Press, 1952.

de la Cruz, Víctor. "Che Gómez y la rebelión de Juchitán: 1911." In *Lecturas históricas del estado de Oaxaca*, vol. 4, *1877-1930*, comp. Ma. Angeles Romero Frizzi, 247-71. Mexico City: Instituto Nacional de Antropología e Historia, 1990.

———. *El General Charis y la pacificación del México posrevolucionario*. Mexico City: Ediciones de la Casa Chata, 1993.

———. *La rebelión de Che Gorio Melendre*. Mexico City: Publicaciones del H. *Ayuntamiento* Popular de Juchitán, 1983.

———. "La rebelión de los juchitecos y uno de sus líderes: Che Gómez." *Historias* 17 (1987): 57-71.

———. "Rebeliones indígenas en el Istmo de Tehuantepec." *Cuadernos Políticos* 38 (October-December 1983): 55-71.

Delgado Aguilar, Francisco Javier. *Jefaturas políticas: Dinámica político y control social en Aguascalientes, 1867-1911*. Aguascalientes: Universidad Autónoma de Aguascalientes, 2000.

Dennis, Philip. *Intervillage Conflict in Oaxaca*. New Brunswick NJ: Rutgers University Press, 1987.

División territorial de los Estados Unidos Mexicanos correspondiente al Censo de 1910: Estado de Oaxaca. Mexico City: Oficina Impresora de la Secretaría de Hacienda, 1918.

Ducey, Michael. "Hijos del pueblo y ciudadanos: Identidades políticas entre los rebeldes indios del siglo XIX." In *Construcción de la legitimidad politica en México en el siglo XIX*, ed. Brian Connaughton, Carlos Illades, and Sonia Pérez Toledo, 127-52. Mexico City: Universidad Nacional Autónoma de México, 1999.

Escalante Gonzalbo, Fernando. *Ciudadanos imaginarios*. Mexico City: El Colegio de México, 1992.

Esparza, Manuel. "Las tierras de los hijos de los pueblos: El distrito de Juchitán en el siglo XIX." In *Lecturas históricas del estado de Oaxaca*, vol. 3, *Siglo XIX*, ed. María de los Angeles Romero Frizzi, 387-434. Mexico City: Instituto Nacional de Antropología e Historia, 1990.

Esposito, Mathew D. "Death and Disorder in Mexico City: The State Funeral of Manuel Romero Rubio." In *Latin American Popular Culture since Independence: An Introduction*, ed. William H. Beezley and Linda A. Curcio-Nagy, 106-20. Wilmington DE: SR Books, 2000.

Fabela, Isidro, ed. *Documentos históricos de la Revolución Mexicana: Revolución y Régimen Maderista*. Vol. 6. Mexico City: Editorial Jus, 1964-65.

Falcón, Romana. "Force and the Search for Consent: The Role of the *Jefaturas Políticas* of Coahuila in National State Formation." In *Everyday Forms of State Formation: Revolution and the Negotiation of Rule in Modern Mexico*, ed. Gilbert M. Joseph and Daniel Nugent, 107-34. Durham: Duke University Press, 1994.

———. "Jefes políticos y rebeliones campesinas: Uso y abuso del poder en el Estado de México." In *Patterns of Contention in Mexican History*, ed. Jaime Rodríguez O., 243-73. Wilmington DE: Scholarly Resources, 1992.

———. *Revolución y caciquismo: San Luis Potosí, 1910–1938*. Mexico City: El Colegio de México, 1984.

Farriss, Nancy. *Maya Society under Colonial Rule: The Collective Enterprise of Survival*. Princeton: Princeton University Press, 1984.

Fortson, James R. *Los gobernantes de Oaxaca*. Mexico City: J. R. Fortson y Cia., S.A., 1985.

Fowler, Will. "Dreams of Stability: Mexican Political Thought during the 'Forgotten Years': An Analysis of the Beliefs of the Creole Inteligentsia (1821–1853)." *Bulletin of Latin American Research* 14, no. 3 (September 1995): 287–312.

French, William E. *A Peaceful and Working People: Manners, Morals, and Class Formation in Northern Mexico*. Albuquerque: University of New Mexico Press, 1996.

Friedrich, Paul. "The Legitimacy of a Cacique." In *Local-Level Politics: Social and Cultural Perspectives*, ed. Marc J. Swartz, 243–69. Chicago: University of Chicago Press, 1968.

———. "A Mexican Cacicazgo." *Ethnology* 4, no. 2 (1965): 190–209.

———. *The Princes of Naranja: An Essay in Anthropological Method*. Austin: University of Texas Press, 1986.

Garner, Paul. *La Revolución en la provincia: Soberanía estatal y caudillismo en las montañas de Oaxaca, 1910–1920*. Mexico City: Fondo de Cultura Económica, 1988.

Gavira, Gabriel. *General de brigada Gabriel Gavira, su actuación político-militar revolucionaria*. Mexico City: Talleres, tipográficos de A. del Bosque, 1933.

Gramsci, Antonio. "The Formation of Intellectuals." In *An Anthology of Western Marxism: From Lukács and Gramsci to Socialist-Femininism*, ed. Roger S. Gottlieb, 113–19. New York: Oxford University Press, 1989.

Guardino, Peter F. *Peasants, Politics, and the Formation of Mexico's National State: Guerrero, 1800–1857*. Stanford: Stanford University Press, 1996.

———. *The Time of Liberty: Popular Political Culture in Oaxaca, 1750–1850*. Durham: Duke University Press, 2005.

Guerra, François Xavier. *México: Del Antiguo Régimen a la Revolución*. Vol. 1. Mexico City: Fonda de Cultura Económica, 1988.

———. "Mexico from Independence to Revolution: The Mutations of Liberalism." In *Cycles of Conflict, Centuries of Change: Crisis, Reform, and Revolution in Mexico*, ed. Elisa Servín, Leticia Reina, and John Tutino, 129–52. Durham: Duke University Press, 2007.

———. "El soberano y su reino: Reflexiones sobre la génesis del ciudadano en América Latina." In *Ciudadanía política y formación de las naciones: Perspectivas históricas de América Latina*, ed. Hilda Sabato, 33–61. Mexico City: El Colegio de Mexico, 1999.

Guerrero, Julio. *La génesis del crimen en México: Estudio de psiquiatría social*. Mexico City: Librería de la Vda. de Ch. Bouret, 1901.

Guha, Ranajit. *Elementary Aspects of Peasant Insurgency in Colonial India*. Delhi: Oxford University Press, 1983.

———. "The Prose of Counterinsurgency." In *Selected Subaltern Studies*, ed. Guha and Gayatri Chravorty Spivak, 45–86. New York: Oxford University Press, 1988.

Guha, Ranajit, and Gayatri Spivak, eds. *Selected Subaltern Studies*. New York: Oxford University Press, 1985.

Gurrión, Evaristo C. "Memorias que, a grandes rasgos, escribe Evaristo C. Gurrión, acerca de la vida política de su hermano Adolfo del mismo apellido." In *Biografía de Adolfo C. Gurrión*, 3–20. Juchitán: H. Ayuntamiento Popular de Juchitán, Oax., 1983.

Gutiérrez Montes, Rodolfo. "La Revolución Mexicana en Juchitán, Oaxaca: El movimiento chegomista de 1911." Master's thesis. Universidad Autónoma Metropolitana, Unidad Iztapalapa, 1986.

Habermas, Jürgen. "Three Normative Models of Democracy." In *Democracy and Difference: Contesting the Boundaries of the Political*, ed. Seyla Benhabib, 21–30. Princeton: Princeton University Press, 1996.

Hale, Charles. *Mexican Liberalism in the Age of Mora, 1821–1853*. New Haven: Yale University Press, 1968.

———. *The Transformation of Liberalism in Late Nineteenth-Century Mexico*. Princeton NJ: Princteon University Press, 1989.

Hamnett, Brian. *Politics and Trade in Southern Mexico, 1750–1821*. London: Cambridge University Press, 1971.

Hart, John Mason. *Revolutionary Mexico: The Coming and Process of the Mexican Revolution*. Berkeley: University of California Press, 1987.

Henderson, Peter V. N. *Félix Díaz, the Porfirians, and the Mexican Revolution*. Lincoln: University of Nebraska Press, 1981.

———. "Un gobernador maderista: Benito Juárez y la Revolución en Oaxaca." *Historia Mexicana* 24, no. 3 (1975): 372–89.

———. *In the Absence of Don Porfirio: Francisco León de la Barra and the Mexican Revolution*. Wilmington DE: Scholarly Resources Books, 2000.

Henestrosa de Webster, Cibeles. *Juchitán: Un pueblo singular*. Mexico City: Alcravan, 1985.

Hernández Chávez, Alicia. "From res publicae to Republic: The Evolution of Republicanism in Early Mexico." In *The Divine Charter: Constitutionalism and Liberalism in Nineteenth-Century Mexico*, ed. Jaime E. Rodríguez O., 35–63. Lanham MD: Rowman and Littlefield, 2005.

———. "La querella de Coahuila, municipios y jefes políticos en el siglo XIX." In *Catálogo del Fondo Jefatura Política, 1885–1893*, edited by Martha Rodríguez, 1–19. Mexico City: Archivo Municipal de Saltillo, 1985.

———. *La tradición republicana del buen gobierno*. Mexico City: Colegio de México, 1993.

Hobsbawm, Eric. *Primitive Rebels*. Manchester: University of Manchester Press, 1959.

Hu-DeHart, Evelyn. *Yaqui Resistance and Survival: The Struggle for Land and Autonomy, 1821–1910*. Madison: University of Wisconsin Press, 1984.

Iglesias González, Román, comp. *Planes políticos, proclamas, manifiestos y otros documentos de la Independencia al México moderno, 1812–1940*. Mexico City: Universidad Nacional Autónoma de México, 1998.

Iturriaga, José E. *La estructura social y cultural de México*. Mexico City: Fondo de Cultura Económica, 1994.

Iturribarria, Jorge Fernando. *Oaxaca en la historia: De la época precolombiana a los tiempos actuales*. Mexico City: Editorial "Benito Juárez" de Oaxaca, 1955.

Jiménez López, Gonzalo. *Historia de Juchitán*. Oaxaca City: Colegio de Bachilleres de Oaxaca, 2000.

Joseph, Gilbert M., and Daniel Nugent, eds. *Everyday Forms of State Formation: Revolution and the Negotiation of Rule in Modern Mexico*. Durham: Duke University Press, 1994.

Juárez, Benito. *Documentos, discursos y correspondencias*. Ed. Jorge L. Tamayo. 15 vols. Mexico City: Editorial Libros de México, 1972–75.

Karush, Matthew. *Workers or Citizens: Democracy and Identity in Rosario, Argentina (1912–1930)*. Albuquerque: University of New Mexico Press, 2002.

Katz, Friedrich. "The Liberal Republic and the Porfiriato, 1867–1910." In *Mexico since Independence*, ed. Leslie Bethell, 49–124. Cambridge: Cambridge University Press, 1991.

———. *The Life and Times of Pancho Villa*. Stanford: Stanford University Press, 1998.

———. *The Secret War in Mexico: Europe, the United States, and the Mexican Revolution*. Chicago: University of Chicago Press, 1981.

Knight, Alan. "Caciquismo in Twentieth-Century Mexico." In *Caciquismo in Twentieth-Century Mexico*, ed. Alan Knight and Wil Pansters, 3-48. London: Institute for the Study of the Americas, 2005.
———. *The Mexican Revolution*. 2 vols. Lincoln: University of Nebraska Press, 1986.
Krauze, Enrique. *Emiliano Zapata: El amor a la tierra*. Mexico City: Fondo de Cultura Económica, 1987.
LaFrance, David G. "Many Causes, Movements, Failures, 1910-1913." In *Provinces of the Revolution: Essays on Regional Mexican History, 1910-1929*, ed. Thomas Benjamin and Mark Wasserman, 17-40. Albuquerque: University of New Mexico Press, 1990.
———. *The Mexican Revolution in Puebla, 1908-1913: The Maderista Movement and the Failure of Liberal Reform*. Wilmington DE: SR Books, 1989.
Lempéiere, Annick. "Reflexiones sobre la terminología del liberalismo." In *Construcción de la legitimidad política en México en el siglo XIX*, ed. Brian Connaughton, Carlos Illades, and Sonia Pérez Toledo, 35-56. Mexico City: Universidad Nacional Autónoma de México, 1999.
Lewis, Stephen. *The Ambivalent Revolution: Forging State and Nation in Chiapas, 1910-1945*. Albuquerque: University of New Mexico Press, 2005.
Lombroso, Cesare. *Criminal Man*. Trans. Mary Gibson and Nicole Hahn Rafter. Durham: Duke University Press, 2006.
Lomnitz, Claudio. *Deep Mexico, Silent Mexico: An Anthropology of Nationalism*. Minneapolis: University of Minnesota Press, 2001.
———. *Exits from the Labyrinth: Culture and Ideology in the Mexican National Space*. Berkeley: University of California Press, 1992.
López de Gómara, Francisco. *Cortés: The Life of the Conqueror by His Secretary*. Trans. and ed. Leslie Byrd Simpson. Berkeley: University of California Press, 1964.
López Gurrión, Ricardo. *Efeméridas Istmeñas*. San Luis Potosí, 1982.
López Monjardin, Adriana. "Juchitán: Histories of Discord." In *Zapotec Struggles: Histories, Politics, and Representations from Juchitán, Oaxaca*, ed. Howard Campbell, Leigh Binford, Miguel Bartolomé, and Alicia Barabas, 65-79. Washington DC: Smithsonian Institution Press, 1993.
Madero, Francisco I. *La sucesión presidencial*. Mexico City: Clío, 1994.
Mallon, Florencia. *Peasant and Nation: The Making of Postcolonial Mexico and Peru*. Berkeley: University of California Press, 1995.
Maqueo Castellanos, Esteban. *Algunos problemas nacionales*. Mexico City: Eusebio Gómez de la Puente, 1909.

Marcus, Joyce, and Kent Flannery. "An Introduction to the Late Postclassic." In *The Cloud People: Divergent Evolution of the Zapotec and Mixtec Civilizations*, ed. Marcus and Flannery, 217–27. New York: Academic Press, 1983.

Martínez Medina, Héctor. "La campaña electoral para gobernador del Estado de Oaxaca en 1910." In *Lecturas históricas del estado de Oaxaca*, vol. 4, *1877–1930*, ed. María de los Angeles Romero Frizzi, 171–95. Mexico City: Instituto Nacional de Antropología e Historia, 1990.

———. "Génesis y desarrollo del maderismo en Oaxaca." In *La Revolución en Oaxaca, 1900–1930*, edited by Víctor Raúl Martínez Vásquez, 88–158. Mexico City: Instituto de Administración Pública de Oaxaca, 1985.

Martínez Medina, Héctor, and Francie Chassen-López. "El maderismo en Oaxaca." In *Memorias: La Revolución en las regiones*, 197–241. Guadalajara: Universidad de Guadalajara, 1986.

Matus Gutiérrez, Macario. "La Revolución en Juchitán, Oaxaca." In *Mi pueblo durante la Revolución*, ed. Eleazar Zavala, 75–167. Mexico City: Instituto Nacional de Antropología e Historia, 1985.

Meyer, Michael C. *Mexican Rebel: Pascual Orozco and the Mexican Revolution, 1910–1915*. Lincoln: University of Nebraska Press, 1967.

Neza. Facsimile ed. Mexico City: Ediciones Toledo, 1987.

Nuñez Ríos, Herón. *Apuntes biográficos de José F. Gómez y de Gregorio Meléndez*. Mexico City, 1969.

———. "Apuntes geográficos sobre el ex-Distrito de Juchitán, Oaxaca." *Neza* 2, nos. 16–20 (1936).

Orozco, Gilberto. *Tradiciones y leyendas del Istmo de Tehuantepec*. Mexico City: Revista Musical Mexicana, 1946.

Overmyer-Velázquez, Mark. *Visions of the Emerald City: Modernity, Tradition, and the Formation of Porfirian Oaxaca, Mexico*. Durham: Duke University Press, 2006.

Pagden, Anthony. *The Fall of Natural Man: The American Indian and the Origins of Comparative Ethnology*. Cambridge: Cambridge University Press, 1982.

Piccato, Pablo. *City of Suspects: Crime in Mexico City, 1900–1931*. Durham: Duke University Press, 2001.

———. *The Tyranny of Opinion: Honor in the Construction of the Mexican Public Sphere*. Durham: Duke University Press, 2010.

Pick, Daniel. *Faces of Degeneration: A European Disorder, c. 1848–1918*. Cambridge: Cambridge University Press, 1996.

Pitt-Rivers, Julian. "Honour and Social Status." *Honour and Shame: The Values of Mediterranean Society*, ed. J. G. Peristiany, 21–77. Chicago: University of Chicago Press, 1965.
Prida, Ramón. *From Despotism to Anarchy: Porfirio Díaz to Victoriano Huerta*. El Paso: El Paso Printing Company, 1914.
Purnell, Jennie. "The Chegomista Rebellion in Juchitán, 1911–1912: Rethinking the Role of Traditional Caciques in Resisting State Power." In *Caciquismo in Twentieth-Century Mexico*, ed. Alan Knight and Wil Pansters, 51–70. London: Institute for the Study of the Americas, 2005.
Raat, W. Dirk. *Revoltosos: Mexico's Rebels in the United States, 1903-1923*. College Station: Texas A&M University Press, 1981.
Ramírez, Alfonso Francisco. *Historia de la Revolución Mexicana en Oaxaca*. Mexico City: Talleres Gráficos de la Nación, 1970.
Ramírez Castañeda, Elisa. *Cuarenta días que conmovieron al Istmo: Hemerografía, documentos y testimonios del movimiento chegomista, Juchitán, 1911*. Oaxaca City: Seculta-IAGO, 2010.
Ríos Pineda, Alfa. "Descripción de Xavishende." *Nesha* 1, no. 3 (August 1935).
Reina, Leticia. "Local Elections and Regime Crises: The Political Culture of Indigenous Peoples." In *Cycles of Conflict, Centuries of Change: Crisis, Reform, and Revolution in Mexico*, edited by Elisa Servín, Leticia Reina, and John Tutino, 92–125. Durham: Duke University Press, 2007.
———. "Raíces y fuerza de la autonomía indígena." *Los retos de la etnicidad en los estados-nación del siglo XXI*, ed. Reina, 245–77. Mexico City: CIESAS-INI-Miguel Ángel Porrúa, 2000.
———. "Sin propiedad comunal pero apropiación del desarrollo económico: Istmo de Tehuantepec, México. Siglos XVII–XIX." Paper presented at XIII Congreso de la Historia Agraria, Congreso Internacional de la SEHA, 2011.
Reina, Leticia, and Fransisco Abardía. "Cien años de rebelión." In *Lecturas históricas del estado de Oaxaca*, vol. 3, *Siglo XIX*, ed. María de los Angeles Romero Frizzi, 435–92. Mexico City: Instituto Nacional de Antropología e Historia, 1990.
Rojas, Basilio. *Efemérides oaxaquenas 1911*. Mexico City, 1962.
Ross, Stanley R. *Francisco I. Madero: Apostle of the Revolution*. New York: Columbia University Press, 1955.
Rubin, Jeffrey. *Decentering the Regime: Ethnicity, Radicalism, and Democracy in Juchitán, Mexico*. Durham: Duke University Press, 1997.
Rugeley, Terry. *Yucatán's Maya Peasantry and the Origins of the Caste War*. Austin: University of Texas Press, 1996.

Ruiz, Ramón Eduardo. *The Great Rebellion: Mexico, 1905-1924*. New York: Norton, 1980.

Ruiz Cervantes, Francisco José. "El Batallón Sierra Juárez." *Guchachi Reza* 9 (1981): 13-19.

———. "De la bola a los primeros impartos." In *Historia de la cuestión agraria mexicana: Estado de Oaxaca*, vol. 1, *Prehispanico-1924*, ed. Leticia Reina, 333-423. Mexico City: Juan Pablos Ed., 1988.

———, ed. *Manifiestos y planes politicos en la Oaxaca revolucionaria*. Oaxaca City: Casa de la Cultura Oaxaquena, 1988.

———. *La Revolución en Oaxaca: El movimiento de la Soberanía, 1915-1920*. Mexico City: Fondo de Cultura Económica, 1986.

Rutherford, John. *Mexican Society during the Revolution: A Literary Approach*. Oxford: Oxford Press, 1971.

Salinas Sandoval, María del Carmen. *Política y sociedad en el gobierno del estado de México, 1825-1880*. Toluca: Universidad Mexiquense, 1996.

Sánchez Silva, Carlos. "Estructura de las propriedades agrarias de Oaxaca a fines del Porfiriato." In *Lecturas históricas del estado de Oaxaca*, vol. 4, *1877-1930*, ed. María de los Angeles Romero Frizzi, 107-34. Mexico City: Instituto Nacional de Antropología e Historia, 1990.

———. *Indios, comerciantes y burocracia en la Oaxaca poscolonial, 1786-1860*. Oaxaca City: Instituto Oaxaqueño de las Culturas, 1998.

Scott, Joan W. "Gender: A Useful Category of Historical Analysis." *American Historical Review* 91, no. 5 (December 1986): 1053-75.

Sierra, Justo. *The Political Evolution of the Mexican People*. 1940. Reprint, Austin: University of Texas Press, 1969.

Smith, Benjamin T. *Pistoleros and Popular Movements: The Politics of State Formation in Postrevolutionary Oaxaca*. Lincoln: University of Nebraska Press, 2009.

Tamayo, Jorge. *Oaxaca en el siglo XX*. Mexico City, 1956.

Tannenbaum, Frank. *Peace by Revolution: Mexico after 1910*. 1933. Reprint, New York: Columbia University Press, 1966.

Taracena, Angel. "Evocaciones de la vida de ayer." *Libertad*, April 1, 1933.

Taylor, William B. *Landlord and Peasant in Colonial Oaxaca*. Stanford: Stanford University Press, 1972.

Tenorio-Trillo, Mauricio. *Mexico at the World's Fairs: Crafting a Modern Nation*. Berkeley: University of California Press, 1996.

Terrones López, María Eugenia. "Istmeños y subversión en el Pofiriato: 1879-1881." In *Lecturas históricas del estado de Oaxaca*, vol. 4, *1877-*

1930, ed. María de los Angeles Romero Frizzi, 135-70. Mexico City: Instituto Nacional de Antropología e Historia, 1990.

Thomson, Guy P. C. "Bulwarks of Patriotic Liberalism: The National Guard, Philharmonic Corps and Patriotic Juntas in Mexico, 1847-1888." *Journal of Latin American Studies* 22, no. 1 (February 1990): 31-68.

———. "Popular Aspects of Liberalism in Mexico, 1848-1888." *Bulletin of Latin American Research* 10 (1990): 265-92.

Thomson, Guy P. C., and David G. LaFrance. *Patriotism, Politics, and Popular Liberalism in Nineteenth-Century Mexico: Juan Francisco Lucas and the Puebla Sierra*. Wilmington DE: Scholarly Resources, 1999.

Tutino, John. "Ethnic Resistance: Juchitán in Mexican History." In *Zapotec Struggles: Histories, Politics, and Representations from Juchitán, Oaxaca*, ed. Howard Campbell, Leigh Binford, Miguel Bartolomé, and Alicia Barabas, 41-61. Washington DC: Smithsonian Institution Press, 1993.

———. *From Insurrection to Revolution in Mexico: Social Bases of Agrarian Violence, 1750-1940*. Princeton NJ: Princeton University Press, 1986.

Valadés, José C. *Historia general de la Revolución Mexicana*. 10 vols. Mexico City: M. Quesada Brandi, 1963-67.

Vanderwood, Paul. *Disorder and Progress: Bandits, Police, and Mexican Development*. Wilmington, Del.: Scholarly Resources, 1992.

Vázquez Gómez, Emilio. *La reelección indefinida*. Mexico City: Imprenta Ignacio Escalante y Cia, 1908.

Vázquez Gómez, Francisco. *Memorias políticas, 1909-1913*. Mexico City: Imprenta Mundial, 1933.

Von Tempsky, G. F. *Mitla. A Narrative of Incidents and Personal Adventures on a Journey in Mexico, Guatemala, and Salvador*. London: Longman, Brown, Green, Longmans, and Roberts, 1858.

Warren, Richard A. *Vagrants and Citizens: Politics and the Masses in Mexico City from Colony to Republic*. Lanham MD: Scholarly Resources Books, 2000.

Waterbury, Ronald. "Non-revolutionary Peasants: Oaxaca Compared to Morelos in the Mexican Revolution." *Comparative Studies in Society and History* 17, no. 4 (1975): 410-42.

Weber, Max. "Class, Status, Party." In *From Max Weber: Essays in Sociology*, ed. H. H. Gerth and C. Wright Mills, 180-95. London: Oxford University Press, 1958.

Wells, Alan, and Gilbert M. Joseph. *Summer of Discontent, Seasons of Upheaval: Elite Politics and Rural Insurgency in Yucatán, 1876-1915*. Stanford: Stanford University Press, 1996.

Whitecotton, Joseph. *The Zapotecs: Princes, Priests, and Peasants*. Norman: University of Oklahoma Press, 1984.

Williams, J. J. *The Isthmus of Tehuantepec*. New York: D. Appleton and Co., 1852.

Wolf, Eric. "Closed Corporate Peasant Communities in Mesoamerica and Central Java." *Southwest Journal of Anthropology* 13, no. 1 (Spring 1957): 1–18.

Womack, John. *Zapata and the Mexican Revolution*. New York: Vintage Books, 1968.

Zarauz López, Héctor. "El Porfiriato y la Revolución Mexicana (1911–1912) en el Istmo de Tehuantepec." PhD diss., Universidad Nacional Autónoma de México 1993.

Zeitlin, Judith Francis. "Colonialism and the Political Transformation of Isthmus Zapotec Society." In *Five Centuries of Law and Politics in Central Mexico*, ed. Ronald Spores and Ross Hassig, 65–85. Nashville: Vanderbilt University Press, 1984.

———. "Ranchers and Indians on the Southern Isthmus of Tehuantepec: Economic Change and Indigenous Survival in Colonial Mexico." *Hispanic American Historical Review* 69, no. 1 (February 1989): 23–60.

INDEX

Page numbers in italic indicate illustrations.

Acevedo, Herminio, 118
agrarian movements, 12, 13, 53, 96–97, 114, 170–71
agriculture, 47–49, 64, 65, 69, 112
Aguilar, Cándido, 151, 159–62, 166, 177, 179, 180, 184, 190
El Ahuizote, 174, 178, 179, 218, 233, 240
Álvarez, Juan, 32, 39
Argüello, Leonides, 219–20
Arista, Manuel, 34
army, federal: Che Gómez's distrust of, 158–59; after Chegomista Rebellion, 154–56, 161; during Chegomista Rebellion, 144–47, 154; control of, 33, 139, 152, 154, 163–68, 183, 184; disarming of revolutionaries, 134; enforcement of property laws, 33–34; against French, 40; and Gómez assassination, 233, 237–38, 242, 243; in Juchitán, 44, 54, 56, 71, 79, 91, 102, 105–8, 115, 117, 118, 120, 121, 125, 127–28, 132, 136, 141, 142, 151, 163, 164, 173, 185–86, 190, 218–20, 265n13; and peace process, 160, 175, 177, 185–86, 228; in Porfiriato, 20, 28, 50, 56, 74; in postcolonial era, 29, 30; punitive expeditions of, 44, 54; Rosalino Martínez in, 69. *See also* military, irregular; rurales
Asociación Juárez, 83–85, 87–88, 89, 90, 134
El Avance, 76, 128, 171–72, 175, 178, 182, 207, 215, 226
ayuntamientos, 51, 184, 187
Ayutla, 39, 41

Baja California, 90, 94
Baroni, Aldo, 157–58, 206, 212–14, 220
barrio de abajo: Che Gómez in, 97; after Chegomista Rebellion, 156; description of, 18, 25–26, 60, 61; governance of, 21; political interests in, 71–72; population of, 57, 63; rebellion in, 147; socioeconomic status in, 72–73. *See also* indigenous population; popular classes
barrio de arriba, 18, 25–26, 60, 63, 64, 72–73. *See also* gente bien
Barrios, Angel, 87, 134
Battle of Puebla, 41

287

El Bien Público, 88, 89, 134
Binu Gada (Nine Lives). *See* Jiménez, Albino
Bolaños Cacho, Miguel, 182, 187, 189, 212

cabeceras, 15–18, 41, 51, 136
cabecillas, 77–78, 88, 95, 160. *See also* rural population
caciques: Benito Juárez Maza on, 138, 139; influence on indigenous population, 35, 209–10, 212, 214–17, 221–25, 230; and jefes políticos, 6; in Juchitán, 9, 140; in Porfiriato, 50–51; in Rincón Antonio, 235; role in revolution, 4–5, 7–8, 13, 23, 24, 114, 194, 196, 204–9; in Sierra Juárez, 173. *See also* Mexican government
Calero, Manuel, 165–69
camarillas, 19–20, 52–53, 68, 70–73, 90, 190
cannons, 2, 146, 213
Cano, Ventura, 236–39
Carballo, Tomás, 236, 238, 239
Casas Grandes, 186
Castellanos, Matilde, 69
Castillejos, Severo, 89–91, 94, 98, 103, 108, 131, 148
caudillos, 35, 195, 200, 201, 205, 207
Celaya, 134
Central America, 46
Centro Antirreeleccionista, 86–87, 126
El Cerrito, 61
Chapital, Constantino, 180
Chassen-López, Francie, 35, 85, 92, 134
Chegomista Rebellion: aftermath of, 154–59, 191, 225, 235; causes of, 3–4, 13–14, 99, 121, 149, 218, 230; conclusion of, 7; as crime, 214–15, 219, 226–28, 243; death toll of, 156; description of, 143–47; government reports on, 165–70, 176–77, 182; historiography of, 8–9, 10; news coverage of, 23, 24, 154–62, 174–80, 184–87, 196, 203–6, 221–22; and popular sovereignty, 194–96; role in Mexican Revolution, 11–13, 220–21; Vázquez Gómez brothers' role in, 121–22
Chegomistas: amnesty for, 54, 59, 154, 158, 161, 181, 183, 185–86, 193, 194, 225, 227, 228; Che Gómez's influence on, 209–15, 225–28; confrontation with federal army, 132, 136–38, 144–47; demands of, 3, 78–79, 107–14, 119–20, 142, 147, 223–24; methods of, 3, 100, 105, 114, 130–32, 220–21; military support of, 128; news coverage of, 157–58; and peace process, 151–52, 156–57, 160–63, 166, 175–78, 181, 190, 193–94, 225; and Vázquez Gómez brothers, 122. *See also* indigenous population; popular classes; rural population
Cheguigo, 60–61
Chiapas, 34, 41, 45, 129, 137
Chihuahua, 69, 82, 159
científicos: Che Gómez tied to, 101, 109, 205–7; Esteban Maqueo Castellano as, 69; opposition to, 80, 84, 122, 123; political interests of, 68, 69, 202
Cioti, Esteban, 59

Ciudad Juárez, Treaty of. *See* Treaty of Ciudad Juárez
Club Antirreeleccionista, 86
Club Democrático Juchiteco, 102–7
Club Justicia la Unión de la Fuerza, 235–36, 238, 239
Club Liberal Santiago de la Hoz, 89
Coahuila, 81
Coalición Obrera-Campesina-Estudiantíl del Istmo (COCEI), 9–11
Coatzalcoalcos (Veracruz), 46. *See also* Veracruz
Colegio Militar, 69
colorados, 190. *See also* military, irregular
Constitution of 1857: on jefes políticos, 51, 139, 152–53, 168; on military control, 163–67, 170, 181, 183; on sovereignty, 119, 142, 169, 179
Constitution of Cádiz (1812), 51, 197
Córdoba, 127
El Correo del Sur, 175–76, 263n61
Cortés, Hernán, 2, 30
counterinsurgency, 194–203
Covarrubias, Miguel, 37
Creelman, James, 80, 122, 246
Cruz, Victor de la, 10, 95, 260n4
Cuicatlán, 134

El Demócrata Mexicano, 104, 105, 157–58, 204, 206, 212–13, 219, 220, 232–33
El Diario, 180, 204, 232, 242, 244–45
Diario del Hogar, 129, 143
Díaz, Félix, 41, 44, 55, 68, 84, 89, 90, 132–33

Díaz, Porfirio: and Che Gomez, 93, 212; defeat and resignation of, 1, 75, 79–83, 99, 123, 124; economic strategy of, 45–49, 56; on Francisco Madero's revolution, 114; influence on elections, 134; in Juchitán, 20, 88; modernization by, 16–21, 25, 45, 49, 50, 53, 56–58; nephew of, 132–33; opposition to, 89, 90, 204; and partido rojo, 27–28, 55, 67–69, 73; political organization under, 3, 6, 49–56, 84–92, 101, 107, 148, 168, 182, 191, 205, 207; rebellion against Juárez regime, 40–41; supporters of, 185; treatment of popular classes, 4, 7, 202, 217, 228; use of mano dura, 246; and Vazquez Gómez brothers, 123
Díaz Quintas, Heliodoro: appointment of jefes políticos, 99, 103, 106, 128, 133; and arrest of Che Gómez, 235–38; Che Gómez's correspondence with, 109–13; and Chegomista Rebellion, 127, 132; as interim governor, 75–76, 87, 133; on Maqueo Castellanos hacienda, 131; request for military, 105–6
dye market, 30, 31

Echeverría, Francisco Javier, 31, 33, 34
El Barrio, 89, 136
elite liberalism, 37–38, 42, 44, 45, 55, 73–74, 80
Espinal, 146
El Estandarte, 89
Esteva, Josué, 235, 236, 239

Etla, 87
Europe, 46, 70

Flores Magón, Enrique, 211
France, 48
French Intervention, 37, 40, 68, 92, 201, 213, 218
Fuentes, Teófilo, 98

Gallegos, Pedro, 39
García Granados, Alberto, 134, 135, 138, 140
Gavira, Gabriel, 106, 127–28, 137, 151, 159–62
Gavroche, 213
gente bien: attitude toward popular classes, 4, 21, 56–59, 197–98, 229–30; Chegomistas against, 120, 125, 132; in Juchitán, 3, 26, 27, 72–73, 128, 218–19; power of, 108. *See also* barrio de arriba
Gil, Carlos María, 184, 185, 234
Gómez, Chechito, 160
Gómez, Cosme, 92
Gómez, Félix, 160
Gómez, Gregorio, 92
Gómez, José F. "Che": agitation by, 102, 104–5, 107, 110–12, 143–44, 183, 222; arrest and assassination of, 7, 163, 231–47; education and employment of, 92–94; image of, 14, 23–24, 93, 95–96, 100–101, 131, 157, 204–9, 215–16; influence on indigenous population, 218, 220–22, 225–28; as jefe politico, 112, 117, 128, 137–42, 158, 160, 169, 205–9, 211, 222; and peace process, 151, 154, 156–58, 159, 160, 181, 186–87, 189; political career of, 78, 92–93, 98, 99, 134; popularity of, 3, 10, 22, 79, 91–92, 95–97, 100, 128, 141, 209, 211–13; property dispute of, 94; during rebellion, 146; rhetoric of, 107–9, 112–13; and Telèsforo Merodio, 160, 265n13; and Vázquez Gómez brothers, 120–22, 129, 136, 260n4
Gómez, Vázquez, 206
González, Abraham, 159, 187, 245
González, Julio, 128, 131
González, Martín, 84, 89
Great Britain, 48
Guadalajara, 134
Guatemala, 31
Guergué, Juan José, 31–33
Guerrero (state), 32, 93–94
Guha, Ranajit, 194, 196, 257nn34–35
Gulf of Tehuantepec, 14–15
Gurrión, Adolfo, 89–90
Gyves, Fernando de, 71
Gyves, Henry de, 48

Habermas, Jürgen, 251n38
Hacienda La Venta, 48
haciendas, 30, 78, 131. *See also* Marquesado del Valle de Oaxaca
Hernández, Gabriel, 189
Hidalgo, 189
Hotel Central, 145–46
Huerta, Victoriano, 134
Hugo, Victor, 213

El Imparcial: on aftermath of rebellion, 155, 161–62, 174, 177; on arms shipments, 137; on Benito Juárez Maza in Juchitán, 244; on

Che Gómez's influence, 212, 226; on Chegomista Rebellion, 204; on Gómez assassination, 232, 233, 235, 242; interview of Che Gómez, 157–58, 206; interview of rebels, 209; on Vázquez Gómez brothers, 129

India, 194, 196, 197

"Indian problem," 4–5, 21, 29, 37, 229–30

indigenous population: attitude toward Pancho León, 103; and caciques, 204–5; citizenship of, 4, 26–27, 35–39, 56–59, 73, 194–200, 221; distribution of, 26, 58, 61, 66–67; governance of, 6, 19–24, 42; image of, 23–24, 70, 198–99, 209–20, 225–28; in Juchitán, 3–10, 18–21; land rights of, 29–33, 42, 53, 93, 96, 211; political interests of, 67, 73, 78–79, 92, 108–14, 229–30; role in economy, 45; support of Che Gómez, 92–93, 95–97, 107, 110–11. *See also* barrio de abajo; Chegomistas; popular classes; rural population

Instituto de Ciencias y Artes del Estado, 68, 85–87, 89, 92, 182

Isthmus. *See* Tehuantepec, Isthmus of

Jalapa, 179

Jauja, 224

jefes políticos: Che Gómez as, 112, 117, 128, 137–42, 158, 160, 169, 205–11, 222; and Che Gomez's arrest, 237; in Juchitán, 2–7, 18, 20, 28, 69–71, 79, 92, 94, 99–109, 117–21, 127, 137–43, 148–49, 160–61, 166, 187, 190; in Porfiriato, 53, 54, 74, 148; postrevolution, 76–78, 103, 133; power of, 5–6, 19, 20, 51–52, 56, 108; selection and appointment of, 3, 151–54, 158, 160, 162, 165–70, 174–75, 179, 180, 185, 187. *See also* Mexican government

Jiménez, Albino, 41, 42, 44, 115

Jiménez López, Gonzalo, 68

jornaleros, 48, 64, 255n55

Juárez, Benito, 33–35

Juárez Maza, Benito: appointment of jefes políticos, 3, 6, 51, 120–21, 138–42, 149, 153, 161–62, 190; attempt to avoid rebellion, 117–18; control of federal army, 154, 183, 184; disarming of revolutionaries, 134–35; and Gómez assassination, 233–45; as governor, 86–87, 132, 151; ideology of, 81–84, 191; image of, 7; and peace process, 162, 182–89, 193, 226; on reason for 1850 rebellion, 201; rebellion against, 40; on rebellion as crime, 214; and state sovereignty, 151–53, 166, 169, 171–74, 180, 181, 188–91; supporters of, 90; treatment of Juchitán, 39–43

Juchitán: agriculture in, 48–49; battles in, 40, 41; Che Gómez's influence in, 3–4, 78, 94, 129–30, 137–38, 206–8, 212, 213; after Chegomista Rebellion, 7, 155–56, 182, 190, 230; education levels in, 63, 63–64; Enrique León in, 138, 141; ethnic distinctions in, 15–16, 60–63, 62, 107, 218, 250n27; factions

Juchitán (*continued*)
in, 13–14, 19–20, 27, 33–38, 43–44, 55, 67–72, 89–92, 95–101, 111, 119–22, 127, 131, 148–49; geography of, 14–15, 17, 42; after Gómez assassination, 239, 244–45; historiography of, 8–11; modernization in, 25–26, 42–43, 46, 47, 56, 59–60, 66, 70–72; neighborhoods in, 25–26, 59–61; Pancho León in, 103; peace process in, 151–55, 159–71, 178, 180, 187–89, 193, 215–16, 225–28; as political district, 39–42; population of, 48, 56, 59, 62, 88, 140; during Porfiriato, 26–27, 70–74, 88; rebellions in, 2, 9–12, 21, 30–37, 40–41, 53–54, 99, 115, 139–40, 143–47, 152, 177–78, 201, 243, 265n13; salt flats in, 31; social class in, 8–27, 64–67, 88, 96–97, 107–9, 114, 147–49, 255n55; state representatives of, 134; vice-presidential election in, 136

Knight, Alan, 12, 13, 122

Laguna Menor, 137
latifundias, 47
León, Enrique: and Gómez arrest and assassination, 235, 236, 239; as jefe politico, 117, 138, 141–43, 151, 158, 160–63, 183, 187, 190
León, Francisco, 54–56, 59, 90–91, 103
León, Pancho, 70–71, 92, 103, 106, 109, 226–27
León, Pedro, 173
León, Ricardo, 90, 98, 227–28

León de la Barra, Francisco: on bandits, 134; and Chegomista Rebellion, 143; as interim president, 83, 118–20, 122, 124–27, 130–31, 140, 141, 142, 147; and popular sovereignty, 170; Vicente Matus's warning to, 115; in vice-presidential election, 136
Ley fuga, 233
liberalism. *See* elite liberalism; popular liberalism
Limantour, José Yves, 94
Lombroso, Cesare, 219
Lomnitz, Claudio, 21, 112, 195, 199, 213
López, Nicolás, 137
López, Rosalía, 92

Madero, Francisco: and appointment of jefes políticos, 6–7, 76–77, 152–53, 179, 180; criticism of, 154, 171–81; freedom of press under, 203; and Gómez arrest and assassination, 231, 234, 241–45; on governor of Oaxaca, 133; and Juchitán's neighborhoods, 25; and peace process, 151–54, 159, 161, 162, 165–66, 170, 181, 184–85, 188, 191, 227–28; as president, 1–2, 75, 79–83, 135, 140, 147; reaction to Chegomista Rebellion, 4, 5, 146–48, 165; role in revolution, 87, 114, 119, 120, 122–26, 139; supporters of, 1–2, 6–7, 81, 86, 90, 100–101, 110, 123, 127, 130, 158, 190–91, 206, 208–9, 228; treatment of revolutionaries, 120, 140, 170–71, 175–77, 222–24, 228–29

Magonistas, 89, 90, 134, 159
Mallon, Florencia, 19, 37–38, 67
El Mañana, 179–80, 224
mano dura, 153, 246–47
Manzano, José, 146
Maqueo, Esteban, 32–33, 69
Maqueo, José W., 70
Maqueo Castellanos, Esteban, 69–71, 130–31, 182
Maqueo Castellanos, José, 69
Maqueo Castellanos family, 48, 54, 69, 93, 136, 236
Marquesado del Valle de Oaxaca, 30–33, 69. *See also* haciendas
Martínez, Rosalino, 68, 69, 71
Matus, Evaristo, 90
Matus, Germán, 90
Matus, Herminio, 90
Matus, Marcos, 44
Matus, Vicente, 90, 91, 101, 102, 104, 108, 115, 130, 148
Maya, 69
Meléndez, José Gregorio, 32–37, 41, 115, 140
Merodio, Telésforo: on arms shipments, 136, 137; and arrest of Che Gómez, 163, 234, 237, 241, 242; on Che Gómez's nepotism, 208; on Chegomista Rebellion, 143; and peace process, 160, 162, 171, 175, 177, 186, 228; relationship with Che Gómez, 160, 265n13
Mexican civil war, 38, 39
Mexican government: and abolition of jefatura, 103, 133; elections in, 135–36; exploitation of salt flats, 31; factions in postcolonial era, 28–29, 197–98; and indigenous population, 217, 223–25, 230; Polko Rebellion against, 32–33; and popular sovereignty, 197, 202, 220–21, 229; during Porfiriato, 26–27, 49–56; reaction to Chegomista Rebellion, 169–70, 222–23, 230; state power in, 18–19, 28, 29, 36–37, 95, 99, 119, 139, 142, 143, 148–54, 162–69, 174–75, 179, 181–84, 188, 190–91, 201–3, 240–43; threats to, 37; warned about Che Gómez, 103, 105. *See also* caciques; jefes políticos; revolution, democratic
Mexican Revolution. *See* revolution, democratic
Mexico City: anti-Díaz organizations in, 123; Benito Juárez Maza in, 86, 188; Castellanos family in, 69; Che Gómez's travel to, 154, 159, 161, 181, 187, 189, 233–36, 243; Francisco Madero in, 1; French invasion of, 40; Oaxaca representatives in, 242; political factions in, 20; railroad in, 46; rebellion in, 32–33
Mexu Chele. *See* Nicolás, Ignacio
Milan, Italy, 69
military, irregular: Cosme Gómez in, 92; demobilization of, 118–20, 124–26; in Juchitán, 106, 121, 127–29, 190, 208; and popular liberalism, 38–42, 44, 45; for state sovereignty, 33, 171, 173. *See also* army, federal; rurales
Les misérables, 213
Moctezuma, 2

Index 293

Modesto Ramirez, Francisco, 184
Monteleone, Duke of, 31
Morales, Francisco de Paula, 179
Morelos, 134, 147, 156, 170–71

National Guard, 33, 38–39. *See also* army, federal; military, irregular
Nicolás, Ignacio, 54–55, 59, 92, 115
Nicu Dada. *See* López, Nicolás

Oaxaca: Che Gómez's reputation in, 206, 209, 211; cholera outbreak in, 34; economy in, 29–32, 45–49; factions in, 29–30, 33, 45; geography of, 14–15, *15*, *17*; government of, 3, 6–7, 16, 127, 132–34, 139, 160, 215–16, 233; Polko Rebellion in, 32–33; population of, 59; reaction to Gómez assassination in, 242–47; revolution in, 8, 75–76, 83–88; separation of, 33–44, 129, 140, 263n61; signs of civil war in, 173–74; social class in, 10, 85–88; sovereignty of, 152–54, 163–74, 179–88, 190–91; vice-presidential election in, 121, 136
Oaxaca City: Adolfo Gurrión in, 89; Benito Juárez Maza in, 133; capture of, 40; Che Gómez in, 92; Chegomista demands in, 142; political interests in, 86; population of, 59, 140; protests in, 152, 172–73; reaction to Gómez assassination in, 242; Severo Castillejos in, 89
Oaxacan Fraternal Society, 188
Ochoa, Guadalupe, 128, 130–31, 137, 145
Olivera, Faustino, 144
Orizaba, 127

Ortega, Mauro, 90, 108
Ortíz, Sebastian, 87
Oseguera, Manuel, 87
Ostos, Amado, 180

El País, 159–61, 177, 186–87, 204, 206, 208, 214–15
Palomares, 136, 235
Pan American Railway, 46, 161, 177. *See also* railroads
Parragua brothers, 91
Partido Constitucional Progresista (PCP), 126, 129, 135
Partido Democrático, 80, 86, 133, 134, 169
Partido Liberal Mexicano (PLM), 80, 85, 87, 89–90
Partido Nacional Antirreeleccionista, 80–81, 123, 126, 135
Partido Popular Evolucionista, 180
partido rojo: description of, 20; hatred of partido verde, 97; in Juchitán, 27–28, 55, 67–73, 90, 98–99, 182, 190; response to Che Gómez, 92–93; in Rincón Antonio, 235–36
partido verde: hatred of partido rojo, 71–73, 97; in Juchitán, 27–28, 55, 67–68, 92, 96, 97, 99, 107, 111; organization of, 22
Paso Guayabo, 231, 238
Pearson, Weetman, 46–48
Petapa, 136, 231, 235, 238, 243
Pimentel, Emilio, 70, 84–87, 89–90
Pineda, Pablo, 183, 190
Pineda, Rosendo, 67–70, 93–94, 101, 182, 207
Pino Suárez, José María, 135, 136

Plan de 20 de Octubre, 34
Plan de San Luis, 81–82
Plan de Tacubaya, 122, 139
Plan de Texca, 32
Plan de Tuxtepec, 92
police force, 102–5, 130
Polko Rebellion, 32–33
popular classes: Che Gómez's influence over, 209–15, 229; and Chegomista Rebellion, 12–13, 78, 119–20, 147, 247; consequence of rule by, 232; image of, 199–202; in Juchitán, 8, 36, 190; in Mexico, 4–8, 22–24; postrevolution, 76–77, 176; rhetoric of, 107–10; sovereignty of, 153, 165, 168, 180, 187, 194–98, 202–3, 220–25; voting by, 198, 267n7. *See also* barrio de abajo; Chegomistas; indigenous population; rural population
popular liberalism, 22, 37–45, 55, 80, 251n38
Popular Sovereignty Club, 123
The Presidential Succession of 1910 (Madero), 81
PRI, 9
Puebla, 125, 126
Puerto Mexico, 47
Purnell, Jennie, 13–14

railroads, 45–46, 50, 53–54, 56, 57, 94, 140. *See also* Pan American Railway; Tehuantepec National Railway
Ranchería Barrancón, 239
La reelección indefinida, 123
La Reforma wars, 37, 39, 55

Regeneración, 89, 175, 180, 211
revolution, democratic: aftermath of, 1–4, 74–79; expectations of, 223–24, 229; factions in, 23, 24, 26, 55, 100, 119–20; failure of, 7–8, 147–49, 230, 244–47; under Francisco Madero, 153; in Juchitán, 8–14, 73–74, 190–91; and Plan de San Luis, 81–82; responsibility for Mexican, 82, 256n10; rhetoric of, 108–10, 114, 194–95; role of Chegomista Rebellion in, 11–13, 203, 220–21; violence associated with, 82–83, 115, 194, 196–97, 218–22. *See also* Mexican government
Rincón Antonio, 47, 136, 231–33, 235–39, 241, 243
Río Blanco, 69
Río de los Perros, 137
Rio de Perros, 61
Rodríguez, Carlos, 99, 100, 102, 104–5, 127
Romero Rubio, Manuel, 68
Ross, Stanley, 122, 147
Rueda, Victoriano, 90, 108
Ruiz Cervantes, José, 87
rurales, 50, 125, 128, 189, 231–34, 236. *See also* army, federal; military, irregular
rural population, 47, 57, 78, 82, 86, 87, 91, 124. *See also* cabecillas; Chegomistas; indigenous population; popular classes

Salina Cruz, 2, 46, 47, 70, 144, 145, 147, 155, 157
salt, 31, 32, 33, 41, 93, 211

Index 295

San Antonio TX, 81, 124, 127
Sánchez, Juan, 25, 61, 63
Sandoval, Federico, 90, 104–5
San Jerónimo: Benito Juárez Maza in, 189, 193; Che Gómez in, 234; and Che Gómez's arrest, 235, 237–38; Juchitán refugees in, 130, 132; Maqueo Castellanos holdings in, 70; military in, 20, 56, 71, 102, 105–6, 107, 127–28, 136, 138; railroad in, 47; road to Juchitán, 156; White Cross in, 155
San Luis Potosí, 81, 123
San Miguel Chimalapa, 54, 92
Santa Anna, Antonio López de, 34–35, 39
Saynes, Mariano, 69, 71, 98, 99
Saynes, Román, 71, 98
La Semecracia, 89
Sierra Juárez, 173
Sierra Mixteca, 118
Sierra Oriente, 14–15
Siglo XX, 240–41
Sonora, 69, 265n13
Spain, 16, 28, 32, 35, 39, 197–99, 204
Spanish language, 63–64, 111
Sugar Mill of Santo Domingo, 48

Tannenbaum, Frank, 204, 256n10
Tapachula, Chiapas, 137
Tehuantepec (cabecera): Chegomistas in, 105; Juchitán's independence from, 39; Maqueo Castellanos holdings in, 70; militia from, 40, 237, 238; population of, 15–16, 140; Spanish influence in, 31

Tehuantepec, Isthmus of: economy on, 42–43, 48, 140; geography of, 14–15; landownership on, 31–32; military on, 33, 41; political organization of, 16; population of, 59; in postcolonial era, 29–31; rebellion on, 178; separation from Oaxaca, 33–44, 129, 140, 263n61
Tehuantepec National Railway, 46, 48, 235, 236. *See also* railroads
Tepoztlán, 112
Tlacolula, Oaxaca, 92
Tlaxcala, 94
Tovar, Almagino, 236
Treaty of Ciudad Juárez, 78, 83, 106, 118, 122, 124
Trejo y Lerdo de Tejada, Carlos, 184–85
Tutino, John, 11

Unión Hidalgo, 47, 157–58, 163, 186, 234
United States, 46, 47, 48, 121, 124, 137
U.S. Army, 32, 33, 37

Valdés, Augustín, 186
Valdivieso, Aurelio, 182
Vargas, Alberto, 152, 164
Vázquez Gómez, Emilio, 106, 120–29, 134, 135, 137, 139, 260n4
Vázquez Gómez, Francisco, 120–26, 129, 132, 135–37, 139, 260n4
Vazquistas, 121, 122, 135, 158
Velasco, Emilio, 183–84
Veracruz, 47, 54, 106, 127, 128, 129, 151, 159. *See also* Coatzalcoalcos (Veracruz)

Vera Estañol, Jorge, 176, 177, 178, 188, 222–25
Vera family, 146
violence. *See* mano dura
La Voz del Istmo, 98

Warren, Richard, 267n7
Weber, Max, 19
Whitecotton, Joseph, 16
White Cross, 155–57, 220
Womack, John, 134

Xapa, 160

Yucatán, 69, 135

Zapata, Emiliano, 10, 171
Zapatistas, 114, 134, 147, 170–71, 178
Zapotec language, 18, 26, 102, 111, 206
Zapotec Renaissance, 9–11
Zapotec society, 15–16, 213, 214, 218, 250n27
Zaragoza Battalion, 44
Zarauz López, Héctor, 260n4
Zea, Leopoldo, 155, 157–58, 206, 209, 226, 232, 235
Zozaya, Manuel, 141, 143, 144

In The Mexican Experience series

From Idols to Antiquity: Forging the National Museum of Mexico
Miruna Achim

Seen and Heard in Mexico: Children and Revolutionary Cultural Nationalism
Elena Jackson Albarrán

Railroad Radicals in Cold War Mexico: Gender, Class, and Memory
Robert F. Alegre
Foreword by Elena Poniatowska

Mexicans in Revolution, 1910–1946: An Introduction
William H. Beezley and Colin M. MacLachlan

Routes of Compromise: Building Roads and Shaping the Nation in Mexico, 1917–1952
Michael K. Bess

Apostle of Progress: Modesto C. Rolland, Global Progressivism, and the Engineering of Revolutionary Mexico
J. Justin Castro

Radio in Revolution: Wireless Technology and State Power in Mexico, 1897–1938
J. Justin Castro

San Miguel de Allende: Mexicans, Foreigners, and the Making of a World Heritage Site
Lisa Pinley Covert

Celebrating Insurrection: The Commemoration and Representation of the Nineteenth-Century Mexican Pronunciamiento
Edited and with an introduction by Will Fowler

Forceful Negotiations: The Origins of the Pronunciamiento *in Nineteenth-Century Mexico*
Edited and with an introduction by Will Fowler

Independent Mexico: The Pronunciamiento *in the Age of Santa Anna, 1821–1858*
Will Fowler

Malcontents, Rebels, and Pronunciados: *The Politics of Insurrection in Nineteenth-Century Mexico*
Edited and with an introduction by Will Fowler

Working Women, Entrepreneurs, and the Mexican Revolution: The Coffee Culture of Córdoba, Veracruz
Heather Fowler-Salamini

The Heart in the Glass Jar: Love Letters, Bodies, and the Law in Mexico
William E. French

"Muy buenas noches": Mexico, Television, and the Cold War
Celeste González de Bustamante
Foreword by Richard Cole

The Plan de San Diego: Tejano Rebellion, Mexican Intrigue
Charles H. Harris III and Louis R. Sadler

The Inevitable Bandstand: The State Band of Oaxaca and the Politics of Sound
Charles V. Heath

Redeeming the Revolution: The State and Organized Labor in Post-Tlatelolco Mexico
Joseph U. Lenti

Gender and the Negotiation of Daily Life in Mexico, 1750–1856
Sonya Lipsett-Rivera

Mexico's Crucial Century, 1810–1910: An Introduction
Colin M. MacLachlan and William H. Beezley

The Civilizing Machine: A Cultural History of Mexican Railroads, 1876–1910
Michael Matthews

Street Democracy: Vendors, Violence, and Public Space in Late Twentieth-Century Mexico
Sandra C. Mendiola García

The Lawyer of the Church: Bishop Clemente de Jesús Munguía and the Clerical Response to the Liberal Revolution in Mexico
Pablo Mijangos y González

From Angel to Office Worker: Middle-Class Identity and Female Consciousness in Mexico, 1890–1950
Susie S. Porter

¡México, la patria! Propaganda and Production during World War II
Monica A. Rankin

A Revolution Unfinished: The Chegomista Rebellion and the Limits of Revolutionary Democracy in Juchitán, Oaxaca
Colby Ristow

Murder and Counterrevolution in Mexico: The Eyewitness Account of German Ambassador Paul von Hintze, 1912–1914
Edited and with an introduction by Friedrich E. Schuler

Deco Body, Deco City: Female Spectacle and Modernity in Mexico City, 1900–1939
Ageeth Sluis

Pistoleros and Popular Movements: The Politics of State Formation in Postrevolutionary Oaxaca
Benjamin T. Smith

Alcohol and Nationhood in Nineteenth-Century Mexico
Deborah Toner

To order or obtain more information on these or other University of Nebraska Press titles, visit nebraskapress.unl.edu.

www.ingramcontent.com/pod-product-compliance
Lightning Source LLC
Chambersburg PA
CBHW021956220426
43663CB00007B/833